SPIDER-MAN
DOCTOR OCTOPUS

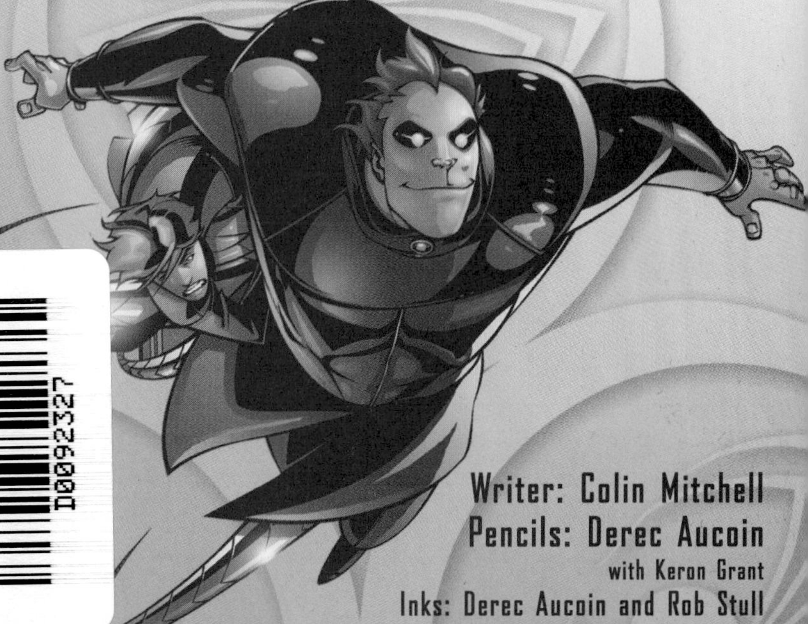

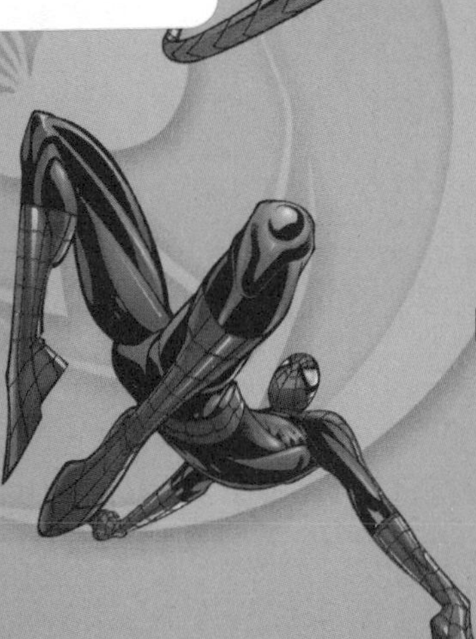

Writer: Colin Mitchell
Pencils: Derec Aucoin
with Keron Grant
Inks: Derec Aucoin and Rob Stull
with Derek Fridolfs & Scott Elmer
Colors: James Rochelle
Letters: Virtual Calligraphy's Cory Petit
Cover Art: Keron Grant & Randy Green
Digital Cover Painting: Brian Haberlin
Assistant Editor: Stephanie Moore
Editors: Cory Sedlmeier & Teresa Focarile

Collections Editor: Jeff Youngquist
Assistant Editor: Jennifer Grünwald
Book Designer: Jeof Vita

Editor in Chief: Joe Quesada
Publisher: Dan Buckley

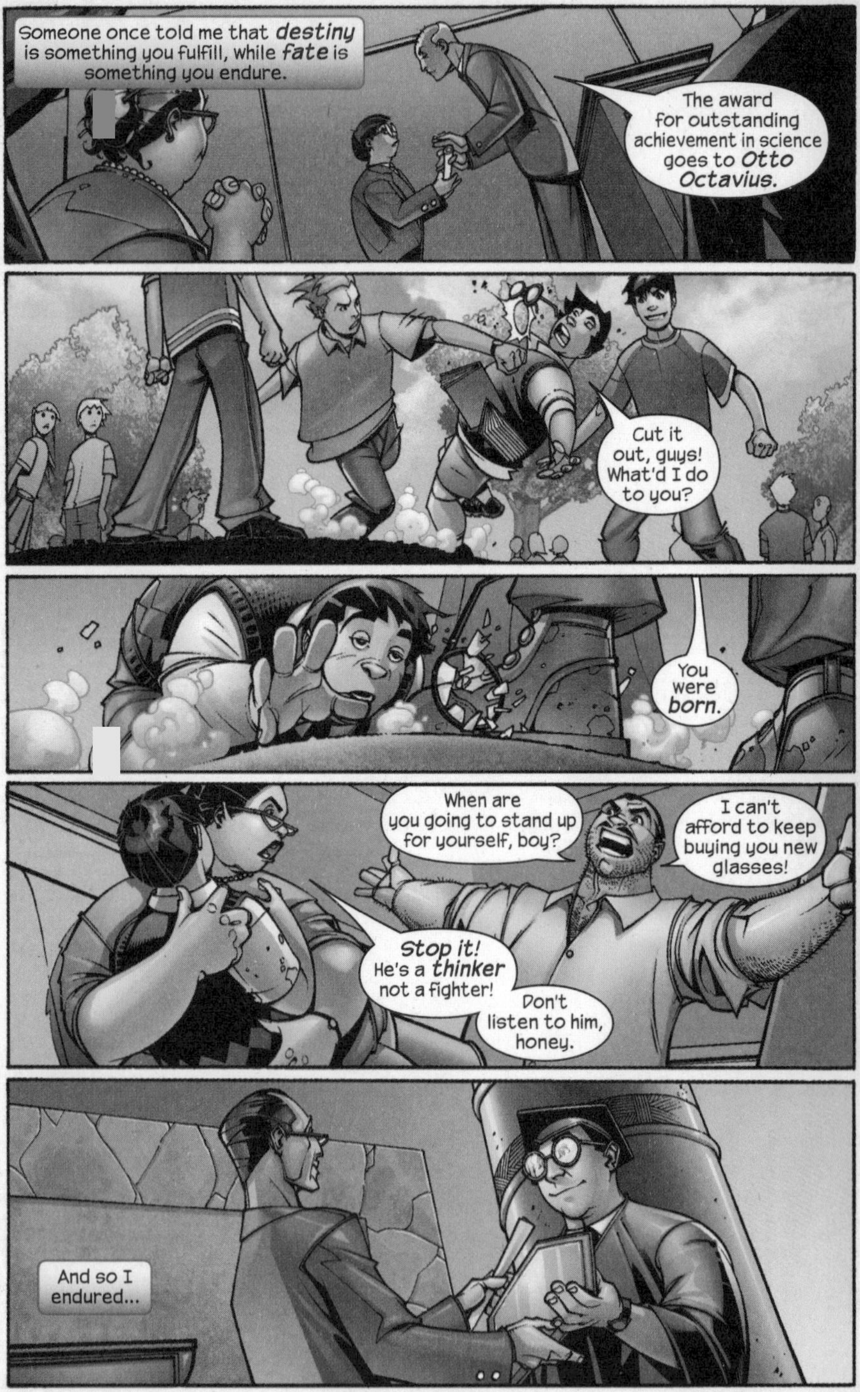
Someone once told me that destiny is something you fulfill, while fate is something you endure.
The award for outstanding achievement in science goes to Otto Octavius.
Cut it out, guys! What'd I do to you?
You were born.
When are you going to stand up for yourself, boy?
I can't afford to keep buying you new glasses!
Stop it! He's a thinker not a fighter!
Don't listen to him, honey.
And so I endured...

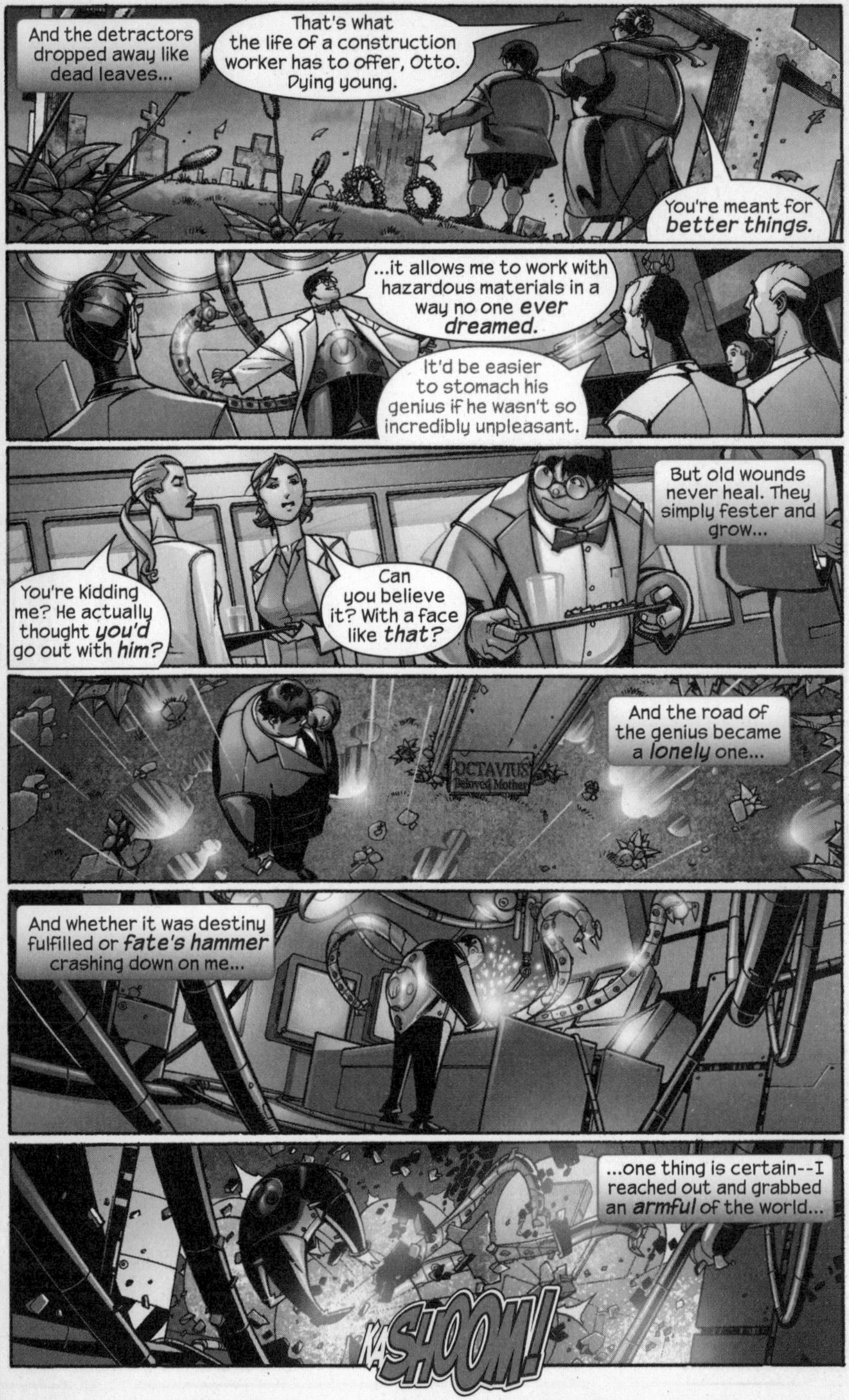
And the detractors dropped away like dead leaves...
That's what the life of a construction worker has to offer, Otto. Dying young.
You're meant for *better things.*
...it allows me to work with hazardous materials in a way no one *ever dreamed.*
It'd be easier to stomach his genius if he wasn't so incredibly unpleasant.
But old wounds never heal. They simply fester and grow...
You're kidding me? He actually thought *you'd* go out with *him*?
Can you believe it? With a face like *that*?
And the road of the genius became a *lonely* one...
OCTAVIUS Beloved Mother
And whether it was destiny fulfilled or *fate's hammer* crashing down on me...
...one thing is certain--I reached out and grabbed an *armful* of the world...
KASHOOM!

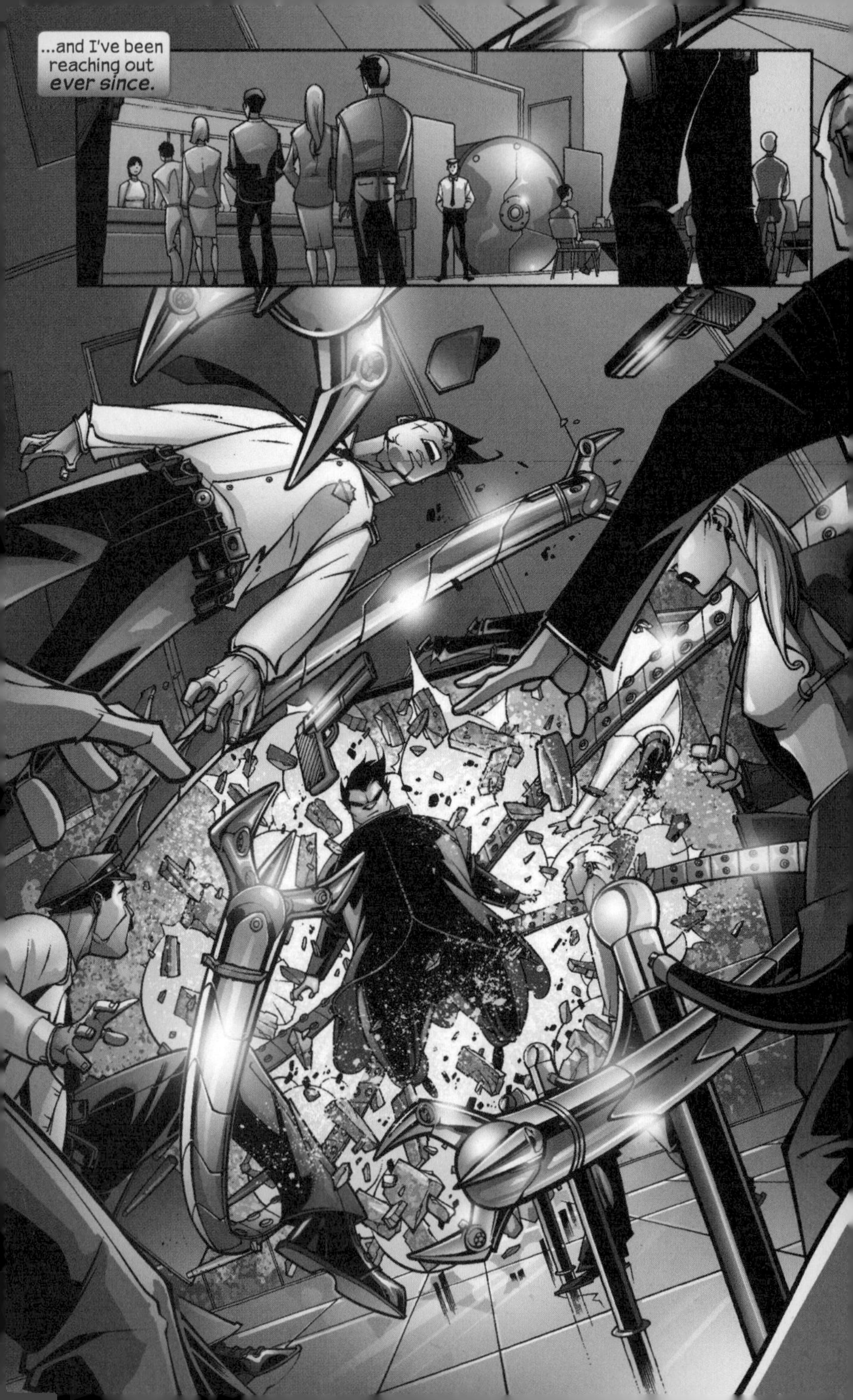
...and I've been reaching out *ever since.*

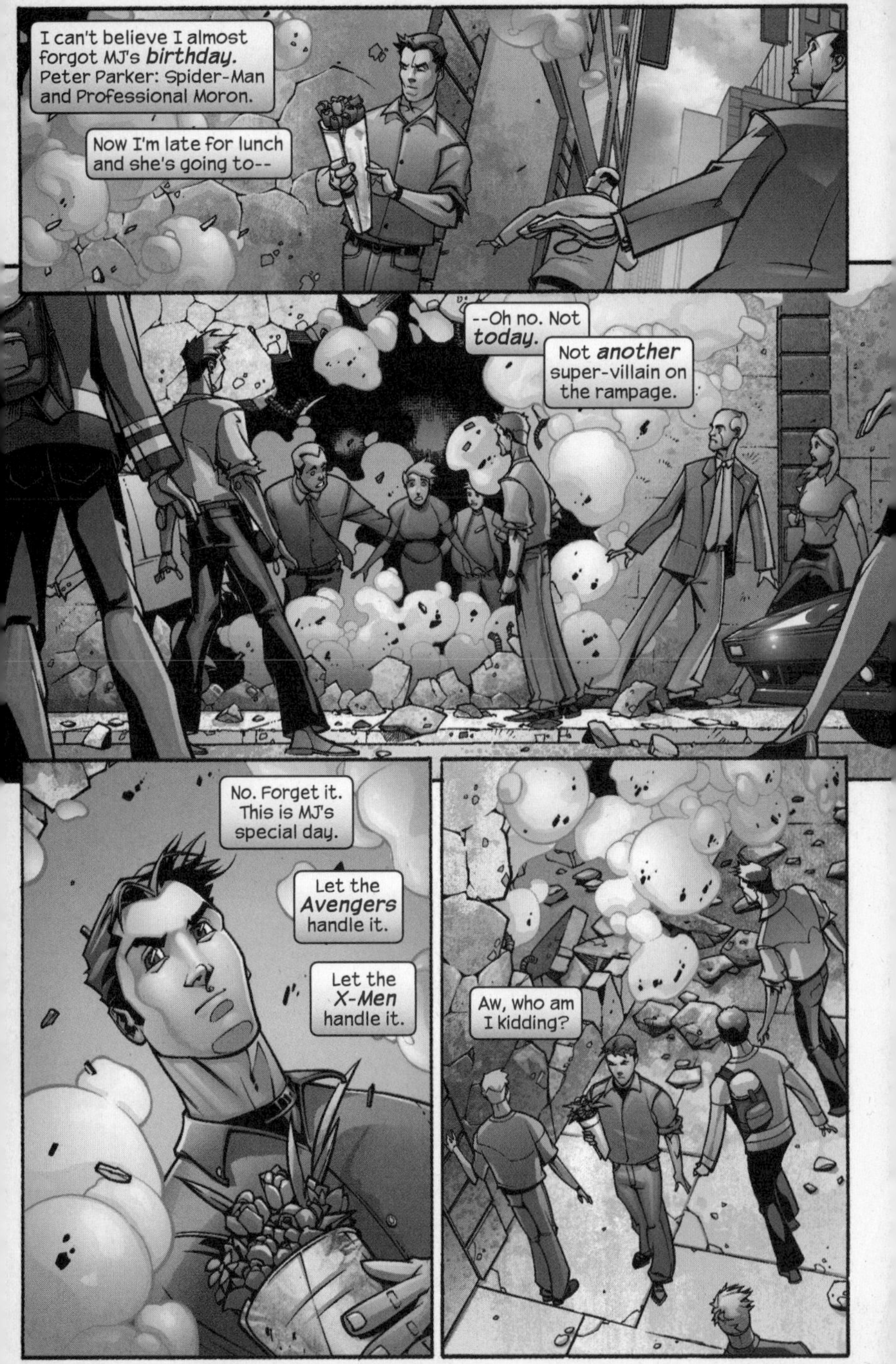

I can't believe I almost forgot MJ's *birthday.* Peter Parker: Spider-Man and Professional Moron.
Now I'm late for lunch and she's going to--
--Oh no. Not *today.*
Not *another* super-villain on the rampage.
No. Forget it. This is MJ's special day.
Let the *Avengers* handle it.
Let the *X-Men* handle it.
Aw, who am I kidding?

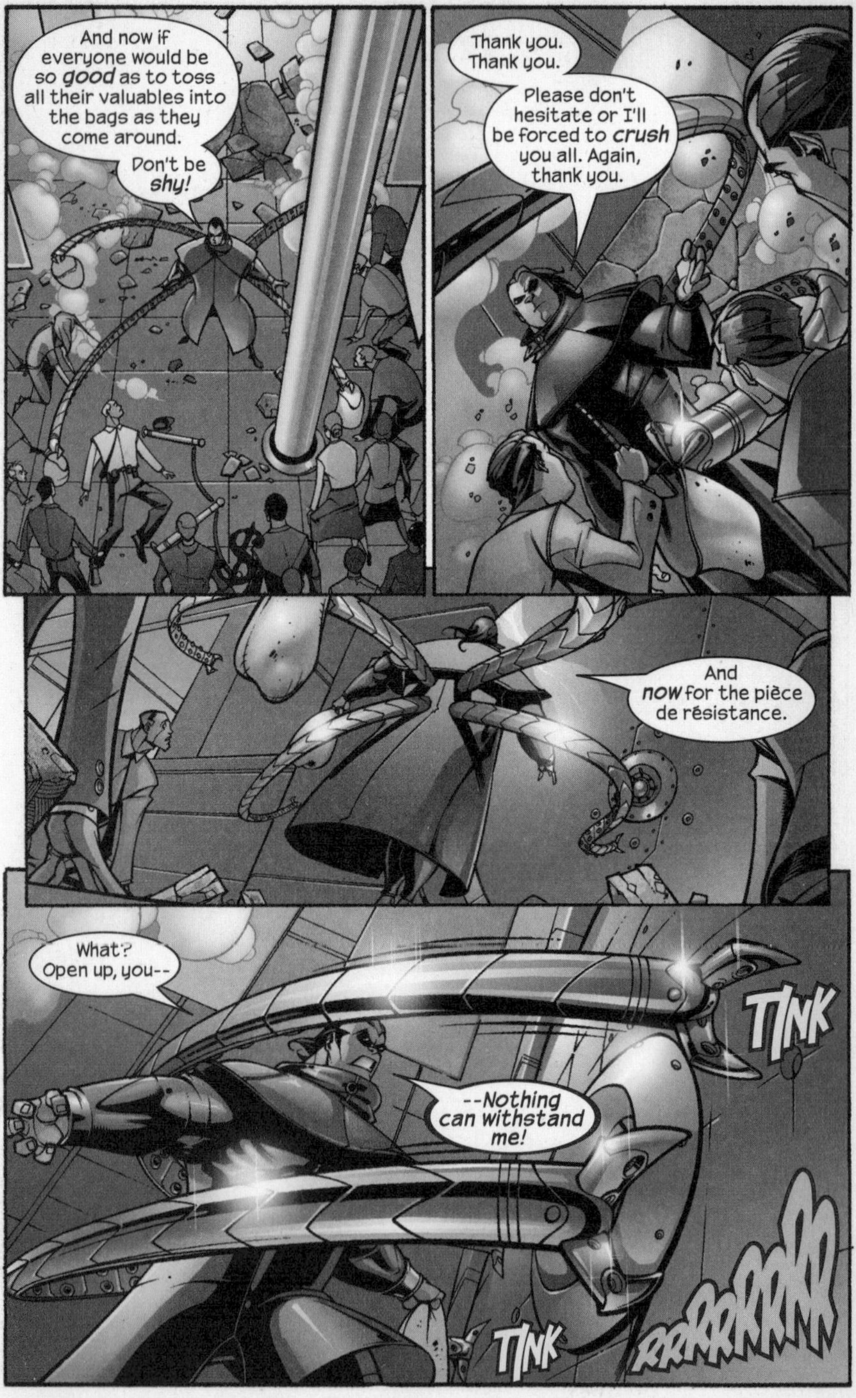
And now if everyone would be so *good* as to toss all their valuables into the bags as they come around.
Don't be *shy!*
Thank you. Thank you.
Please don't hesitate or I'll be forced to *crush* you all. Again, thank you.
And *now* for the pièce de résistance.
What? Open up, you--
--Nothing can withstand me!
TINK
TINK
RRRRRRRRR

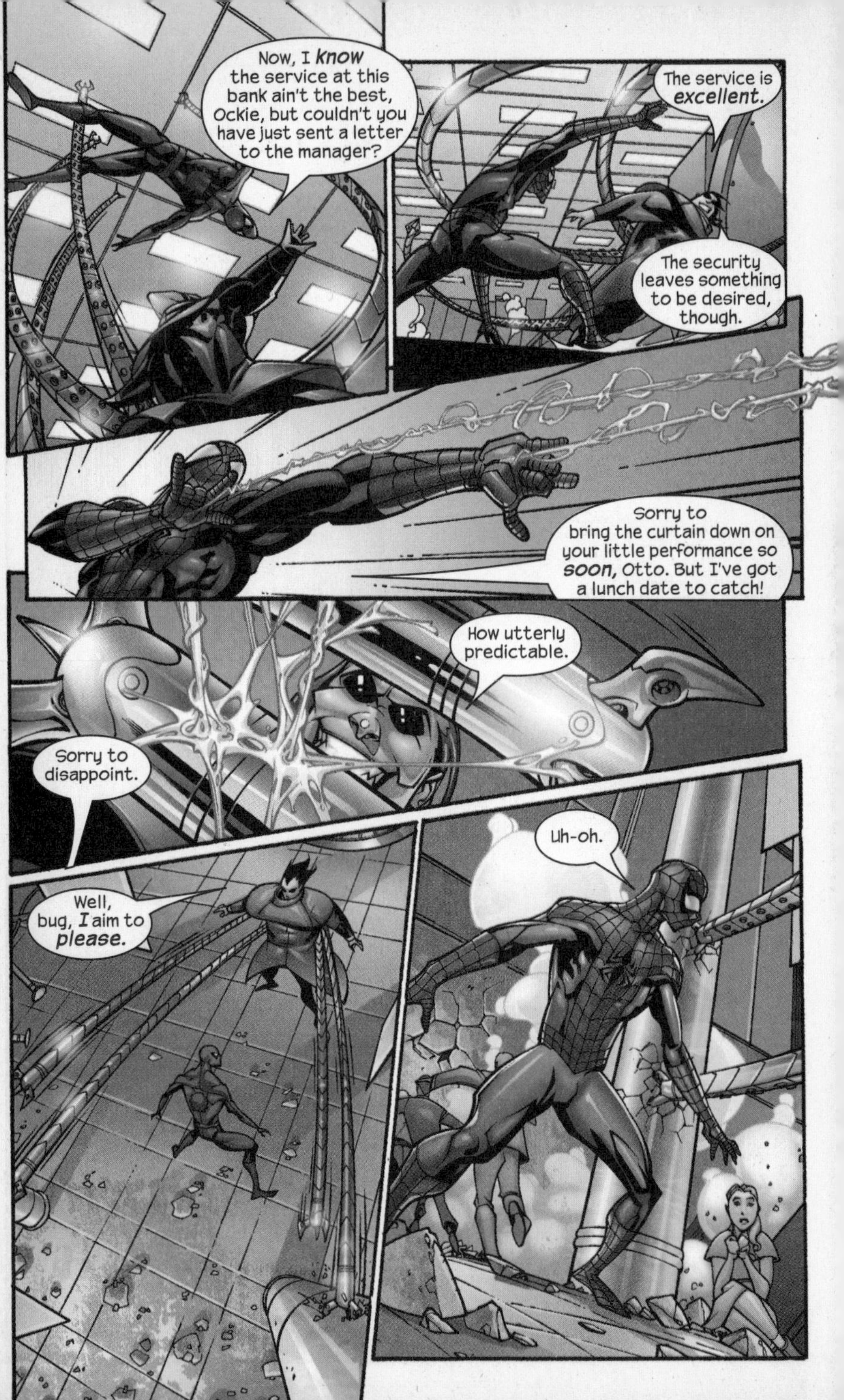
Now, I know the service at this bank ain't the best, Ockie, but couldn't you have just sent a letter to the manager?
The service is excellent.
The security leaves something to be desired, though.
Sorry to bring the curtain down on your little performance so soon, Otto. But I've got a lunch date to catch!
How utterly predictable.
Sorry to disappoint.
Well, bug, I aim to please.
Uh-oh.

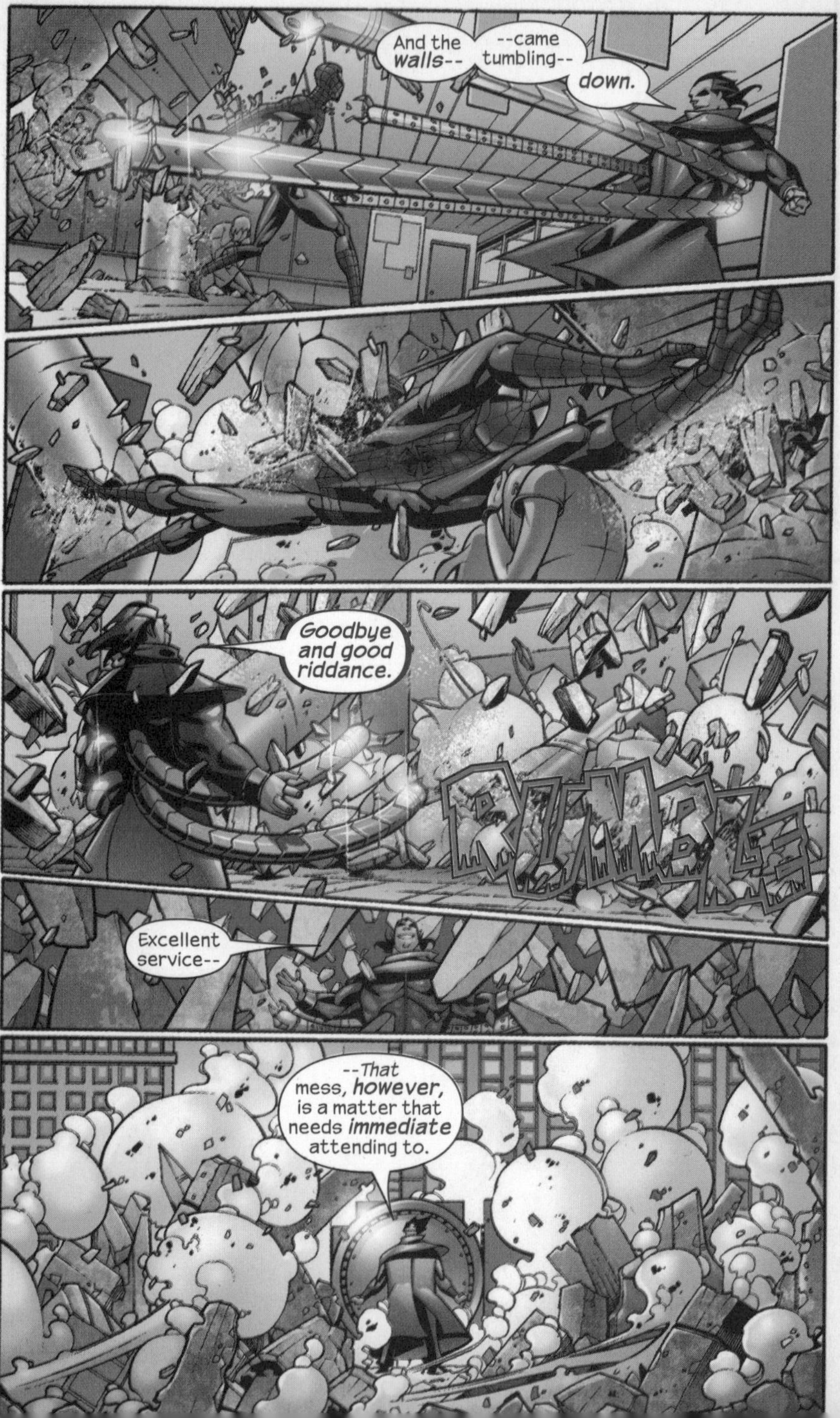
And the walls--
--came tumbling--
down.
Goodbye and good riddance.
Excellent service--
--That mess, however, is a matter that needs immediate attending to.

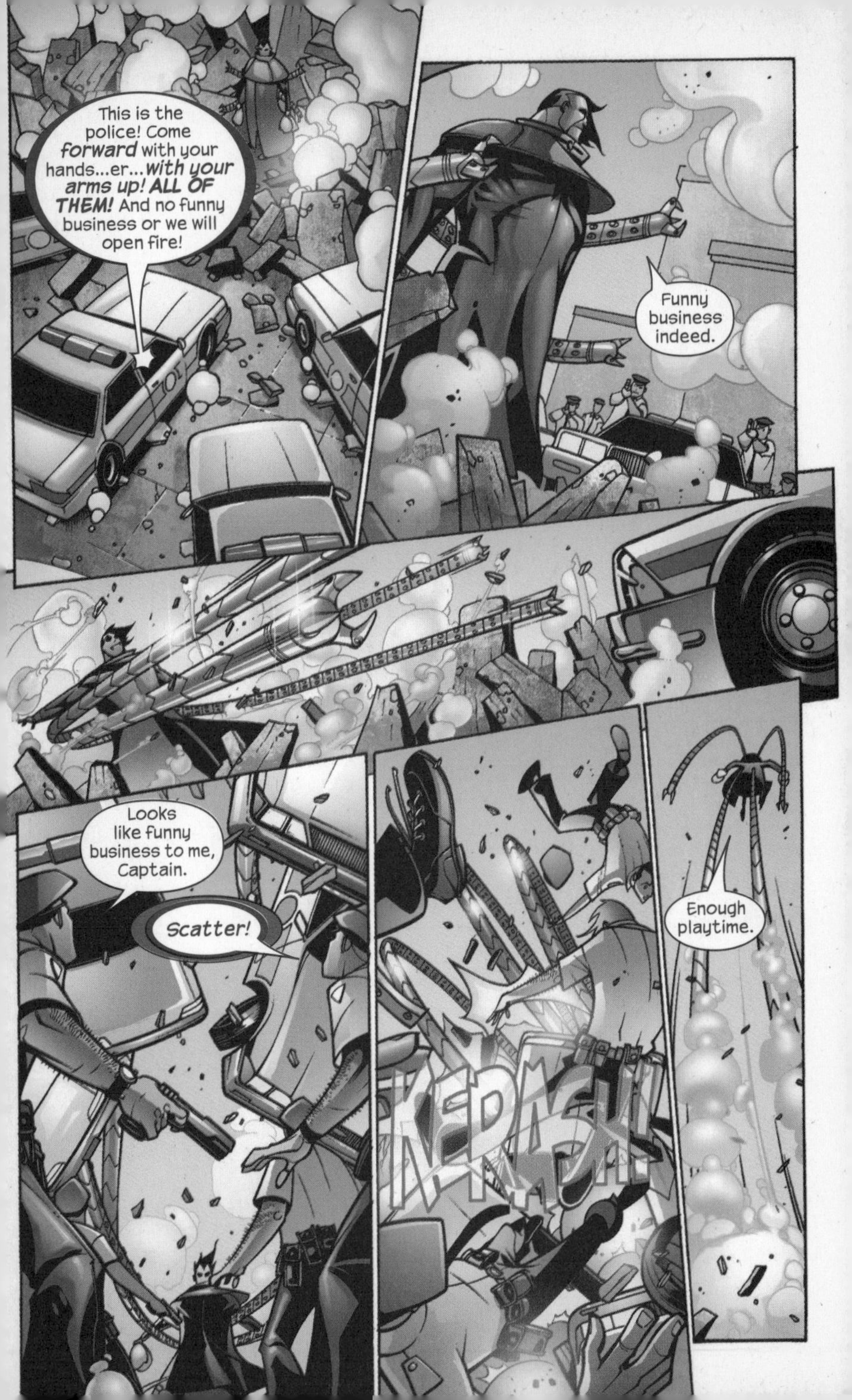
This is the police! Come forward with your hands...er...with your arms up! ALL OF THEM! And no funny business or we will open fire!
Funny business indeed.
Looks like funny business to me, Captain.
Scatter!
KRRNCH!
Enough playtime.

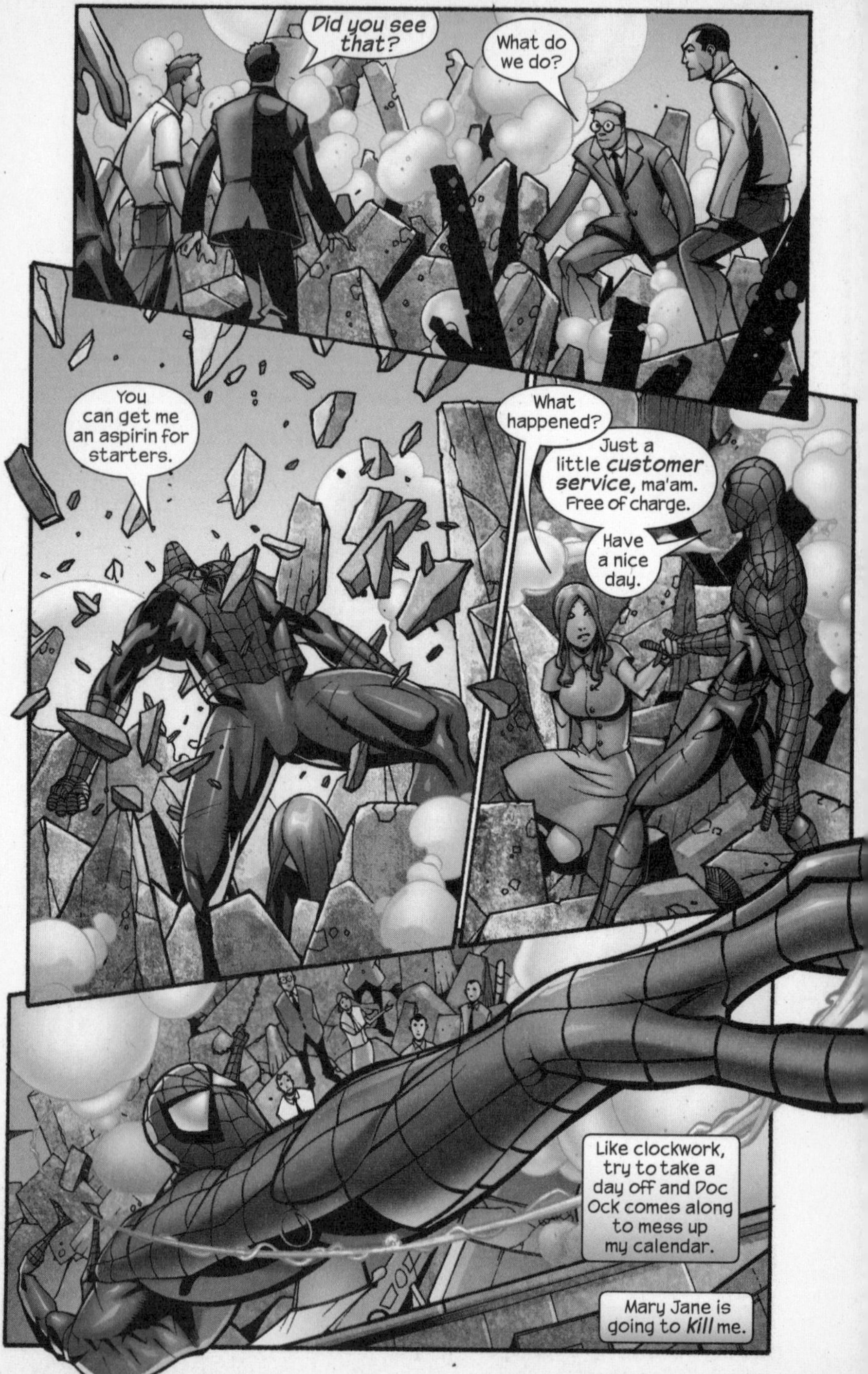
Did you see that?
What do we do?
You can get me an aspirin for starters.
What happened?
Just a little customer service, ma'am. Free of charge.
Have a nice day.
Like clockwork, try to take a day off and Doc Ock comes along to mess up my calendar.
Mary Jane is going to kill me.

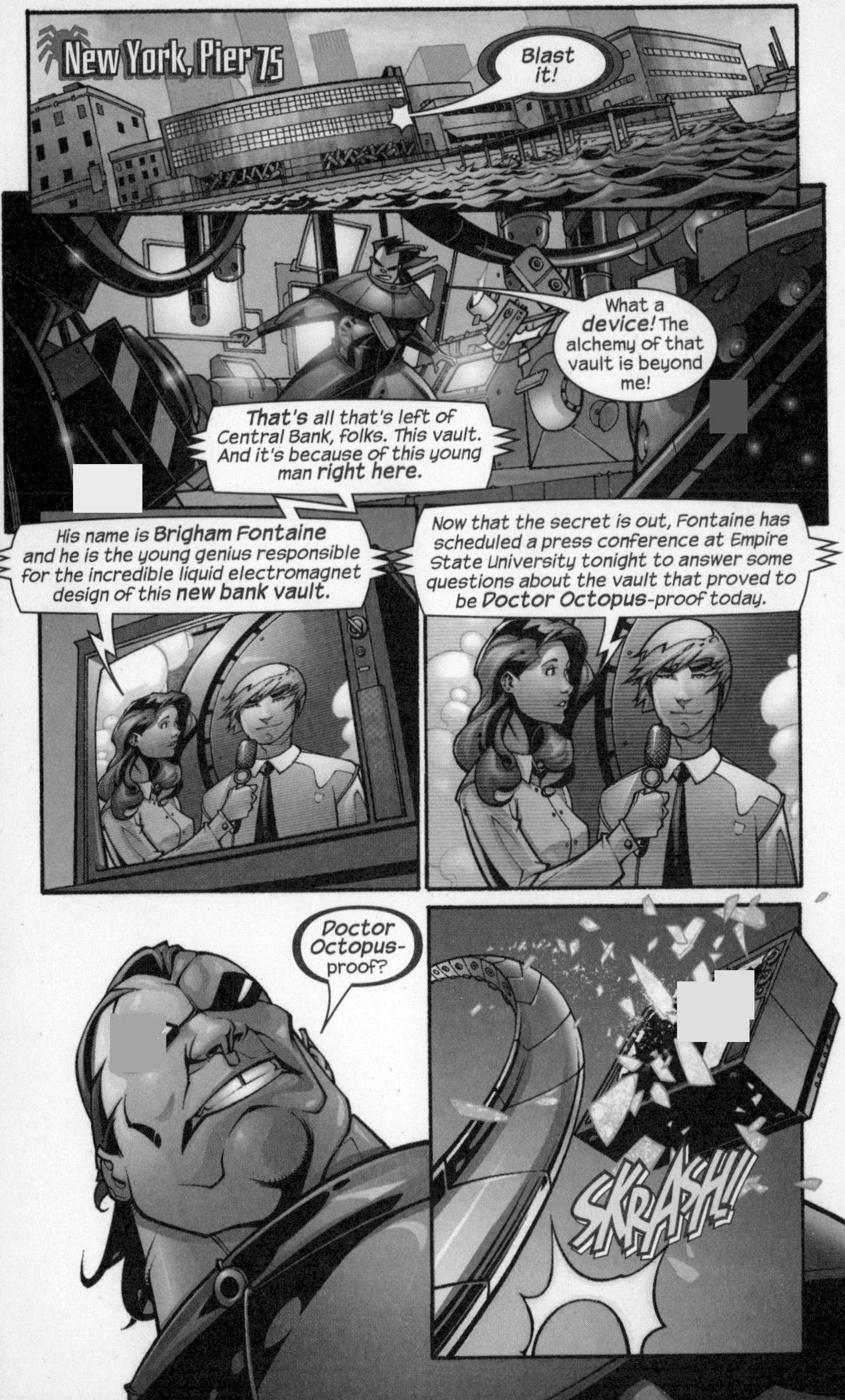

New York, Pier 75
Blast it!
What a device! The alchemy of that vault is beyond me!
That's all that's left of Central Bank, folks. This vault. And it's because of this young man right here.
His name is Brigham Fontaine and he is the young genius responsible for the incredible liquid electromagnet design of this new bank vault.
Now that the secret is out, Fontaine has scheduled a press conference at Empire State University tonight to answer some questions about the vault that proved to be Doctor Octopus-proof today.
Doctor Octopus-proof?
SKRASH!

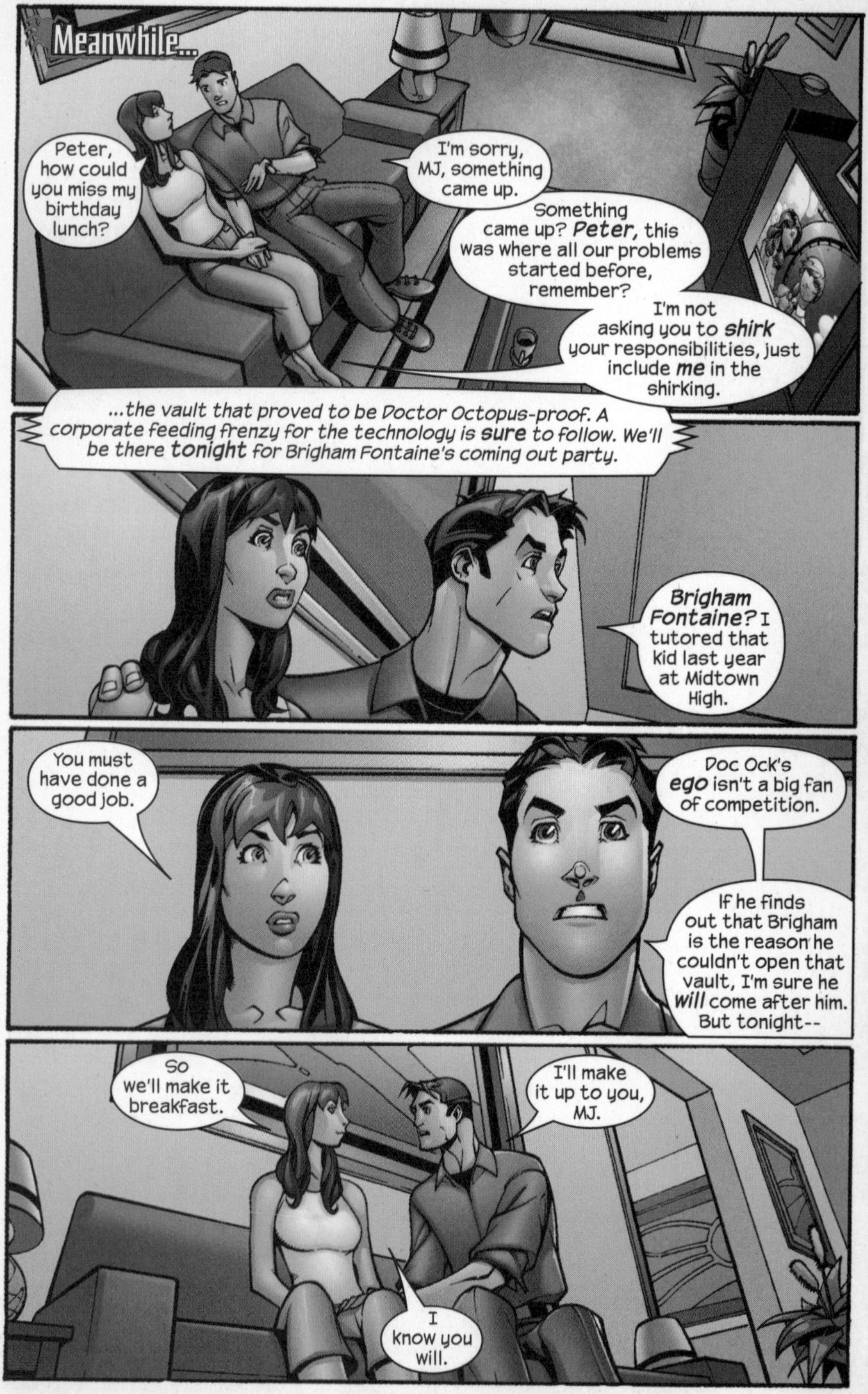
Meanwhile...
Peter, how could you miss my birthday lunch?
I'm sorry, MJ, something came up.
Something came up? Peter, this was where all our problems started before, remember?
I'm not asking you to shirk your responsibilities, just include me in the shirking.
...the vault that proved to be Doctor Octopus-proof. A corporate feeding frenzy for the technology is sure to follow. We'll be there tonight for Brigham Fontaine's coming out party.
Brigham Fontaine? I tutored that kid last year at Midtown High.
You must have done a good job.
Doc Ock's ego isn't a big fan of competition.
If he finds out that Brigham is the reason he couldn't open that vault, I'm sure he will come after him. But tonight--
So we'll make it breakfast.
I'll make it up to you, MJ.
I know you will.

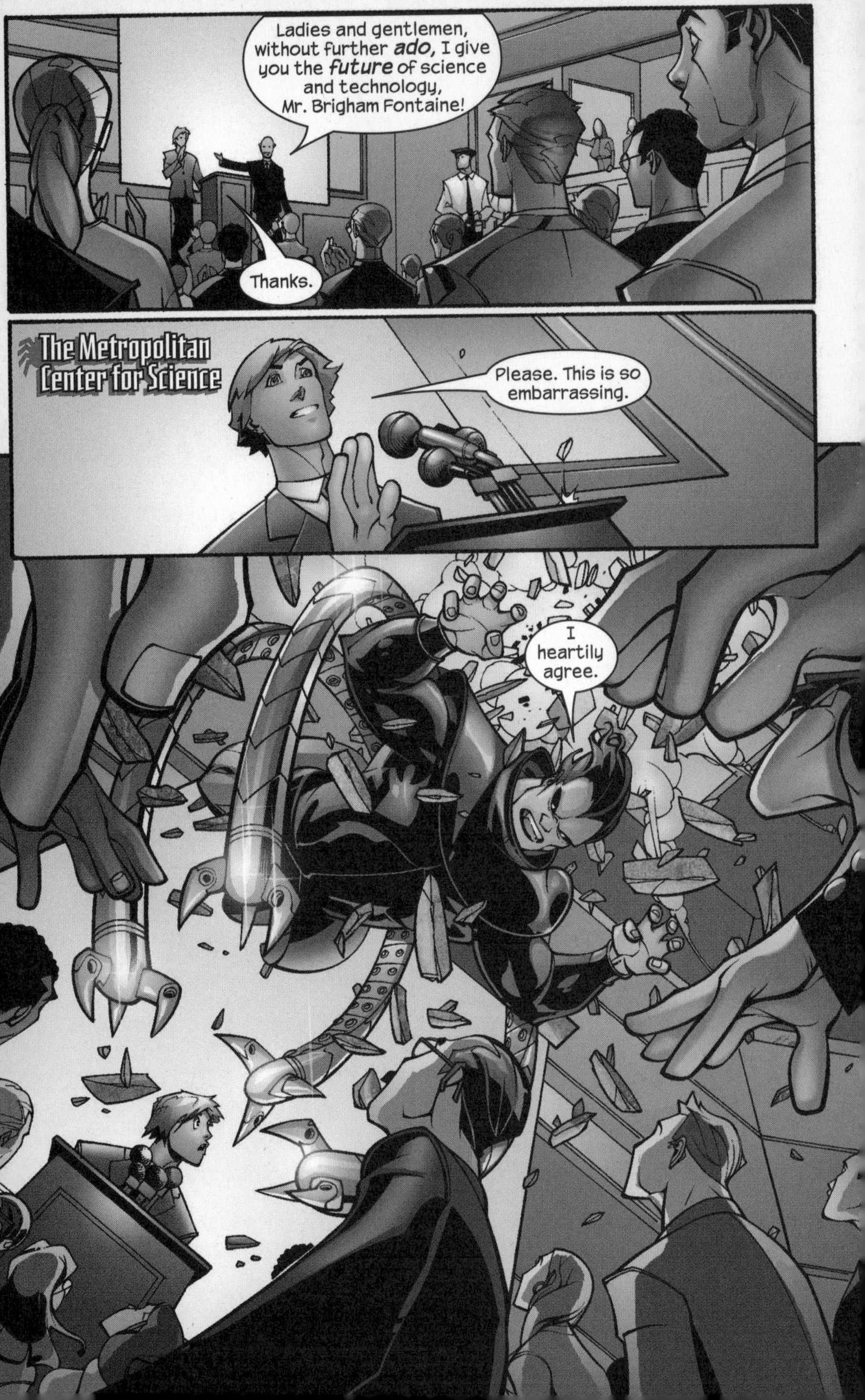

Ladies and gentlemen, without further *ado,* I give you the *future* of science and technology, Mr. Brigham Fontaine!
Thanks.
The Metropolitan Center for Science
Please. This is so embarrassing.
I heartily agree.

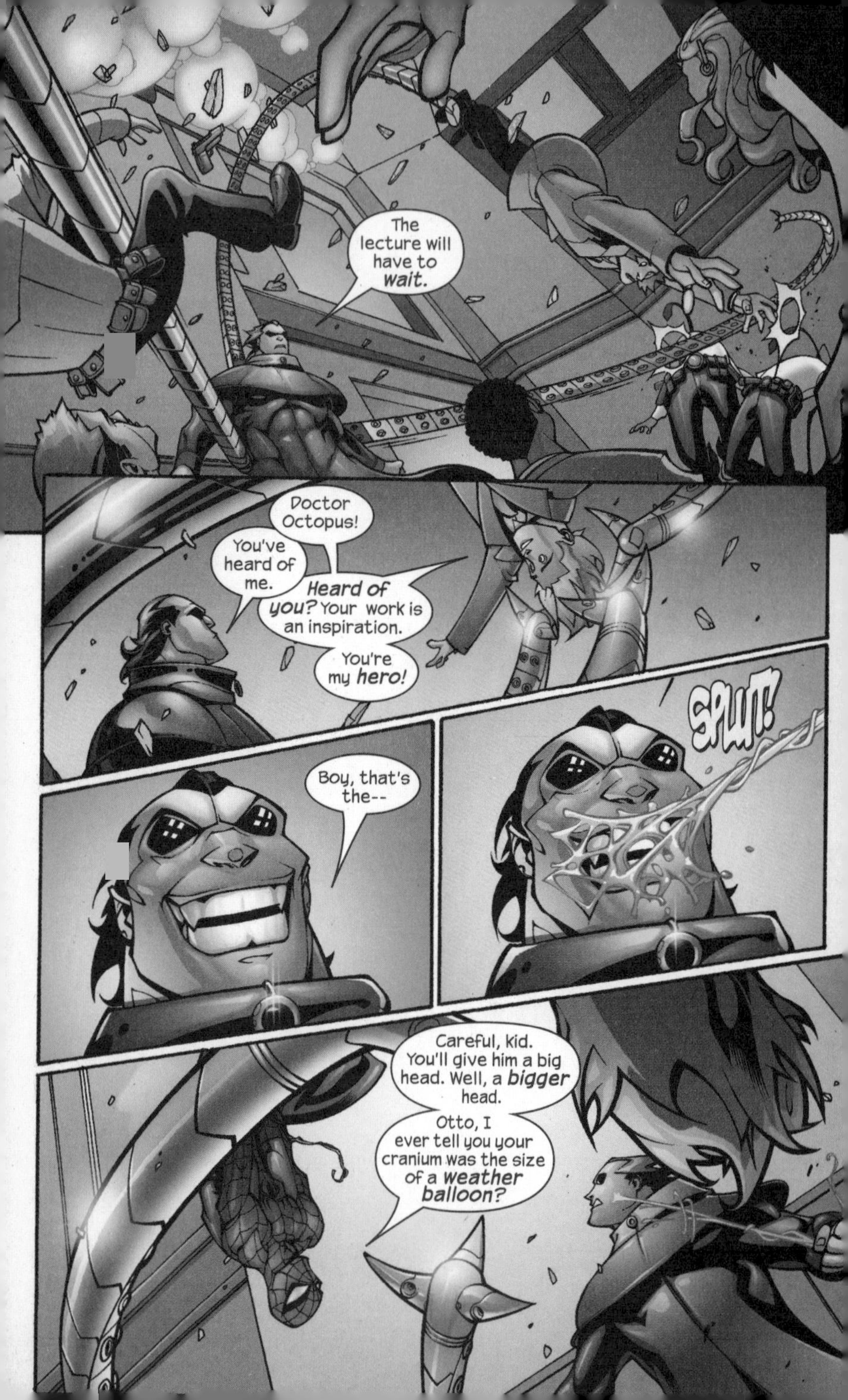
The lecture will have to *wait.*
Doctor Octopus!
You've heard of me.
Heard of you? Your work is an inspiration.
You're my *hero!*
Boy, that's the--
SPLUT!
Careful, kid. You'll give him a big head. Well, a *bigger* head.
Otto, I ever tell you your cranium was the size of a *weather balloon?*

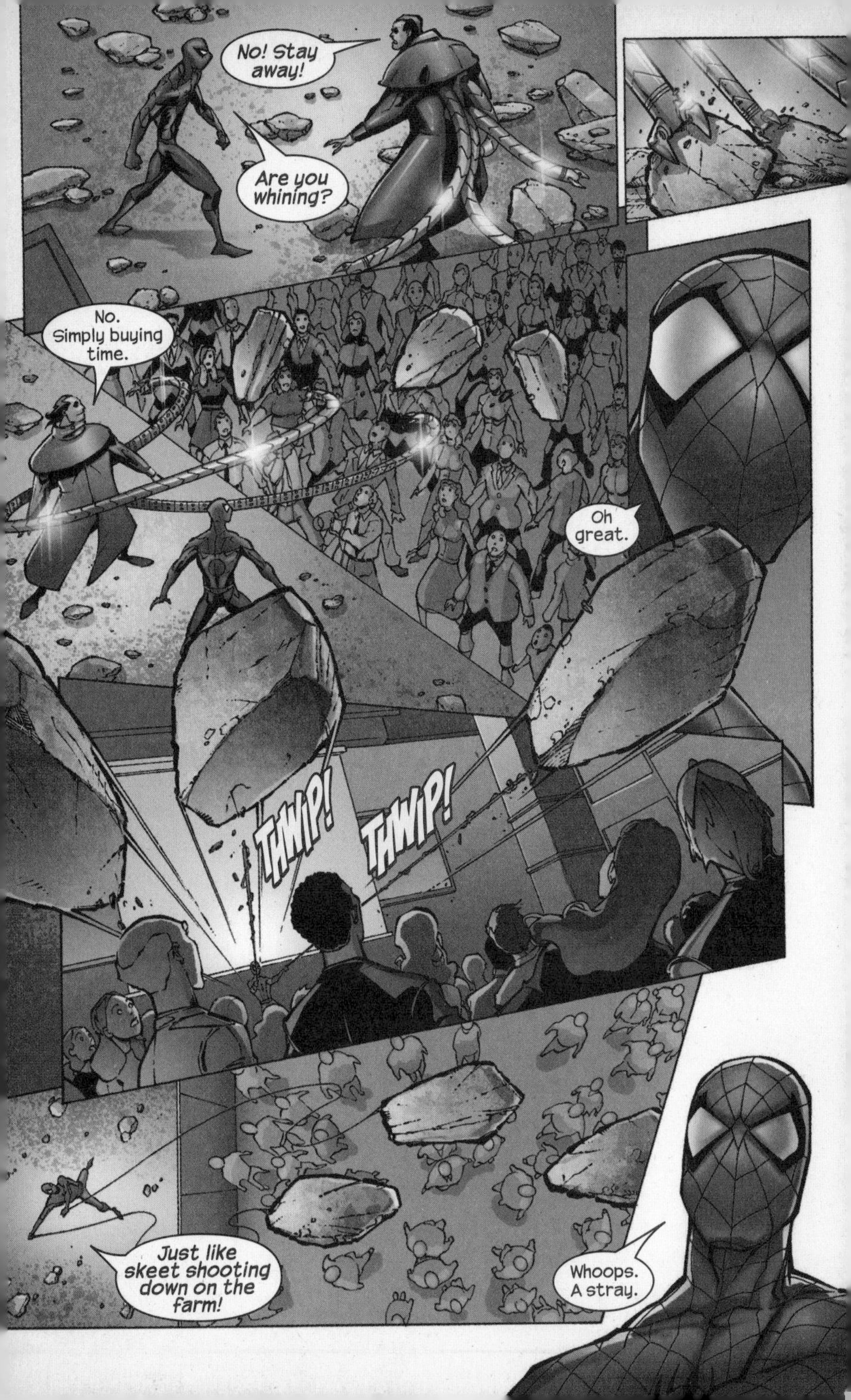
No! Stay away!
Are you whining?
No. Simply buying time.
Oh great.
THWIP!
THWIP!
Just like skeet shooting down on the farm!
Whoops. A stray.

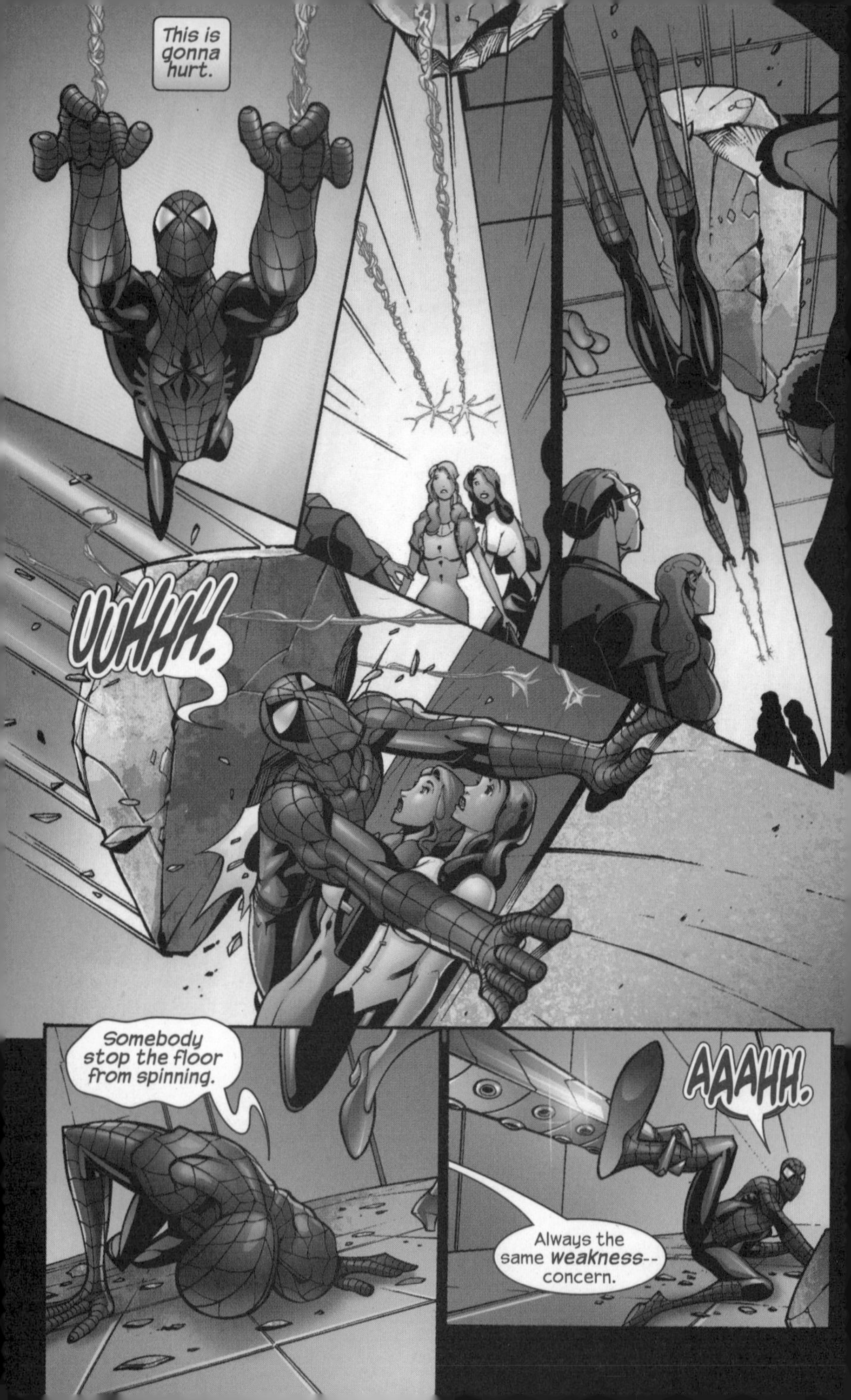
This is gonna hurt.
UUHHH.
Somebody stop the floor from spinning.
AAAHH.
Always the same weakness-- concern.

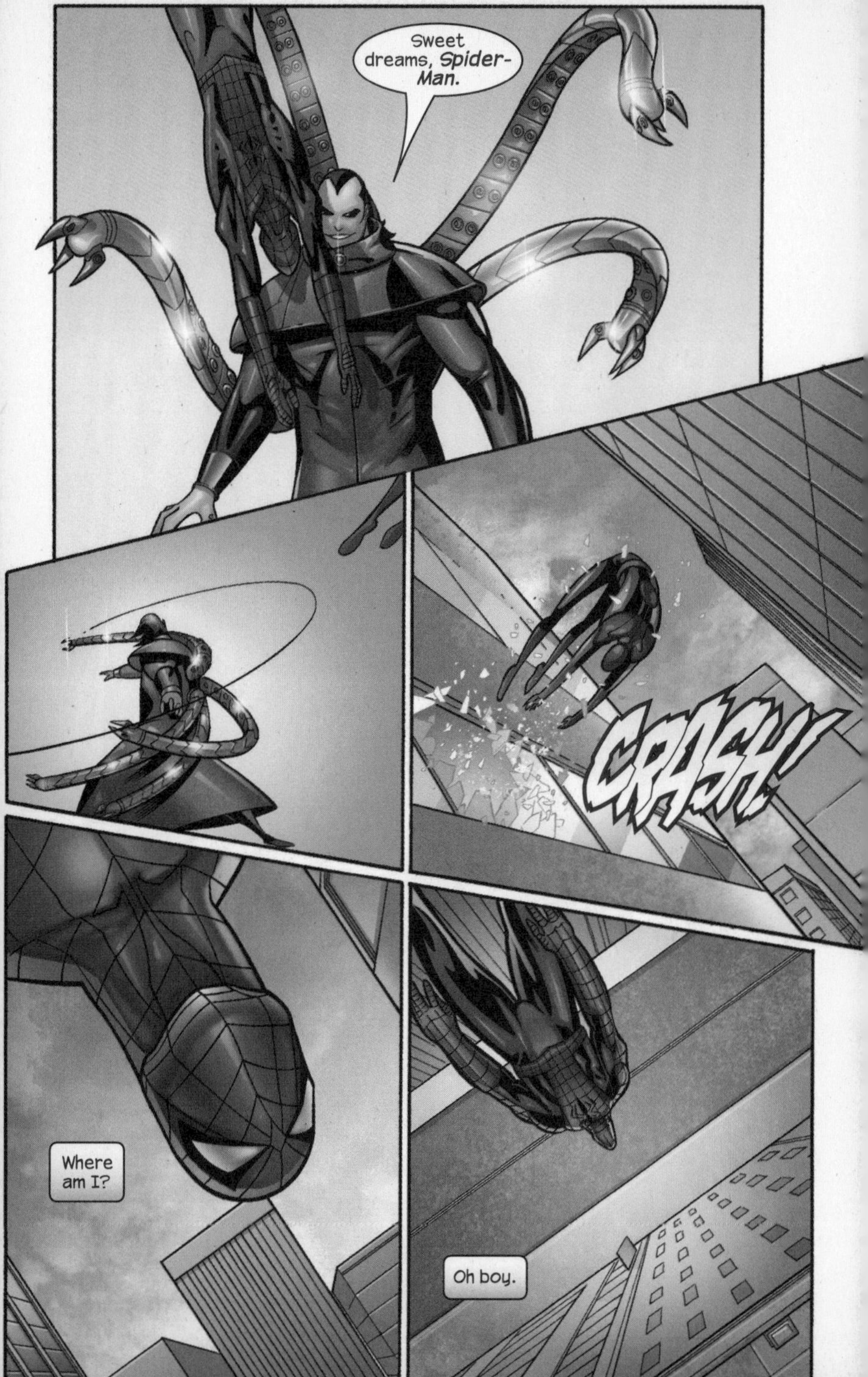
Sweet dreams, Spider-Man.
CRASH!
Where am I?
Oh boy.

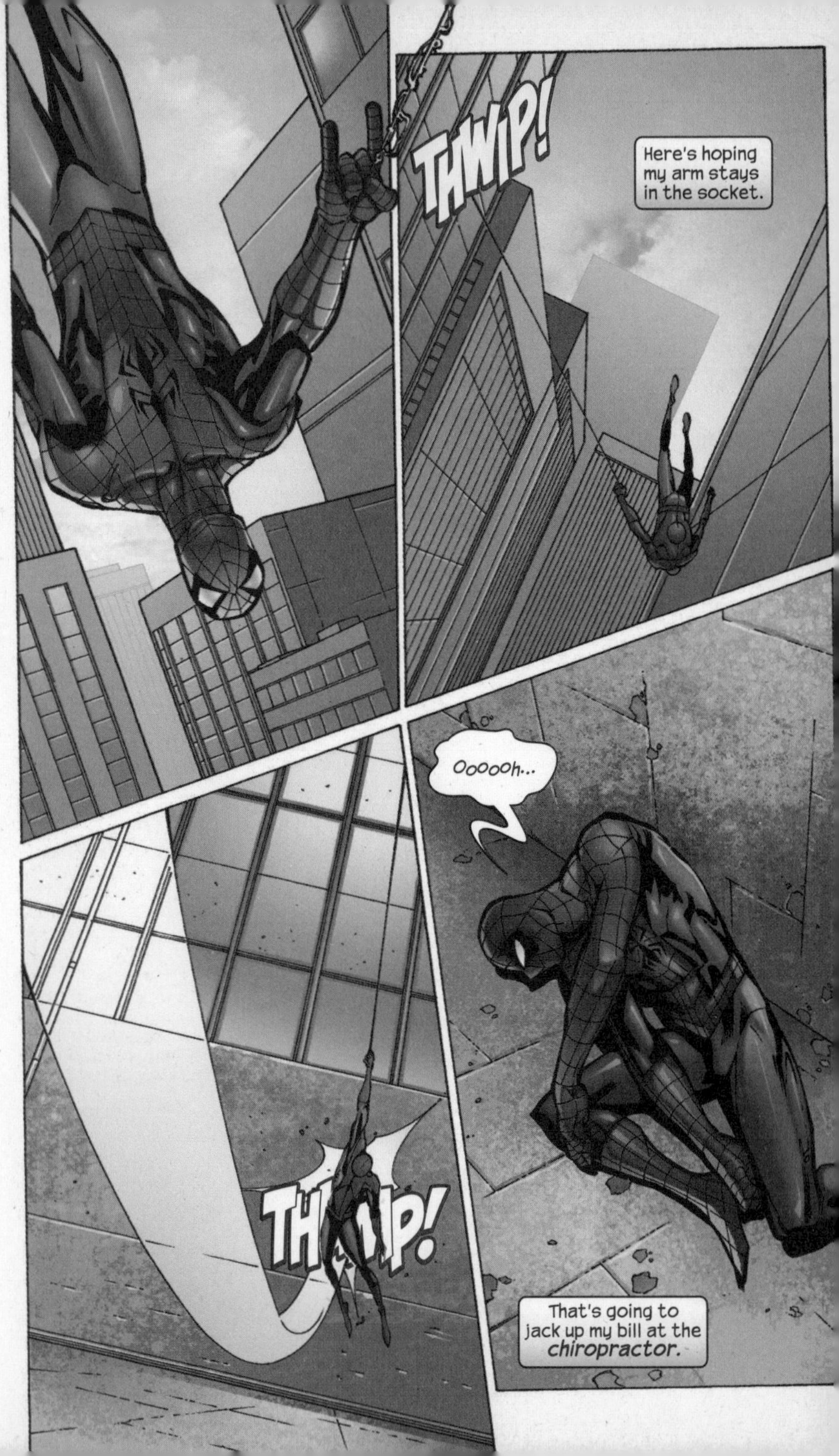
THWIP!
Here's hoping my arm stays in the socket.
THWIP!
Oooooh...
That's going to jack up my bill at the *chiropractor*.

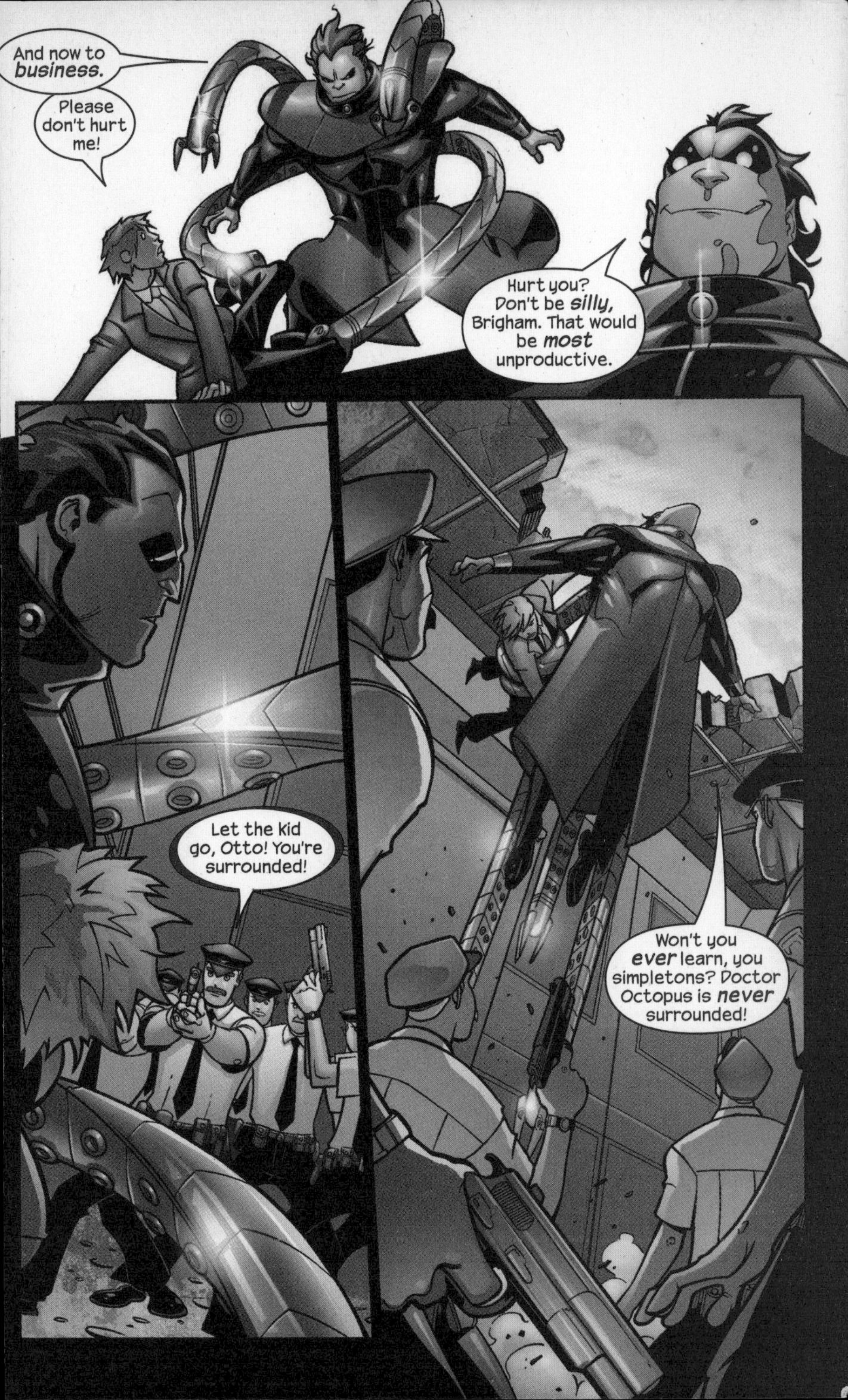
And now to business.
Please don't hurt me!
Hurt you? Don't be silly, Brigham. That would be most unproductive.
Let the kid go, Otto! You're surrounded!
Won't you ever learn, you simpletons? Doctor Octopus is never surrounded!

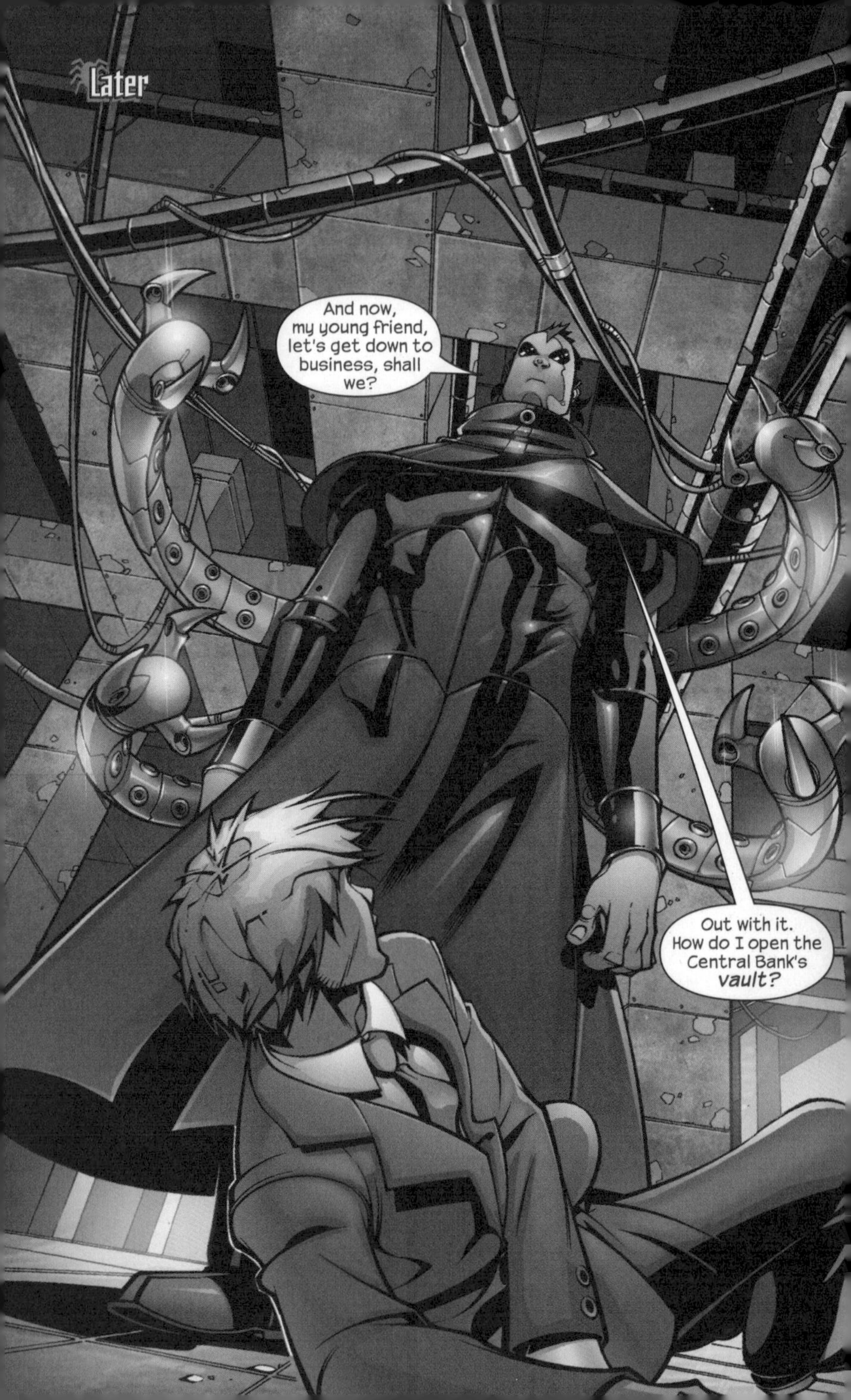
Later
And now, my young friend, let's get down to business, shall we?
Out with it. How do I open the Central Bank's *vault?*

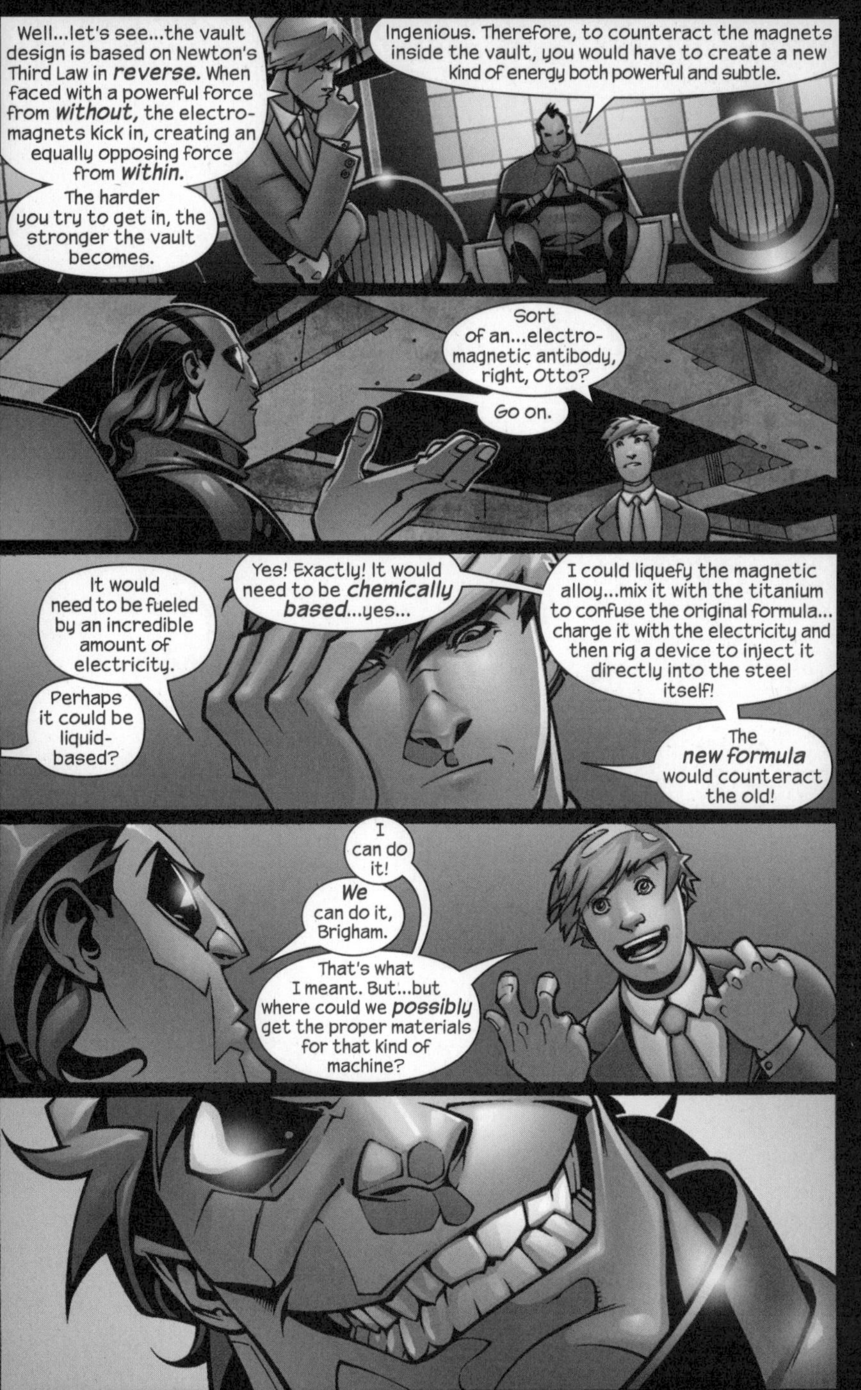
Well...let's see...the vault design is based on Newton's Third Law in *reverse.* When faced with a powerful force from *without,* the electro-magnets kick in, creating an equally opposing force from *within.*
The harder you try to get in, the stronger the vault becomes.
Ingenious. Therefore, to counteract the magnets inside the vault, you would have to create a new kind of energy both powerful and subtle.
Sort of an...electro-magnetic antibody, right, Otto?
Go on.
It would need to be fueled by an incredible amount of electricity.
Perhaps it could be liquid-based?
Yes! Exactly! It would need to be *chemically based*...yes...
I could liquefy the magnetic alloy...mix it with the titanium to confuse the original formula... charge it with the electricity and then rig a device to inject it directly into the steel itself!
The *new formula* would counteract the old!
I can do it!
We can do it, Brigham.
That's what I meant. But...but where could we *possibly* get the proper materials for that kind of machine?

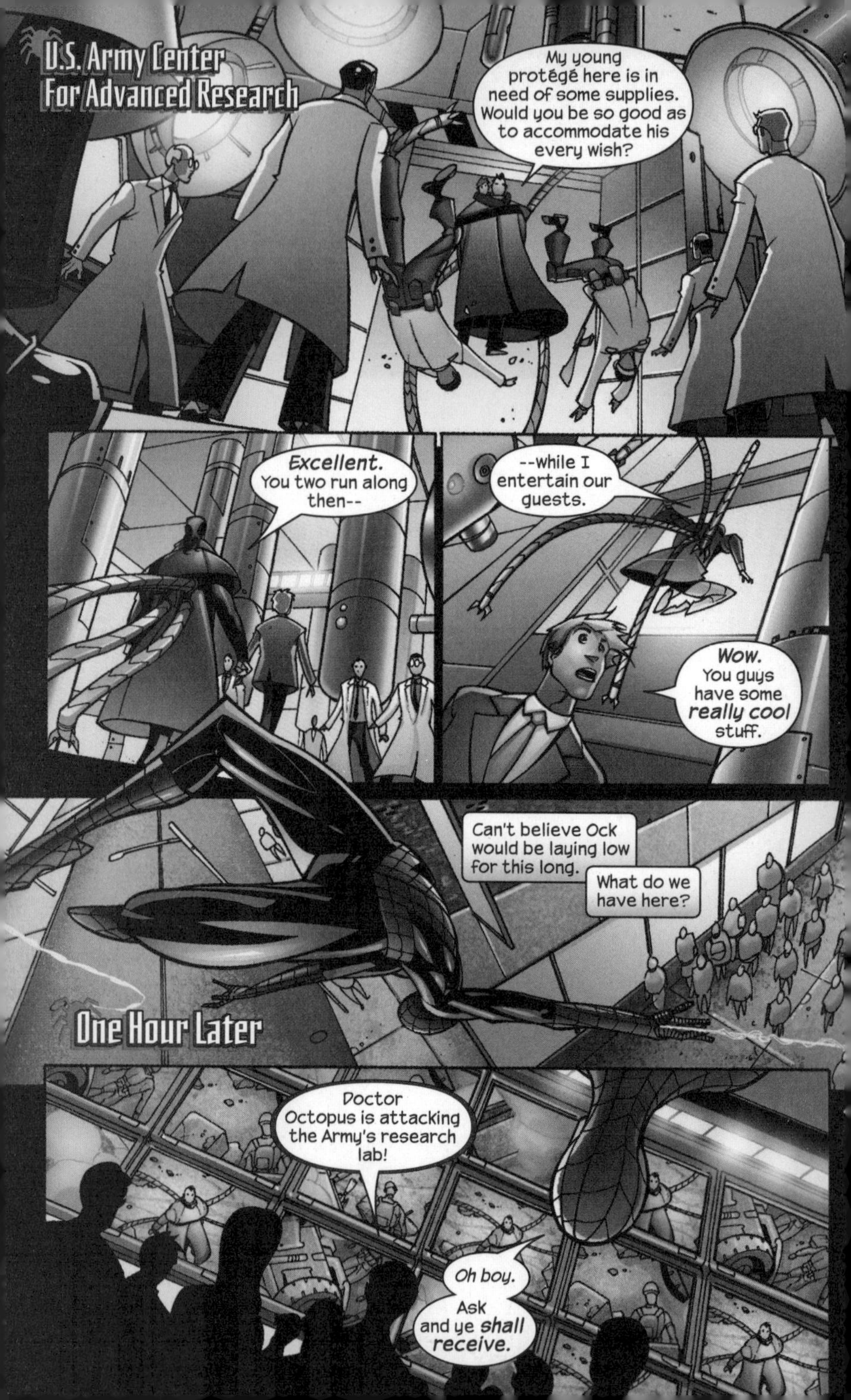
U.S. Army Center For Advanced Research
My young protégé here is in need of some supplies. Would you be so good as to accommodate his every wish?
Excellent. You two run along then--
--while I entertain our guests.
Wow. You guys have some really cool stuff.
One Hour Later
Can't believe Ock would be laying low for this long.
What do we have here?
Doctor Octopus is attacking the Army's research lab!
Oh boy.
Ask and ye shall receive.

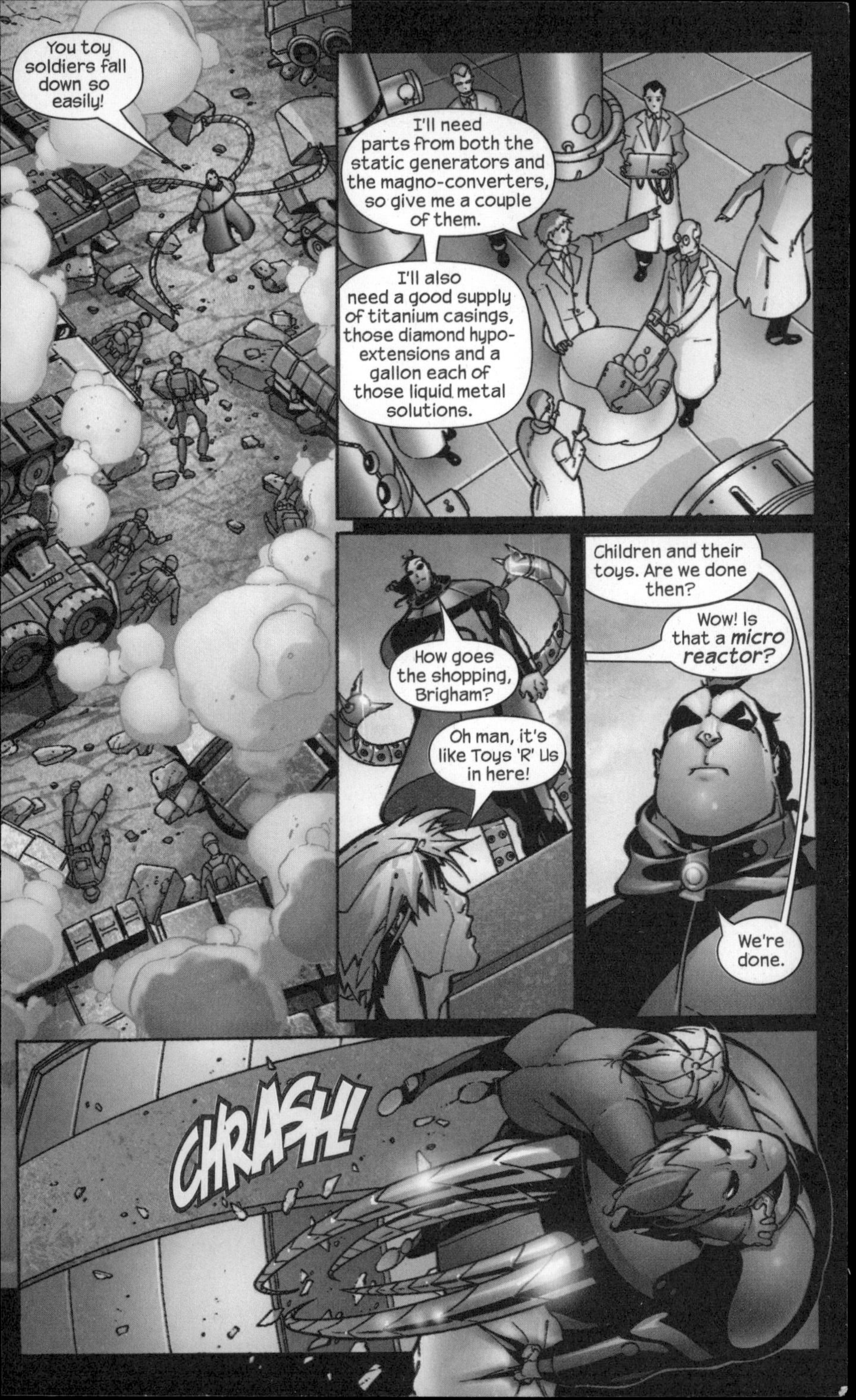
You toy soldiers fall down so easily!
I'll need parts from both the static generators and the magno-converters, so give me a couple of them.
I'll also need a good supply of titanium casings, those diamond hypo-extensions and a gallon each of those liquid metal solutions.
How goes the shopping, Brigham?
Oh man, it's like Toys 'R' Us in here!
Children and their toys. Are we done then?
Wow! Is that a *micro reactor?*
We're done.
CHRASH!

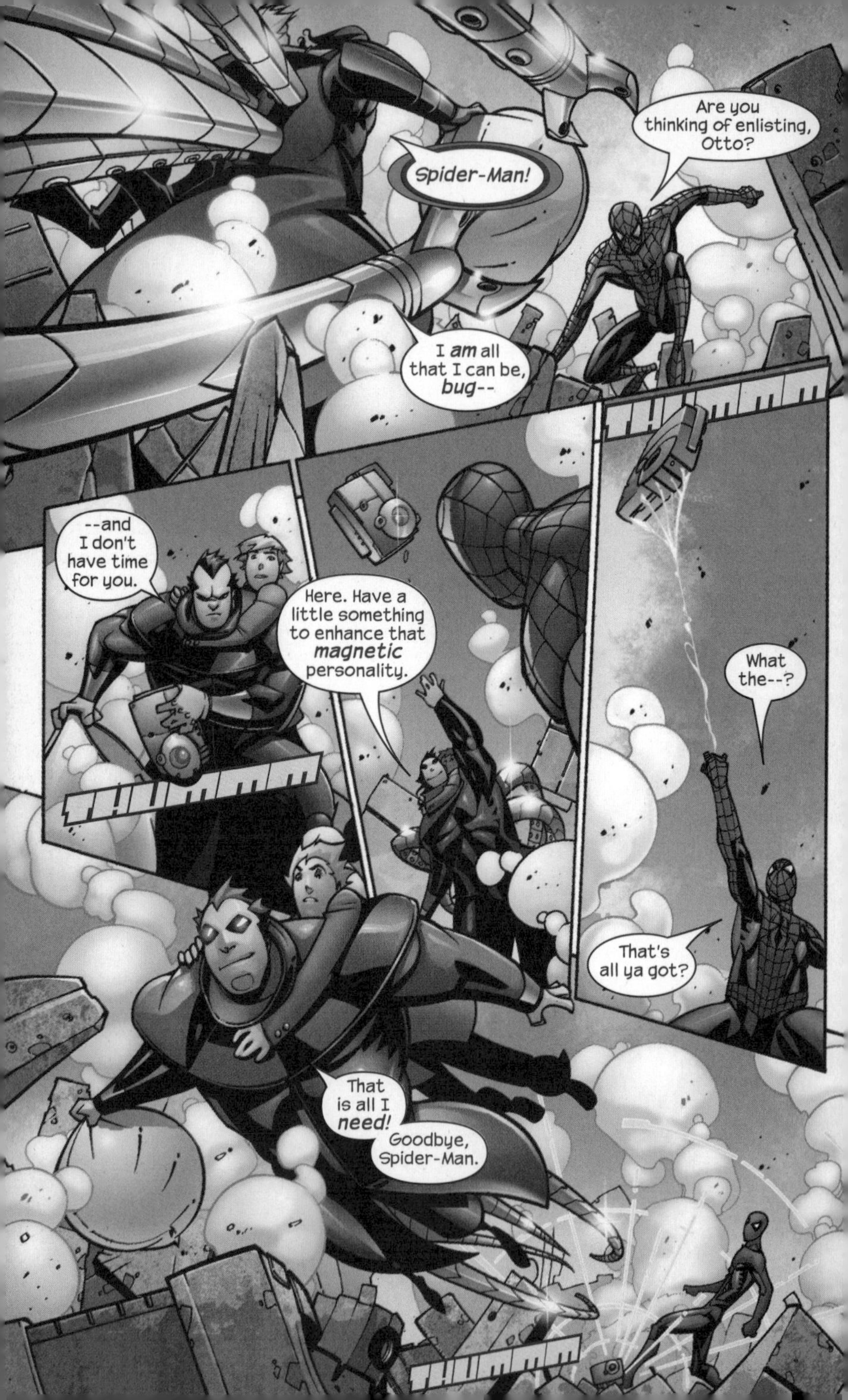
Spider-Man!
Are you thinking of enlisting, Otto?
I *am* all that I can be, *bug*--
THUMMMM
--and I don't have time for you.
Here. Have a little something to enhance that *magnetic* personality.
THUMMMM
What the--?
That's all ya got?
That is all I *need!*
Goodbye, Spider-Man.
THUMMMM

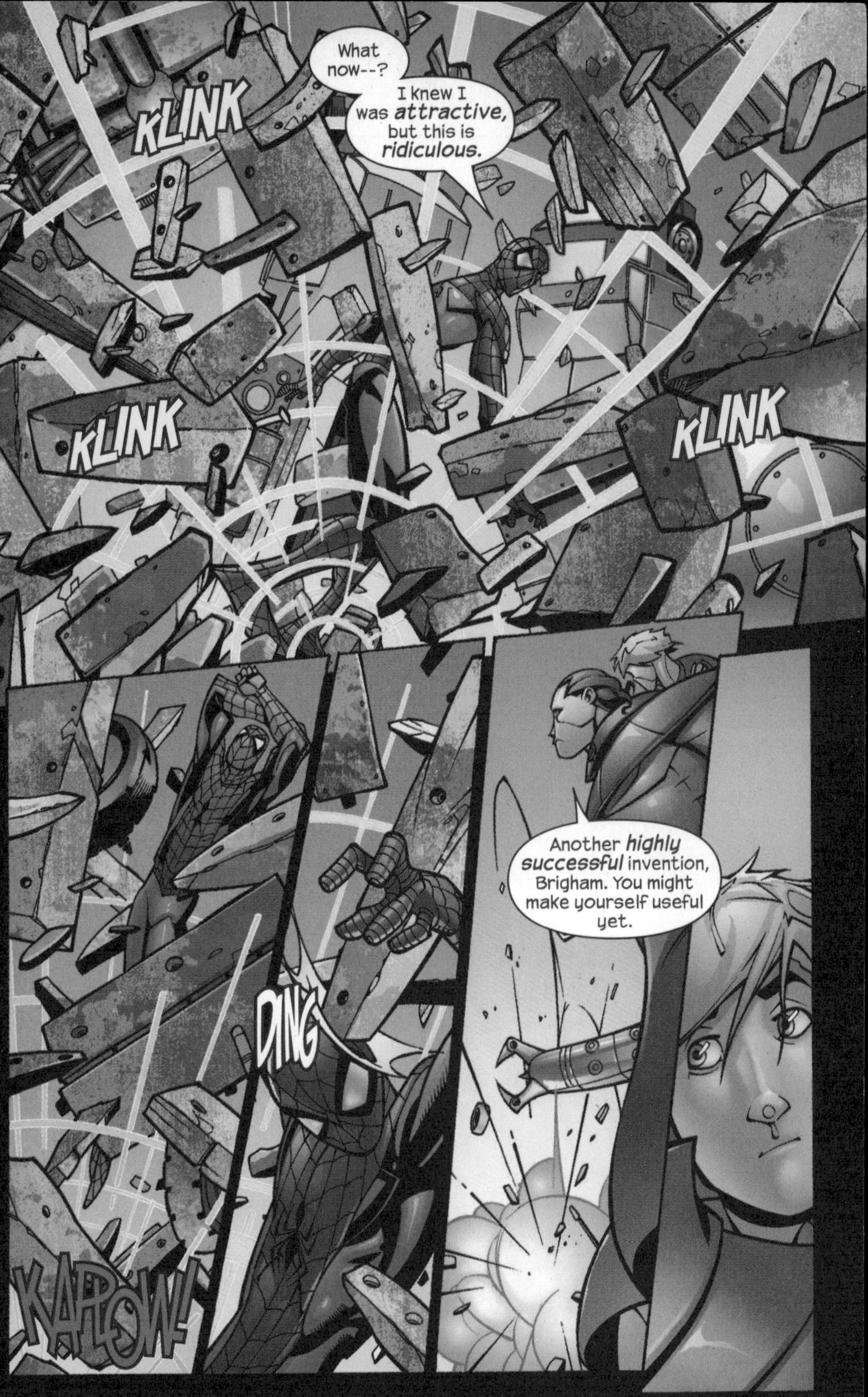

What now--?
I knew I was *attractive*, but this is *ridiculous.*
KLINK
KLINK
KLINK
DING
KAPOW!
Another *highly successful* invention, Brigham. You might make yourself useful yet.

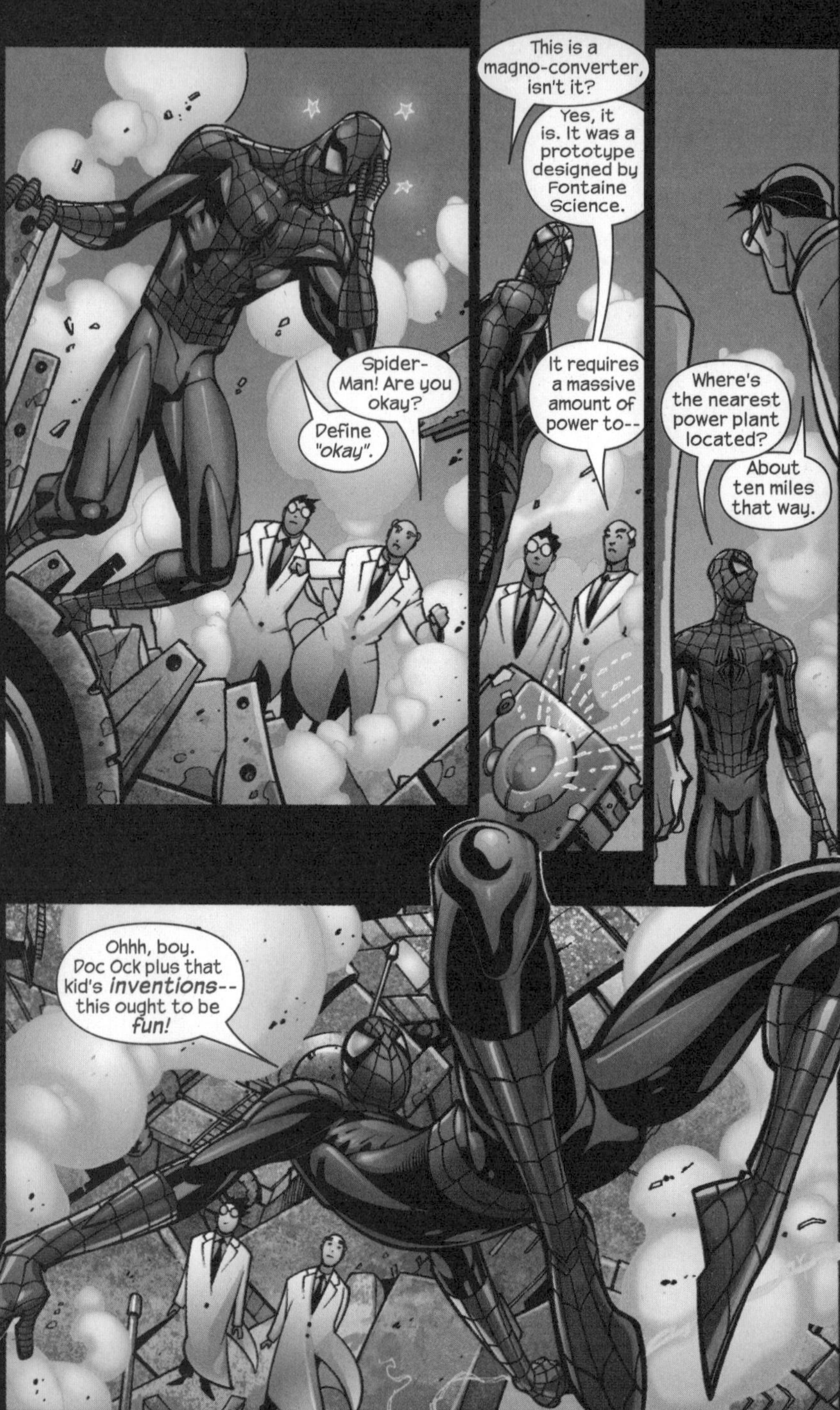
Spider-Man! Are you okay?
Define "okay".
This is a magno-converter, isn't it?
Yes, it is. It was a prototype designed by Fontaine Science.
It requires a massive amount of power to--
Where's the nearest power plant located?
About ten miles that way.
Ohhh, boy. Doc Ock plus that kid's *inventions*-- this ought to be *fun!*

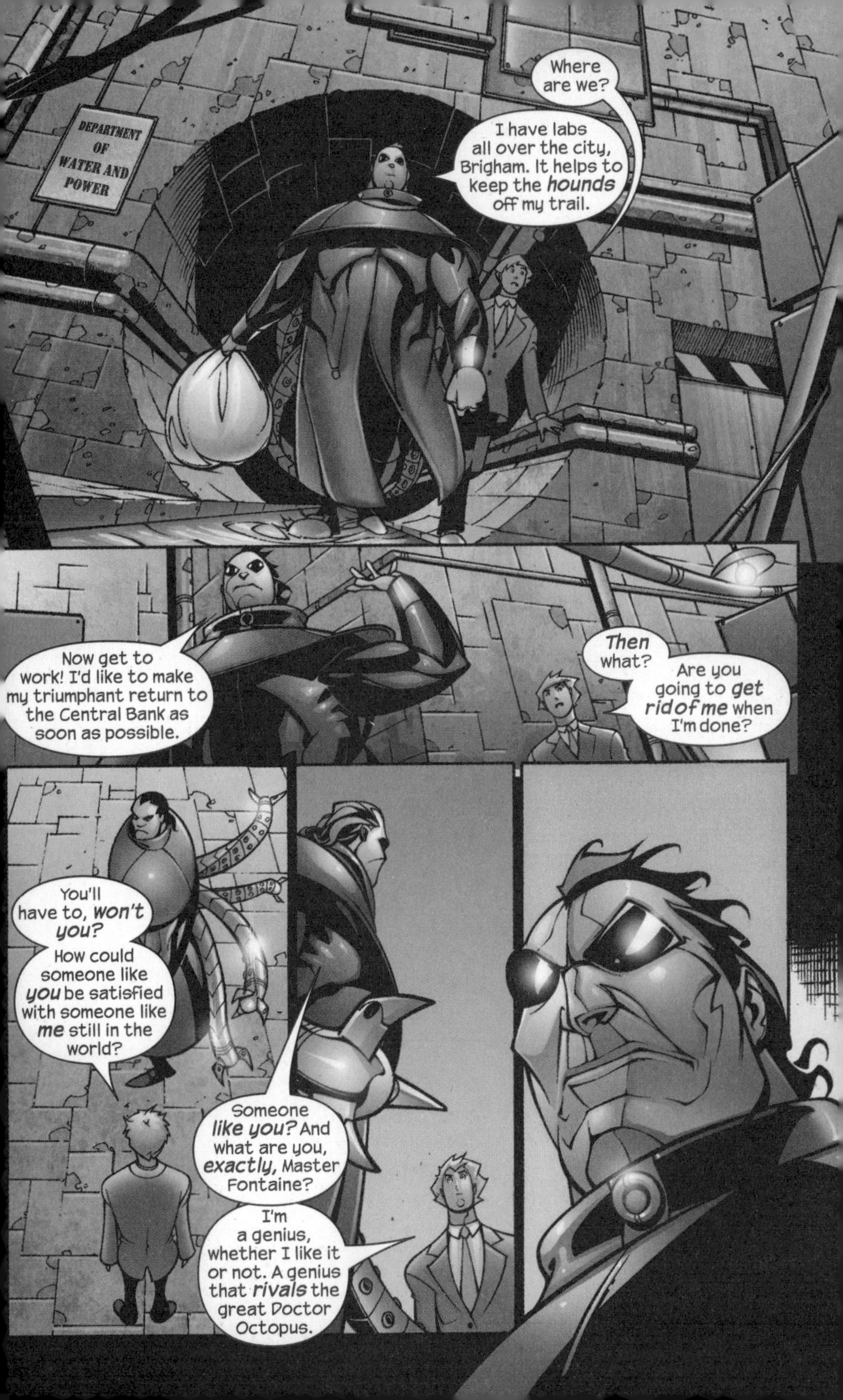
DEPARTMENT OF WATER AND POWER
Where are we?
I have labs all over the city, Brigham. It helps to keep the hounds off my trail.
Now get to work! I'd like to make my triumphant return to the Central Bank as soon as possible.
Then what?
Are you going to get rid of me when I'm done?
You'll have to, won't you?
How could someone like you be satisfied with someone like me still in the world?
Someone like you? And what are you, exactly, Master Fontaine?
I'm a genius, whether I like it or not. A genius that rivals the great Doctor Octopus.

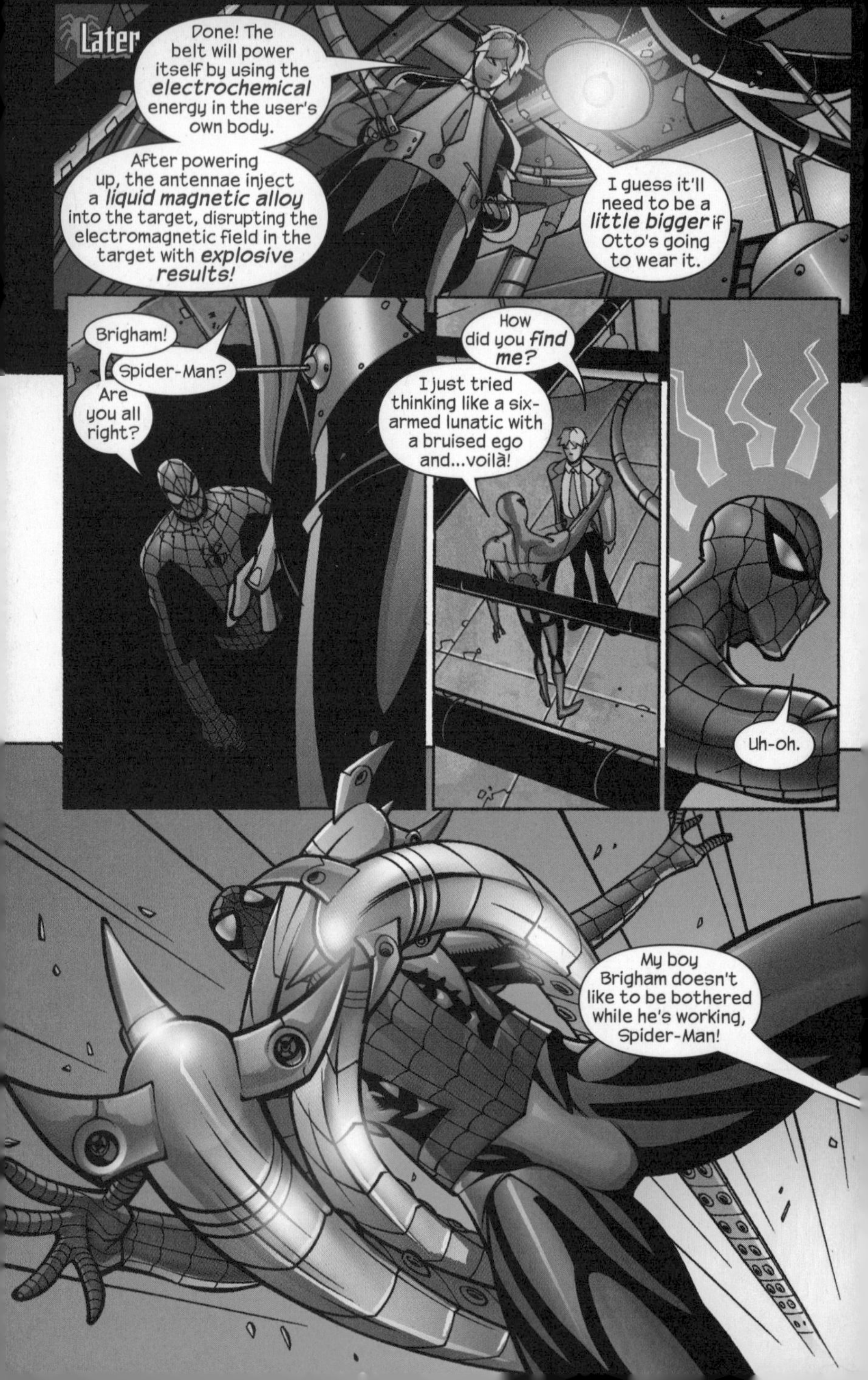
Later
Done! The belt will power itself by using the *electrochemical* energy in the user's own body.
After powering up, the antennae inject a *liquid magnetic alloy* into the target, disrupting the electromagnetic field in the target with *explosive results!*
I guess it'll need to be a *little bigger* if Otto's going to wear it.
Brigham!
Spider-Man?
Are you all right?
How did you *find me?*
I just tried thinking like a six-armed lunatic with a bruised ego and...voilà!
Uh-oh.
My boy Brigham doesn't like to be bothered while he's working, Spider-Man!

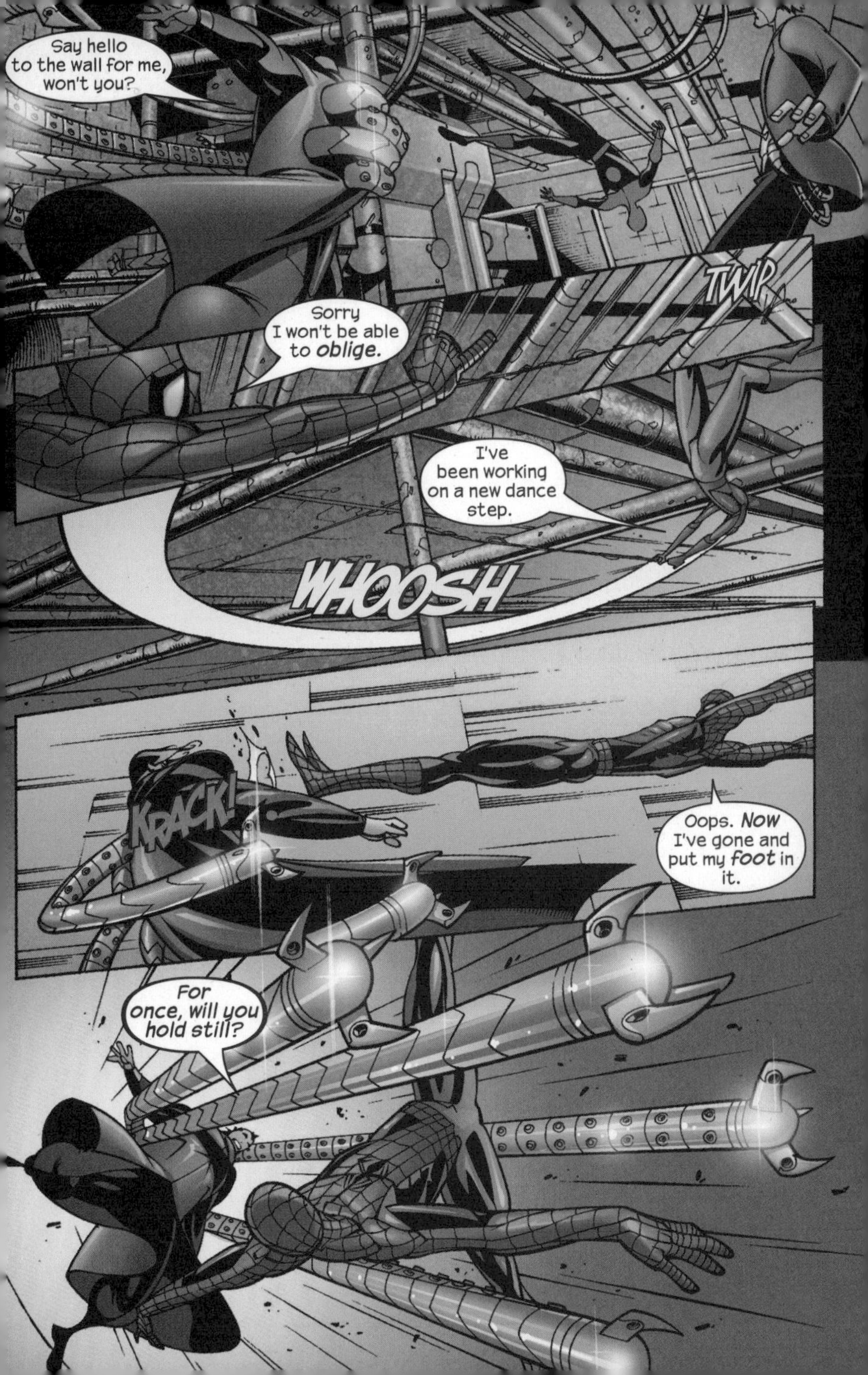
Say hello to the wall for me, won't you?
Sorry I won't be able to *oblige.*
TWIP
I've been working on a new dance step.
WHOOSH
KRACK!
Oops. *NOW* I've gone and put my *foot* in it.
For once, will you hold still?

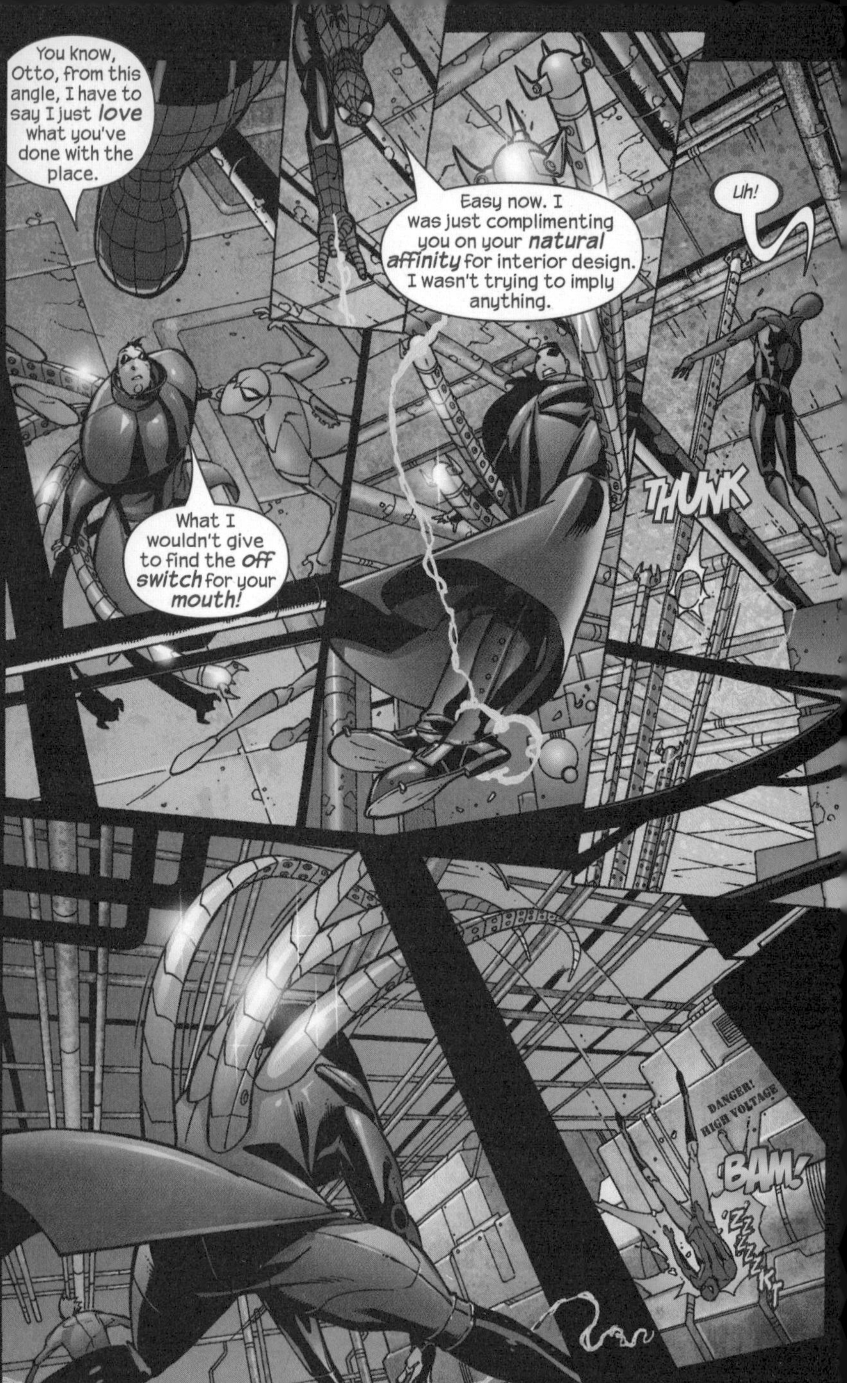
You know, Otto, from this angle, I have to say I just *love* what you've done with the place.
Easy now. I was just complimenting you on your *natural affinity* for interior design. I wasn't trying to imply anything.
Uh!
What I wouldn't give to find the *off switch* for your *mouth!*
THUNK
DANGER! HIGH VOLTAGE
BAM!
ZZZZKT

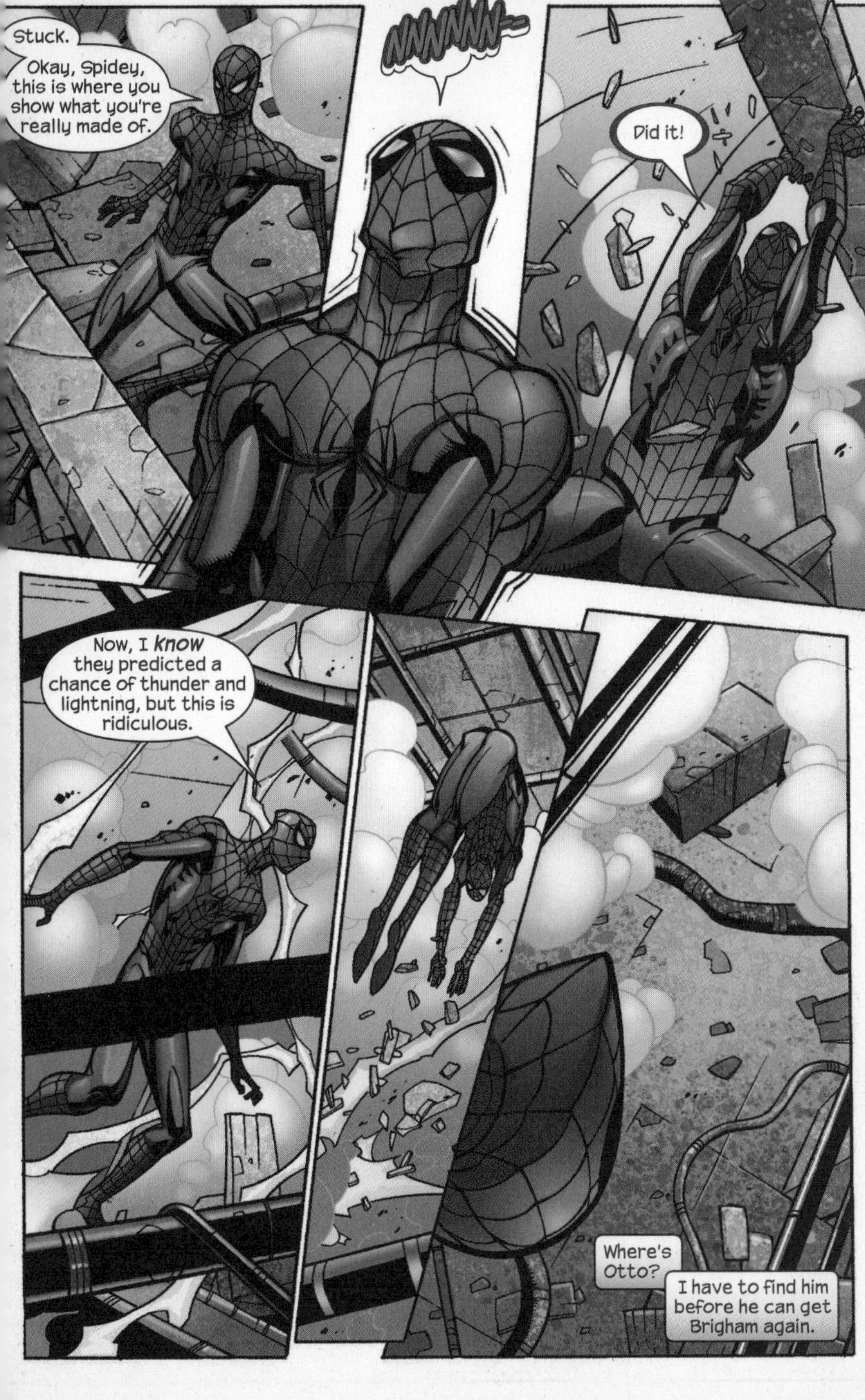
Stuck.
Okay, Spidey, this is where you show what you're really made of.
NNNNNN--
Did it!
Now, I *know* they predicted a chance of thunder and lightning, but this is ridiculous.
Where's Otto?
I have to find him before he can get Brigham again.

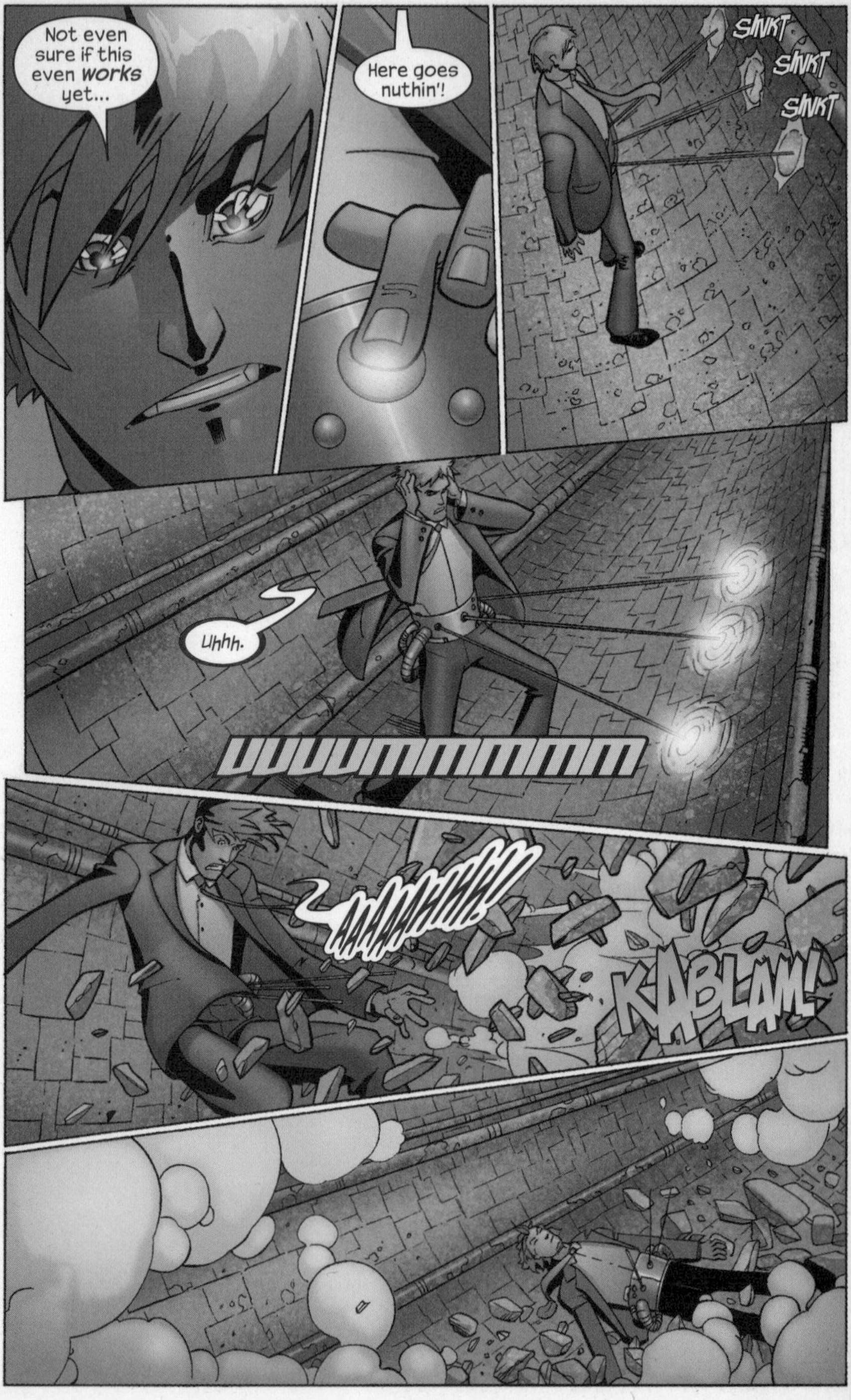
Not even sure if this even works yet...
Here goes nuthin'!
SNKT
SNKT
SNKT
Uhhh.
VVVVMMMMMMM
AAAAAAHHHH!
KABLAM!

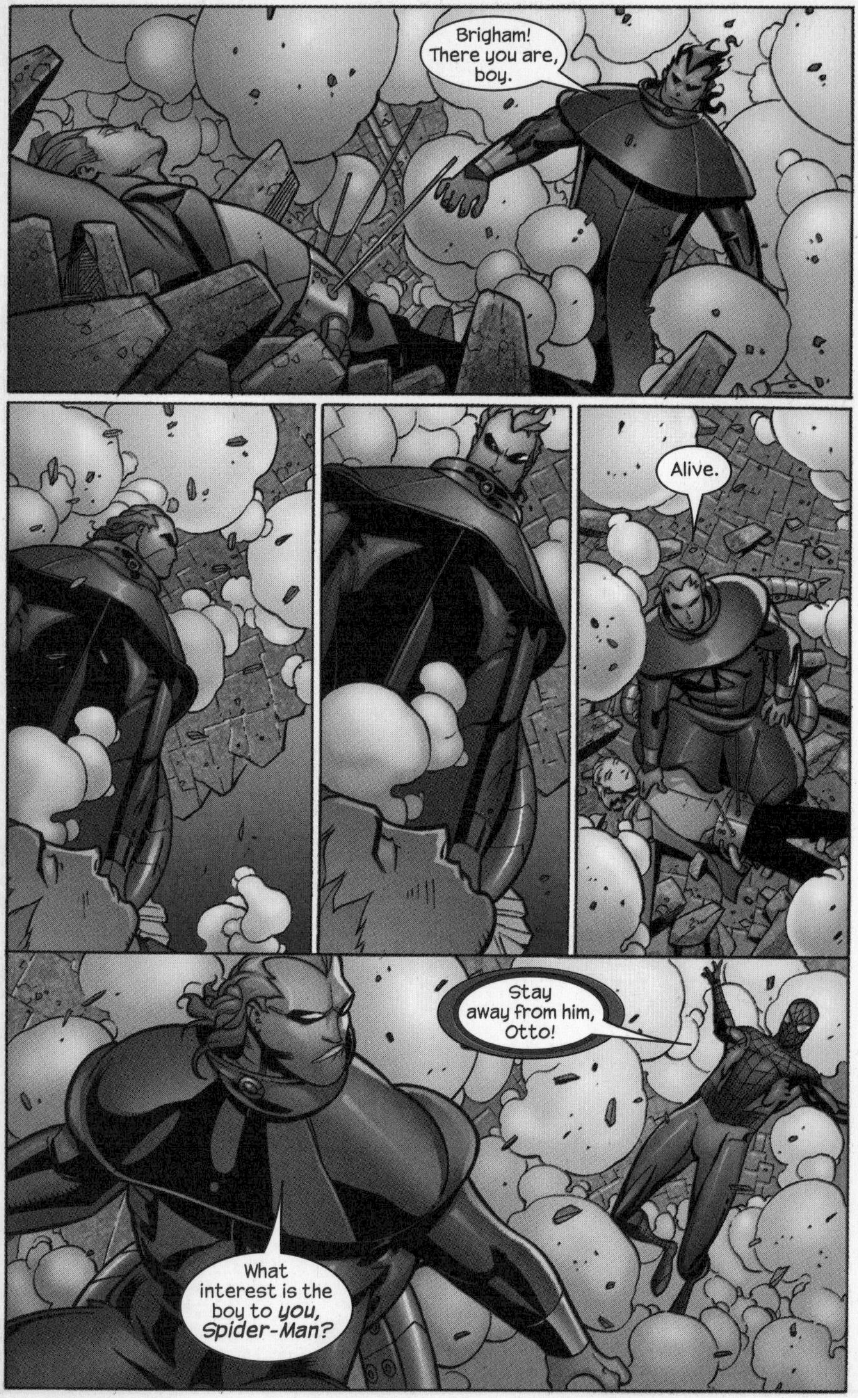
Brigham! There you are, boy.
Alive.
Stay away from him, Otto!
What interest is the boy to *you*, *Spider-Man*?

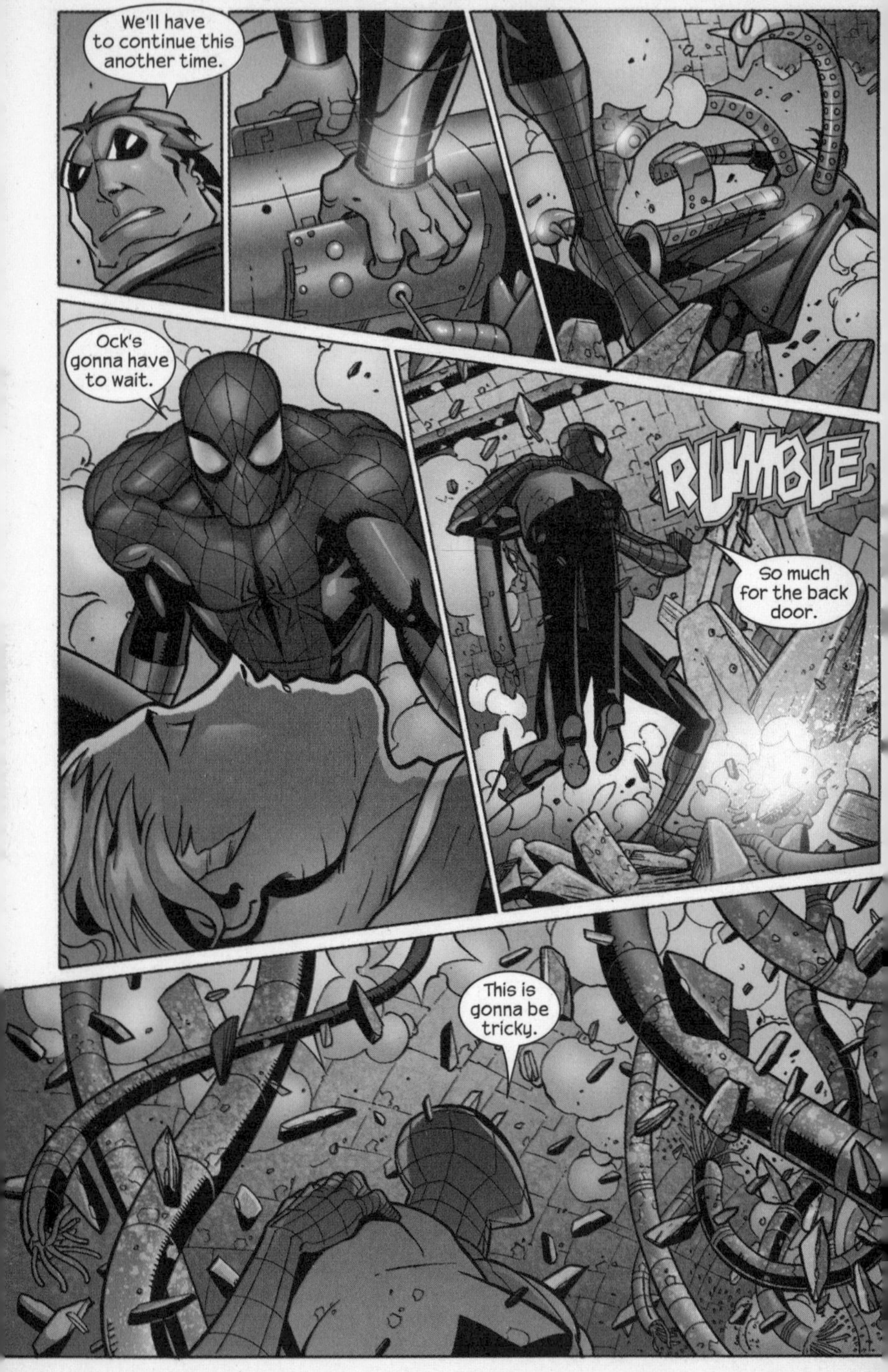
We'll have to continue this another time.
Ock's gonna have to wait.
RUMBLE
So much for the back door.
This is gonna be tricky.

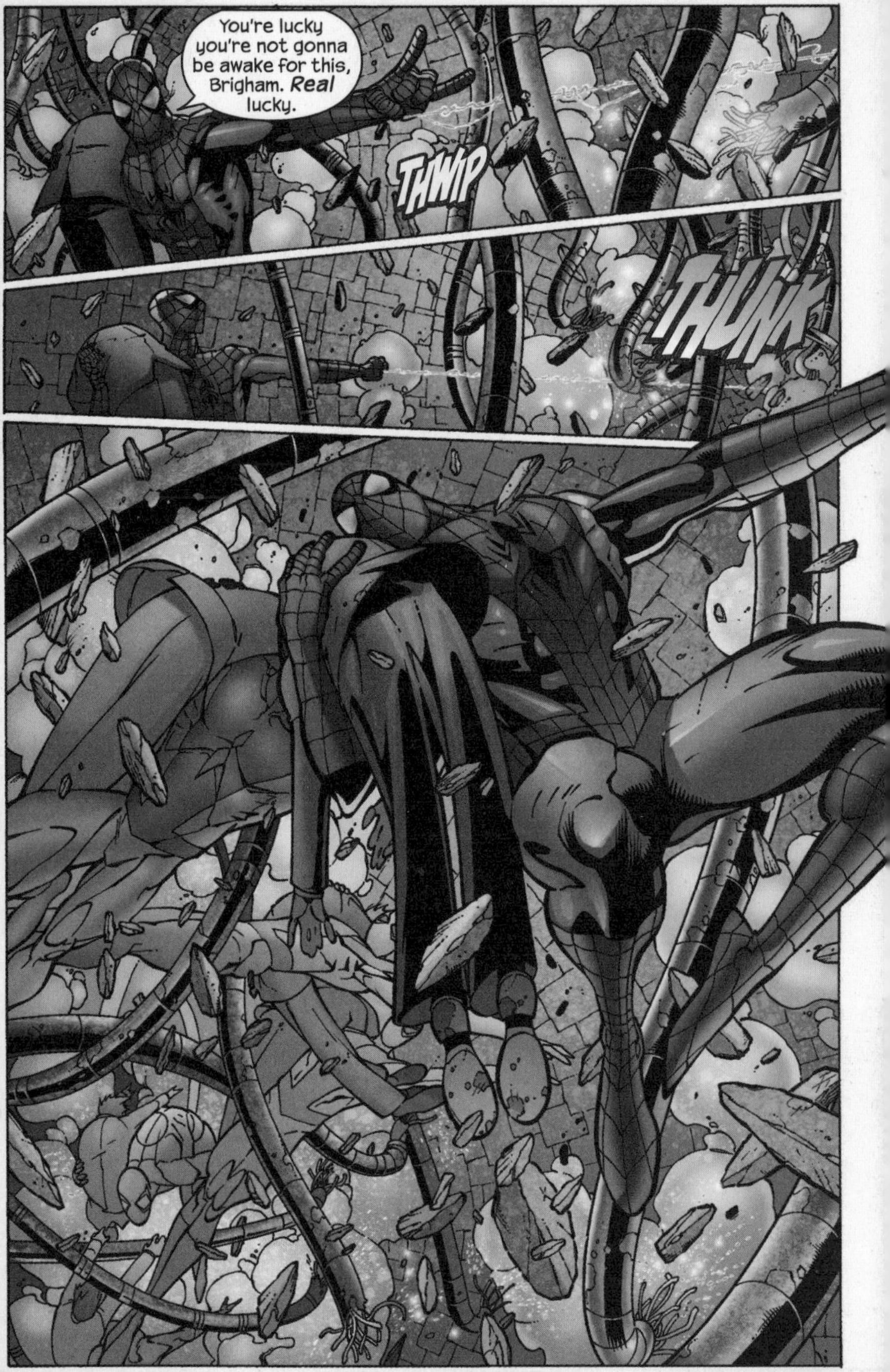
You're lucky you're not gonna be awake for this, Brigham. *Real* lucky.
THWIP
THUNK

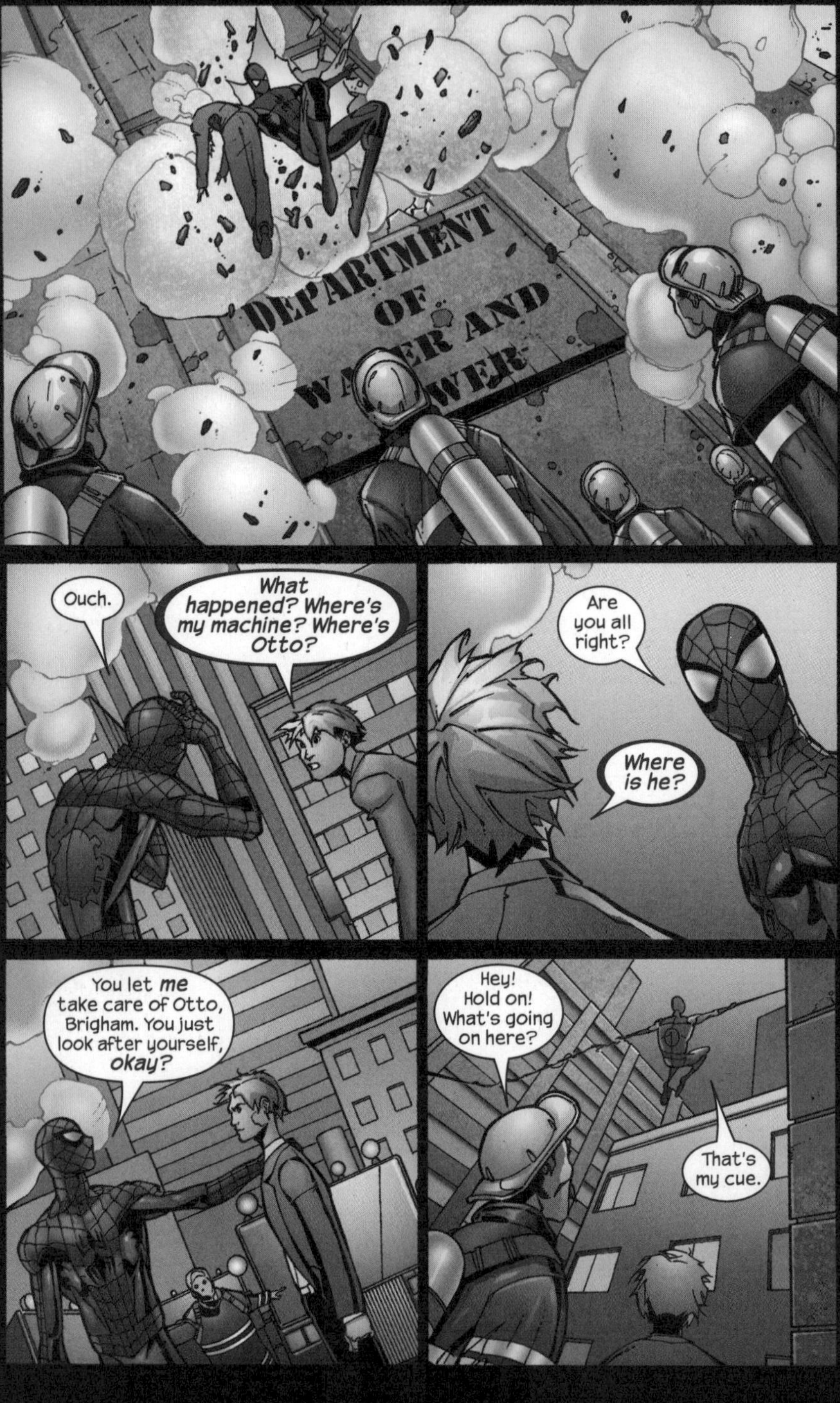
DEPARTMENT OF
Ouch.
What happened? Where's my machine? Where's Otto?
Are you all right?
Where is he?
You let me take care of Otto, Brigham. You just look after yourself, okay?
Hey! Hold on! What's going on here?
That's my cue.

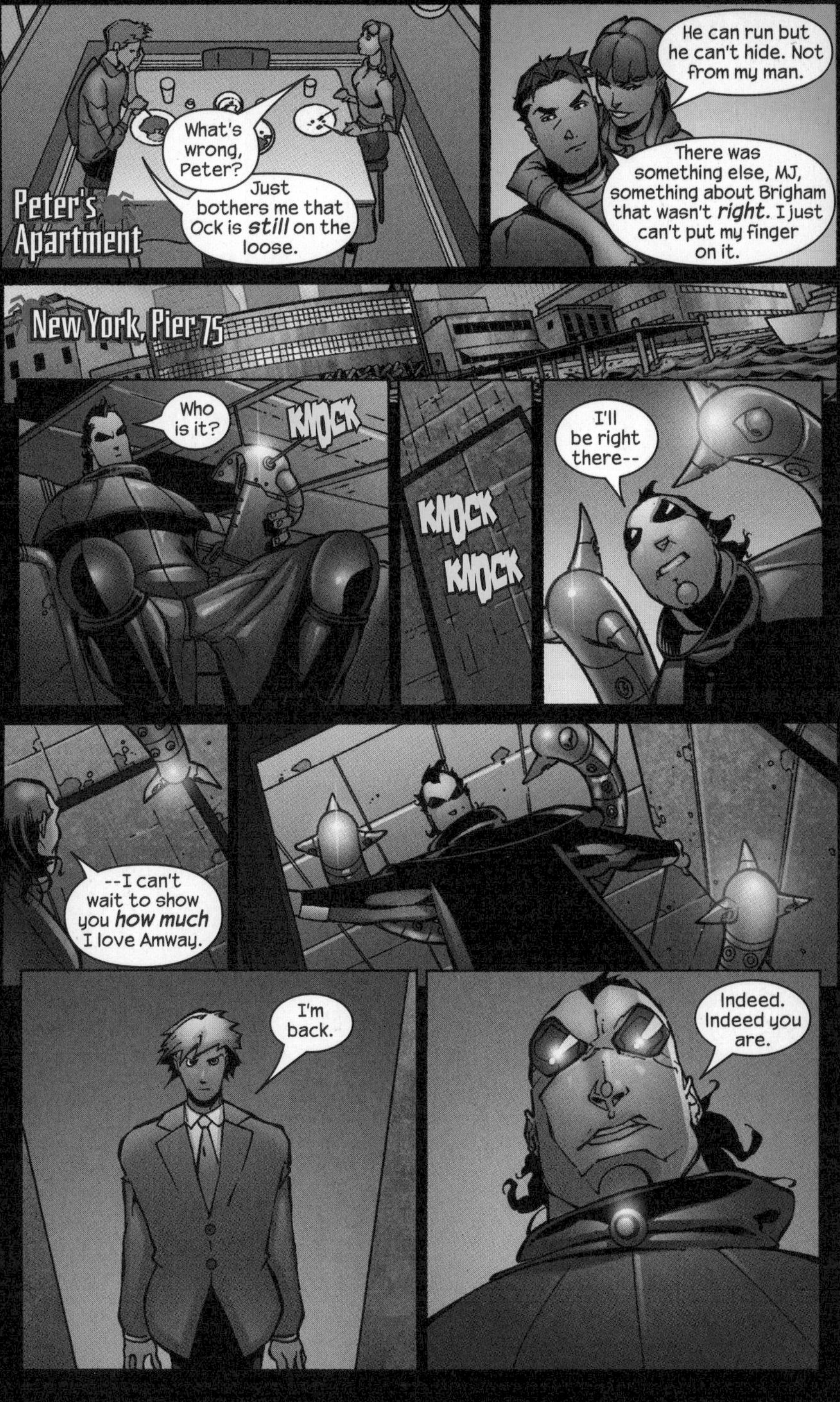
Peter's Apartment
What's wrong, Peter?
Just bothers me that Ock is *still* on the loose.
He can run but he can't hide. Not from my man.
There was something else, MJ, something about Brigham that wasn't *right*. I just can't put my finger on it.
New York, Pier 75
Who is it?
KNOCK
KNOCK
KNOCK
I'll be right there--
--I can't wait to show you *how much* I love Amway.
I'm back.
Indeed. Indeed you are.

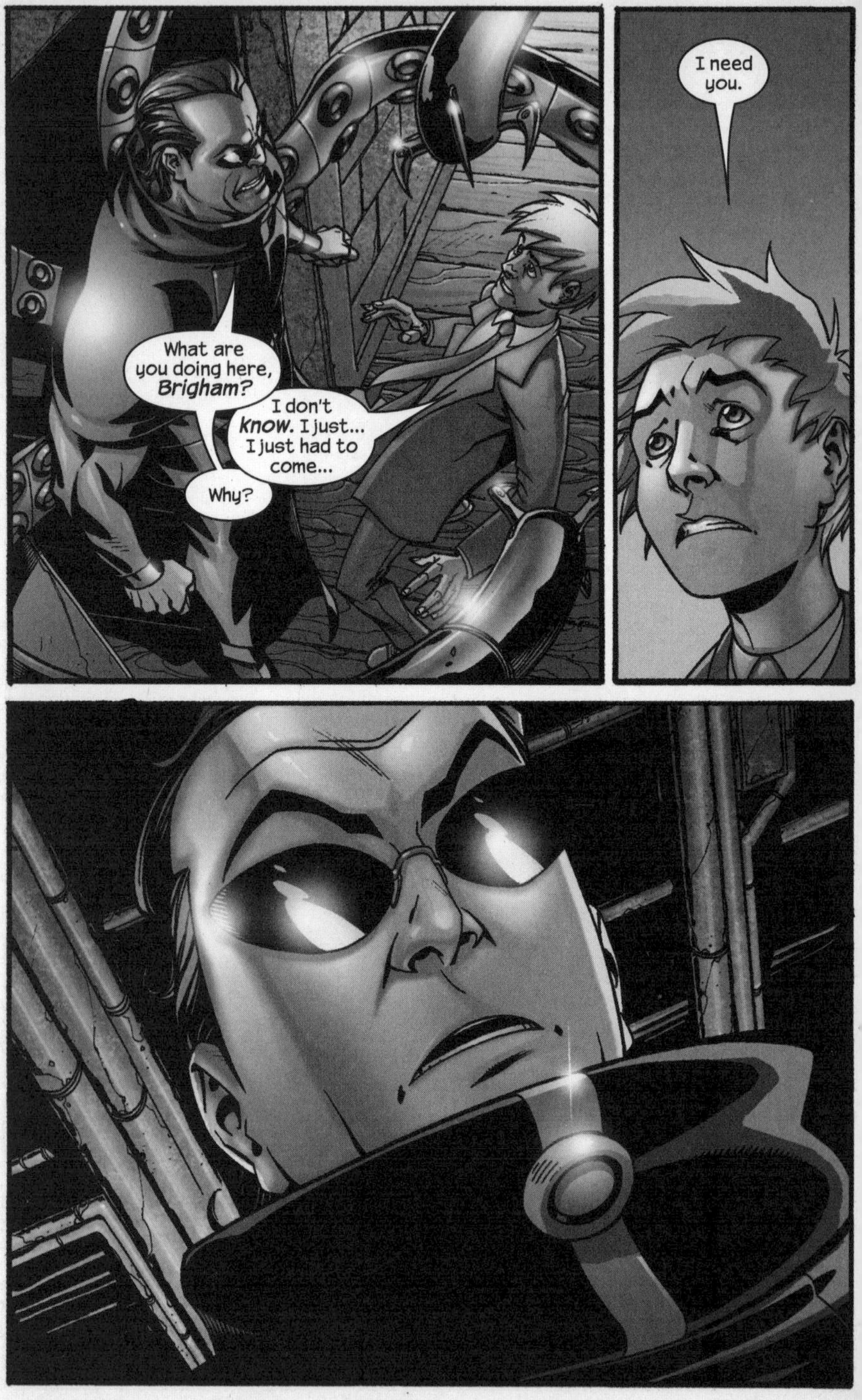
What are you doing here, Brigham?
I don't know. I just... I just had to come...
Why?
I need you.

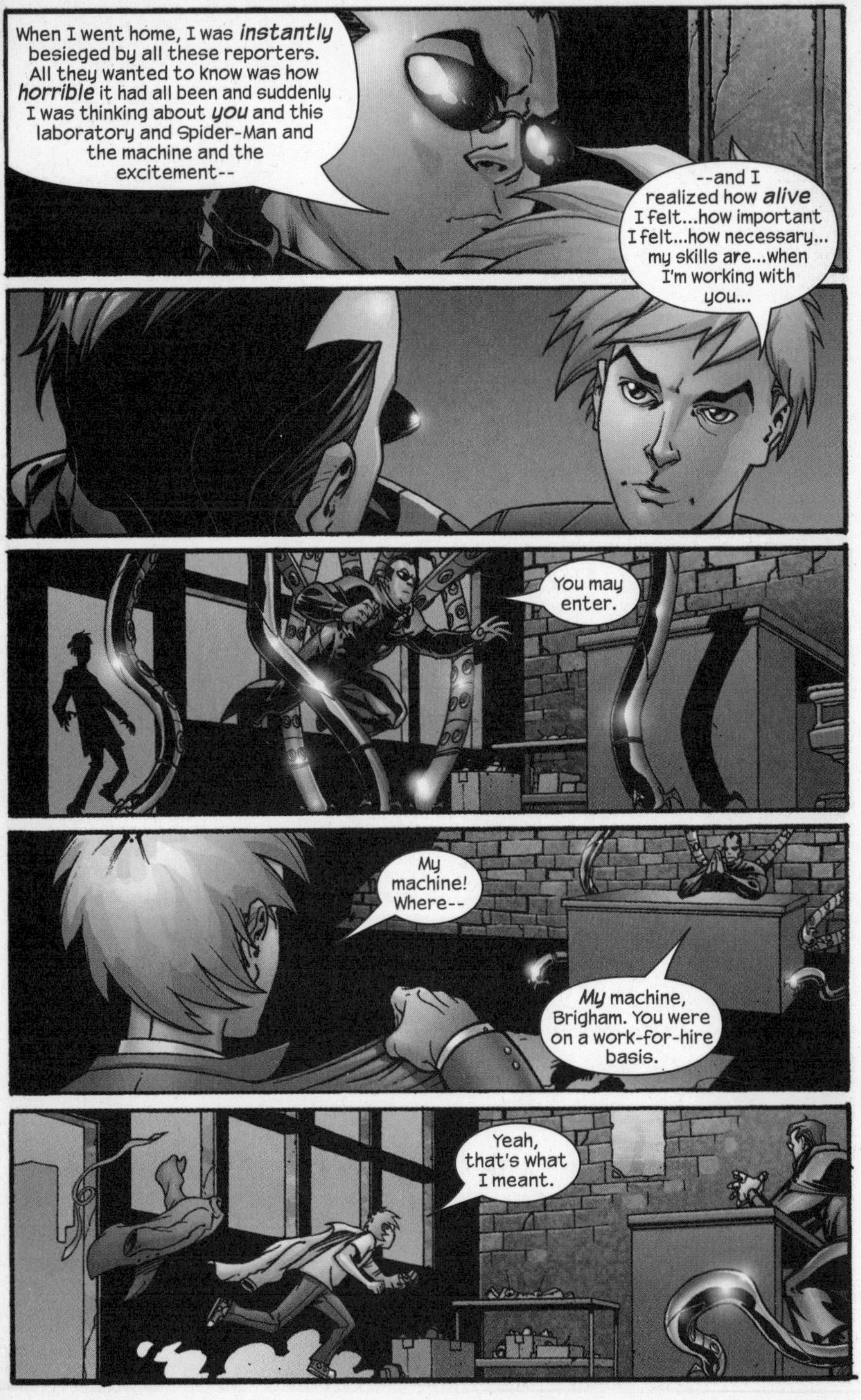
When I went home, I was *instantly* besieged by all these reporters. All they wanted to know was how ***horrible*** it had all been and suddenly I was thinking about ***you*** and this laboratory and Spider-Man and the machine and the excitement--
--and I realized how *alive* I felt...how important I felt...how necessary... my skills are...when I'm working with you...
You may enter.
My machine! Where--
My machine, Brigham. You were on a work-for-hire basis.
Yeah, that's what I meant.

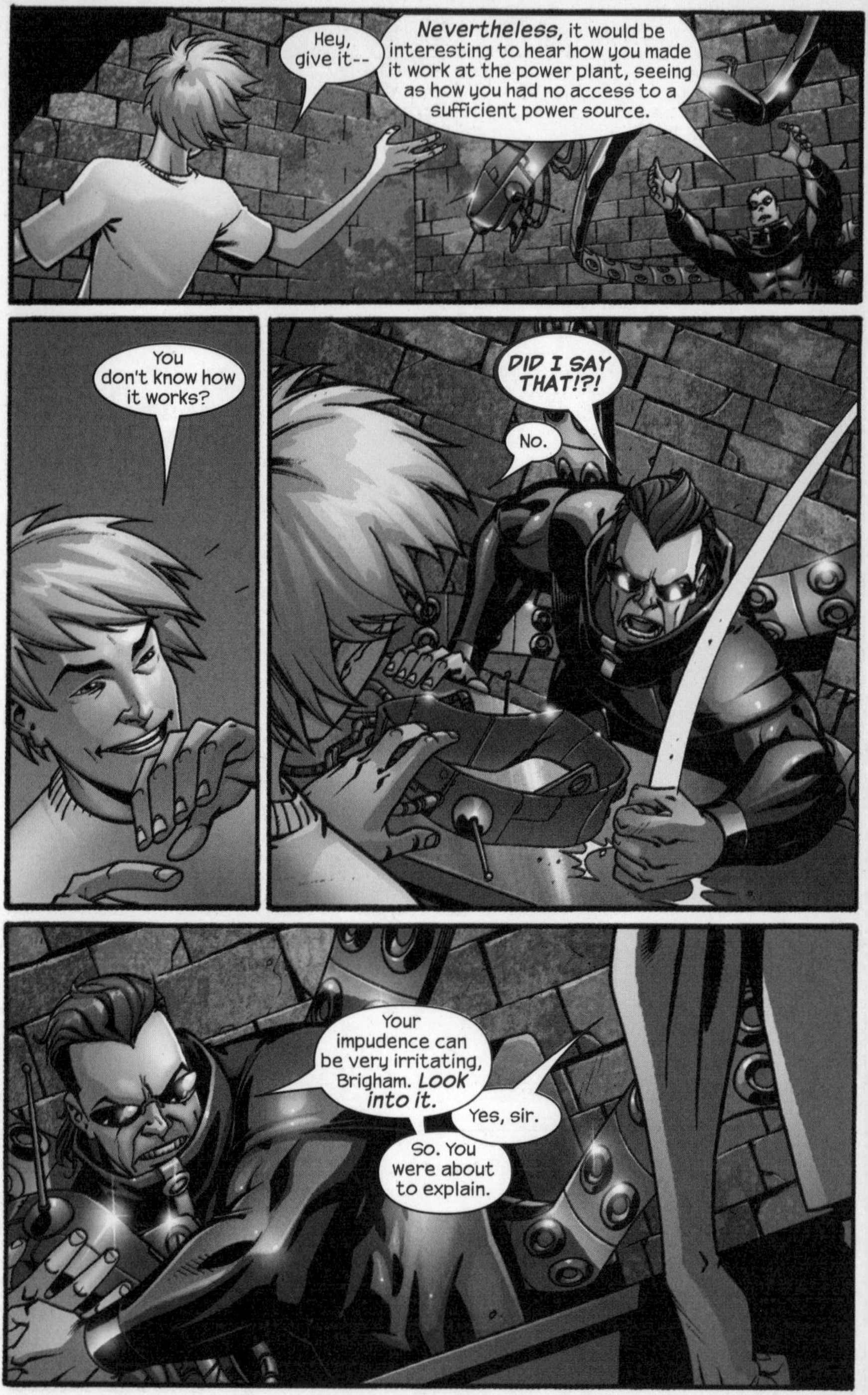
Hey, give it--
Nevertheless, it would be interesting to hear how you made it work at the power plant, seeing as how you had no access to a sufficient power source.
You don't know how it works?
DID I SAY THAT!?!
No.
Your impudence can be very irritating, Brigham. Look into it.
Yes, sir.
So. You were about to explain.

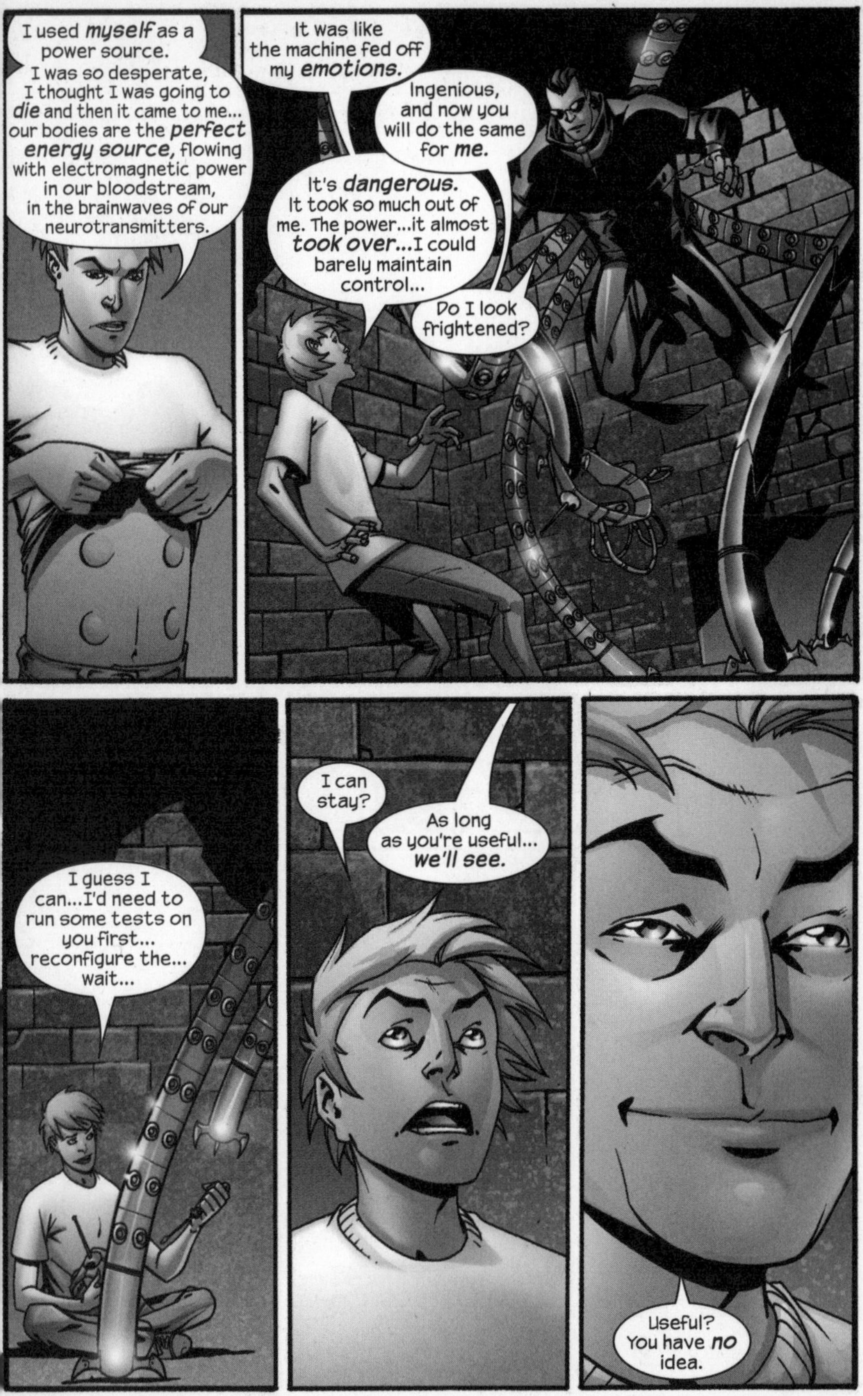

I used *myself* as a power source. I was so desperate, I thought I was going to *die* and then it came to me... our bodies are the *perfect energy source,* flowing with electromagnetic power in our bloodstream, in the brainwaves of our neurotransmitters.
It was like the machine fed off my *emotions.*
Ingenious, and now you will do the same for *me.*
It's *dangerous.* It took so much out of me. The power...it almost *took over...*I could barely maintain control...
Do I look frightened?
I guess I can...I'd need to run some tests on you first... reconfigure the... wait...
I can stay?
As long as you're useful... *we'll see.*
Useful? You have *no* idea.

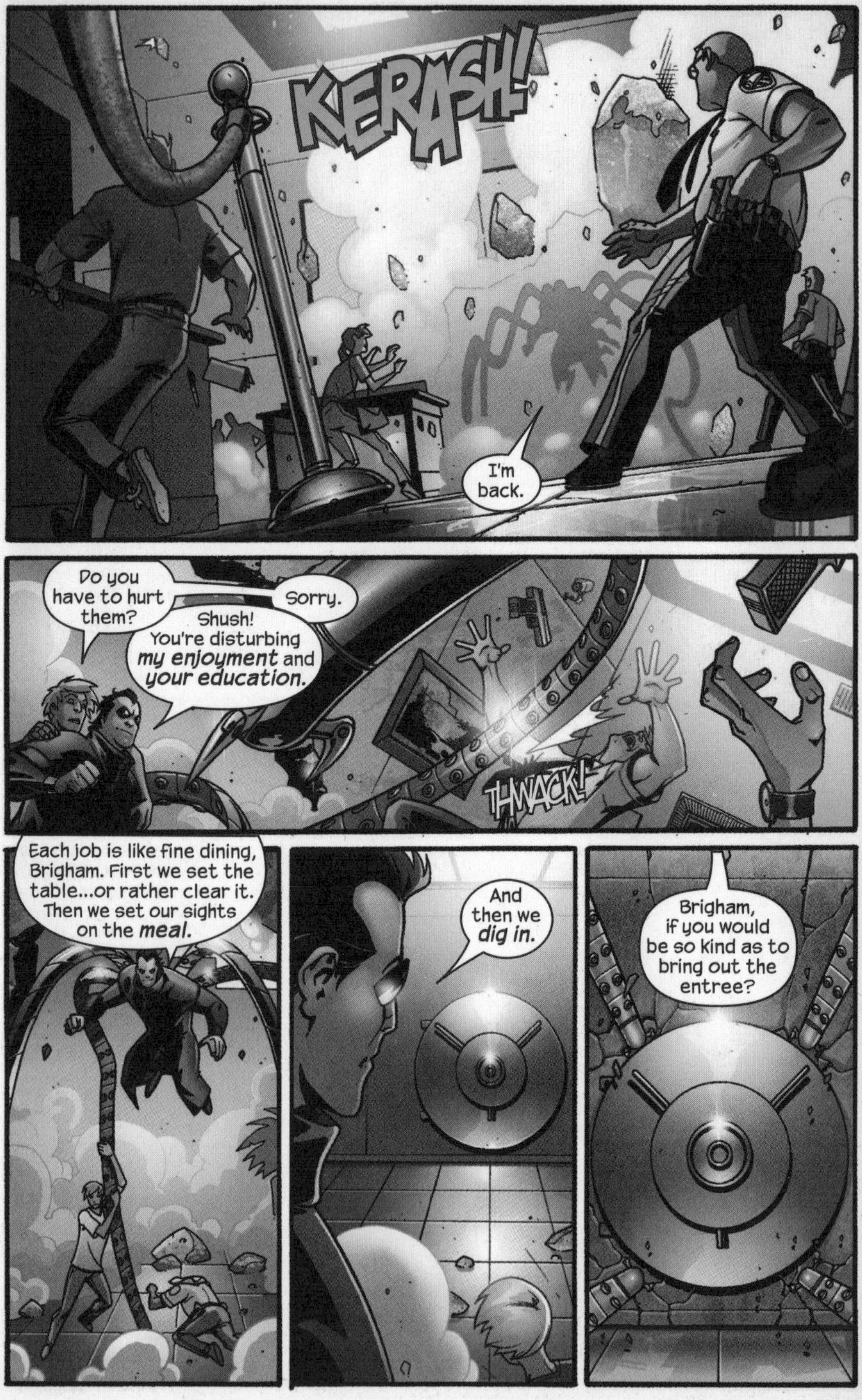
KERASH!
I'm back.
Do you have to hurt them?
Sorry.
Shush! You're disturbing my enjoyment and your education.
THWACK!
Each job is like fine dining, Brigham. First we set the table...or rather clear it. Then we set our sights on the meal.
And then we dig in.
Brigham, if you would be so kind as to bring out the entree?

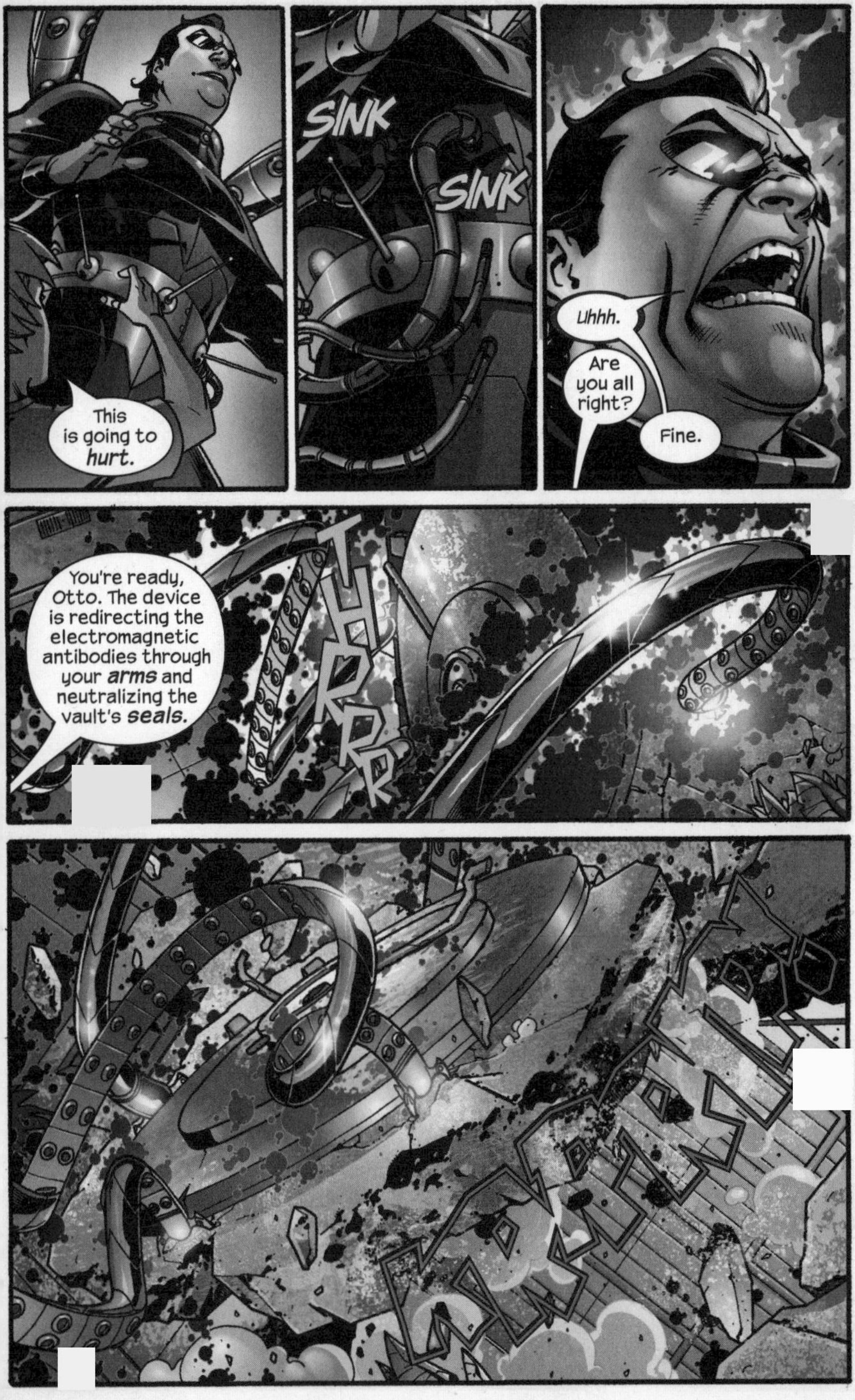
This is going to *hurt.*
SINK
SINK
Uhhh.
Are you all right?
Fine.
You're ready, Otto. The device is redirecting the electromagnetic antibodies through your *arms* and neutralizing the vault's *seals.*
THRRRR

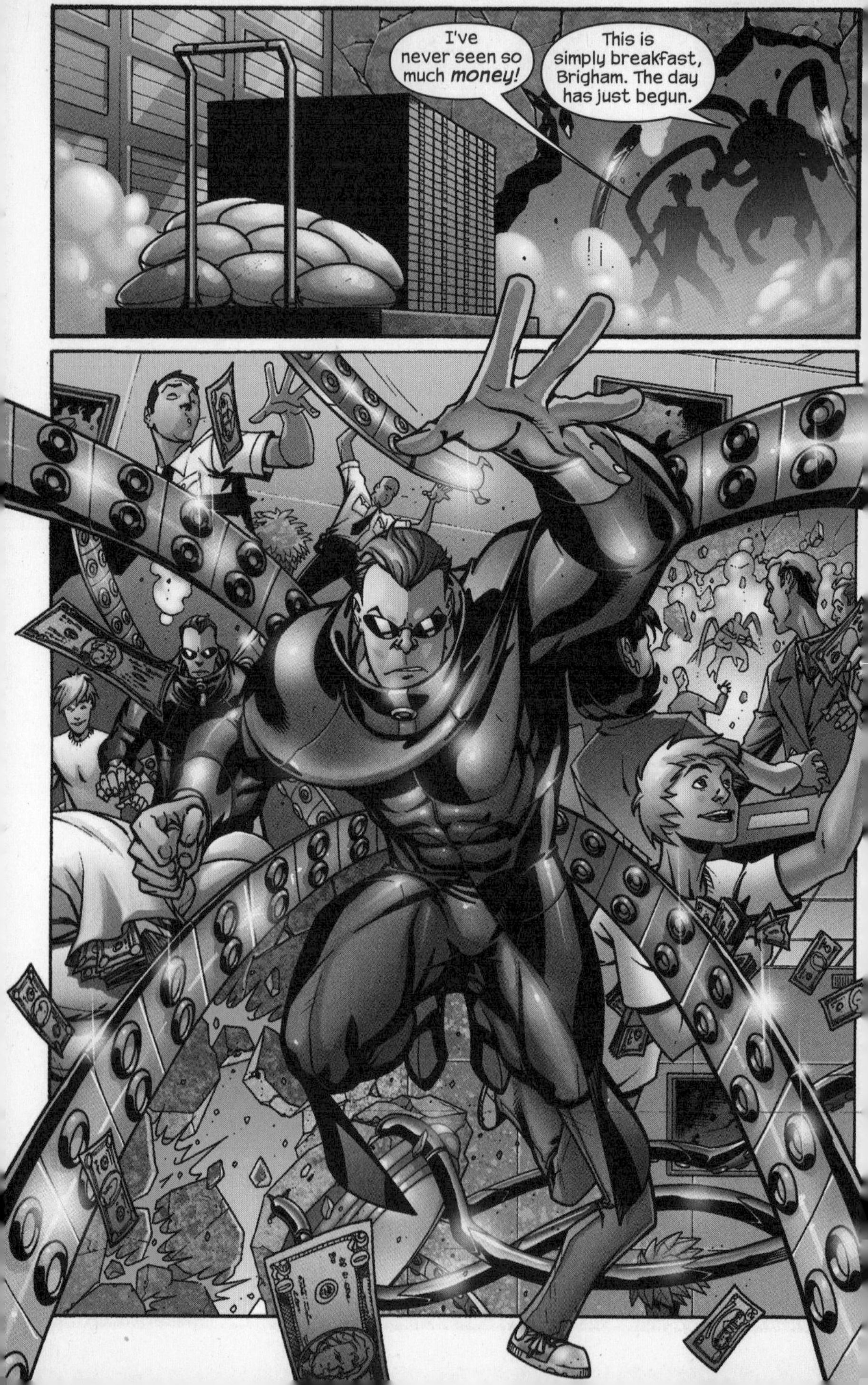
I've never seen so much *money!*
This is simply breakfast, Brigham. The day has just begun.

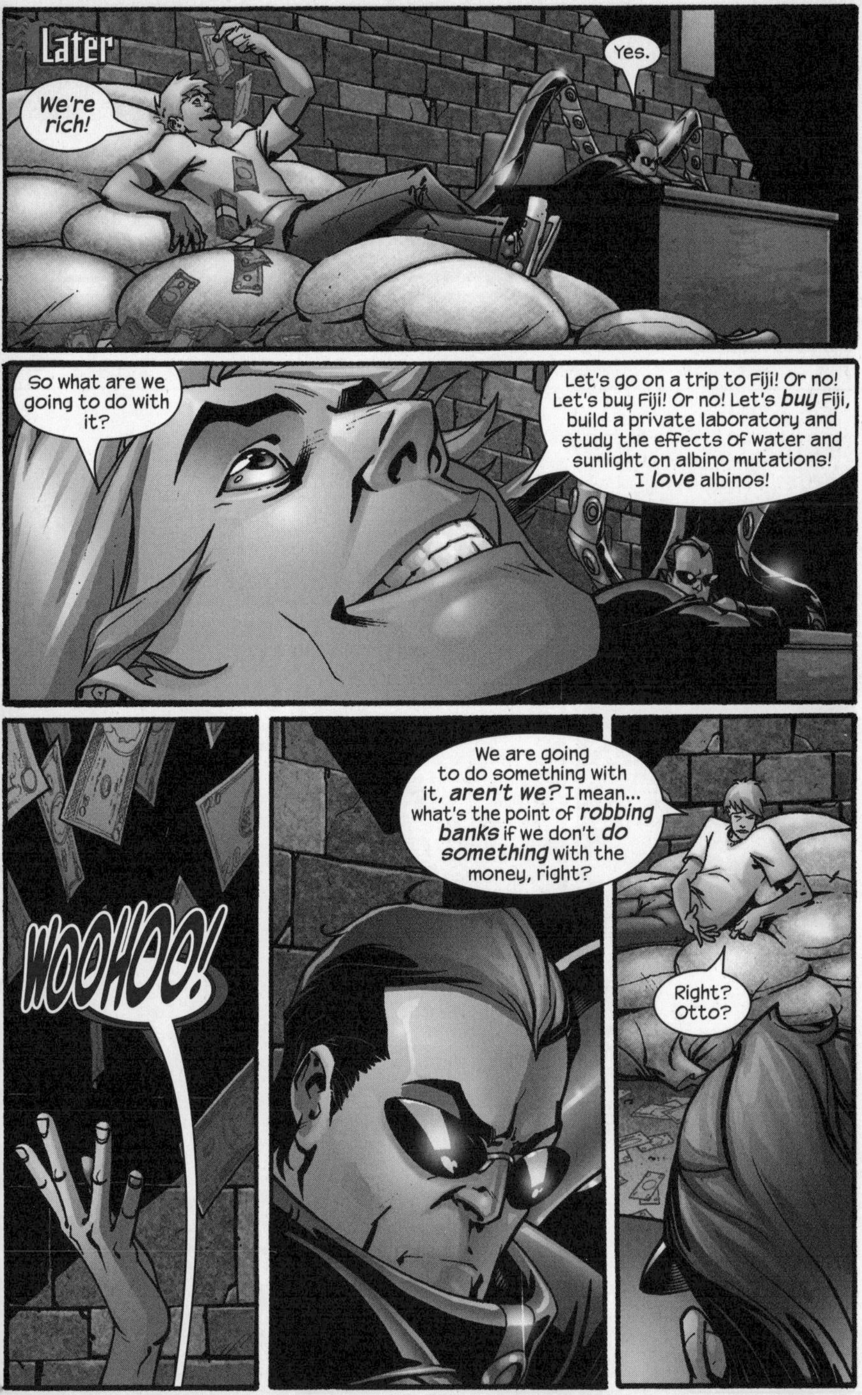
Later
We're rich!
Yes.
So what are we going to do with it?
Let's go on a trip to Fiji! Or no! Let's buy Fiji! Or no! Let's *buy* Fiji, build a private laboratory and study the effects of water and sunlight on albino mutations! I *love* albinos!
WOOHOO!
We are going to do something with it, *aren't we?* I mean... what's the point of *robbing banks* if we don't *do something* with the money, right?
Right? Otto?

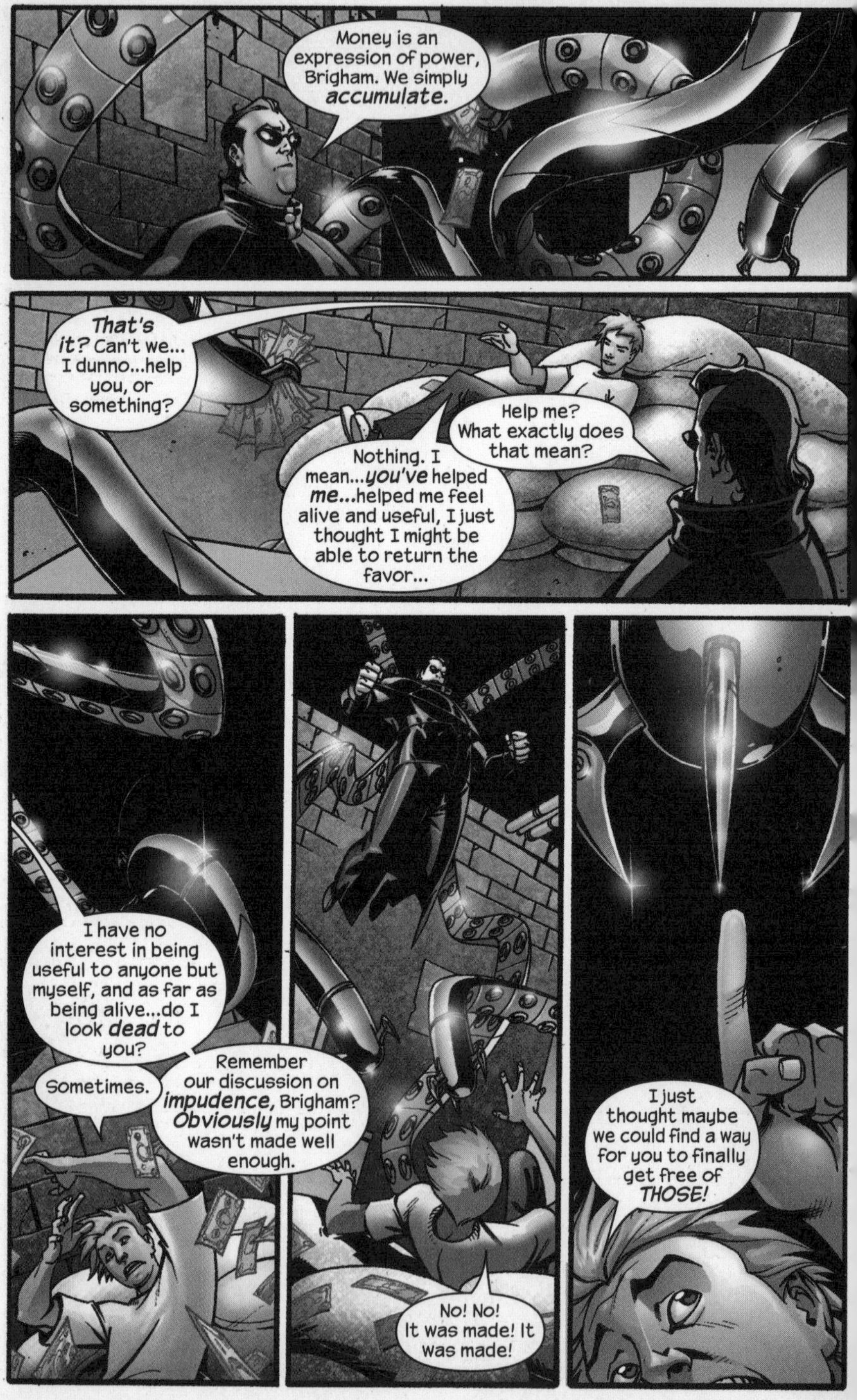
Money is an expression of power, Brigham. We simply *accumulate.*
That's it? Can't we... I dunno...help you, or something?
Help me? What exactly does that mean?
Nothing. I mean...*you've* helped *me*...helped me feel alive and useful, I just thought I might be able to return the favor...
I have no interest in being useful to anyone but myself, and as far as being alive...do I look *dead* to you?
Sometimes.
Remember our discussion on *impudence,* Brigham? *Obviously* my point wasn't made well enough.
No! No! It was made! It was made!
I just thought maybe we could find a way for you to finally get free of *THOSE!*

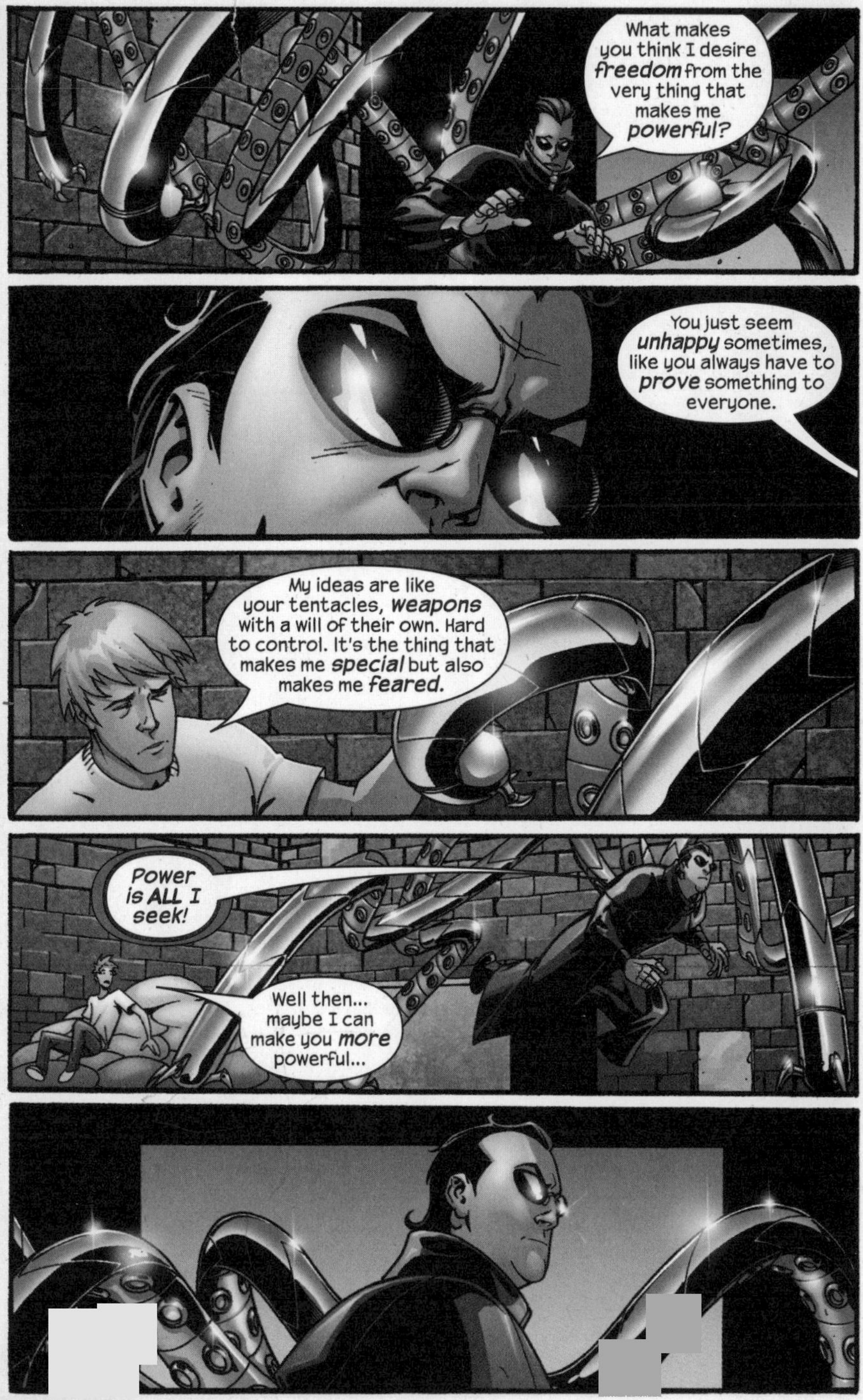
What makes you think I desire freedom from the very thing that makes me powerful?
You just seem unhappy sometimes, like you always have to prove something to everyone.
My ideas are like your tentacles, weapons with a will of their own. Hard to control. It's the thing that makes me special but also makes me feared.
Power is ALL I seek!
Well then... maybe I can make you more powerful...

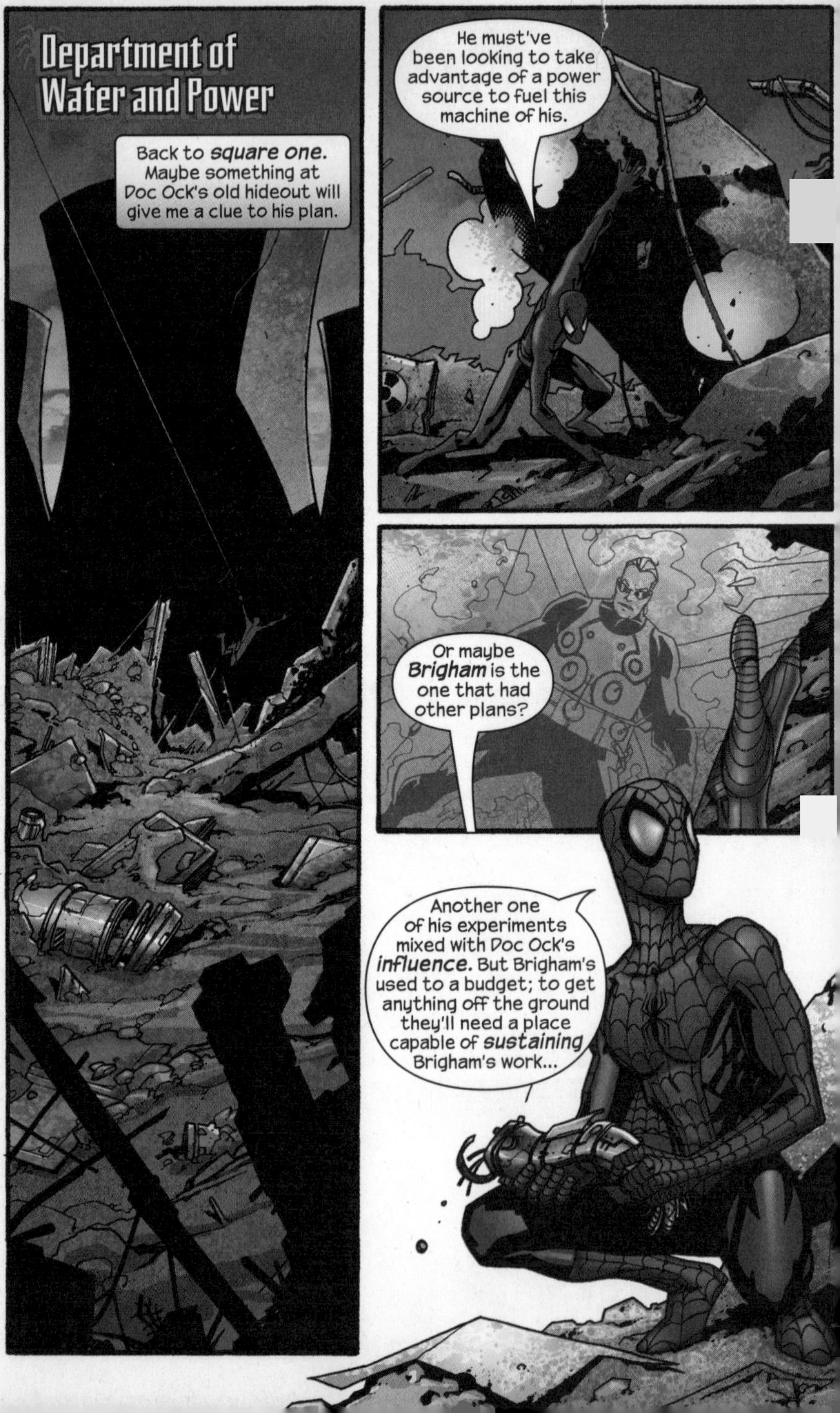
Department of Water and Power
Back to square one. Maybe something at Doc Ock's old hideout will give me a clue to his plan.
He must've been looking to take advantage of a power source to fuel this machine of his.
Or maybe Brigham is the one that had other plans?
Another one of his experiments mixed with Doc Ock's influence. But Brigham's used to a budget; to get anything off the ground they'll need a place capable of sustaining Brigham's work...

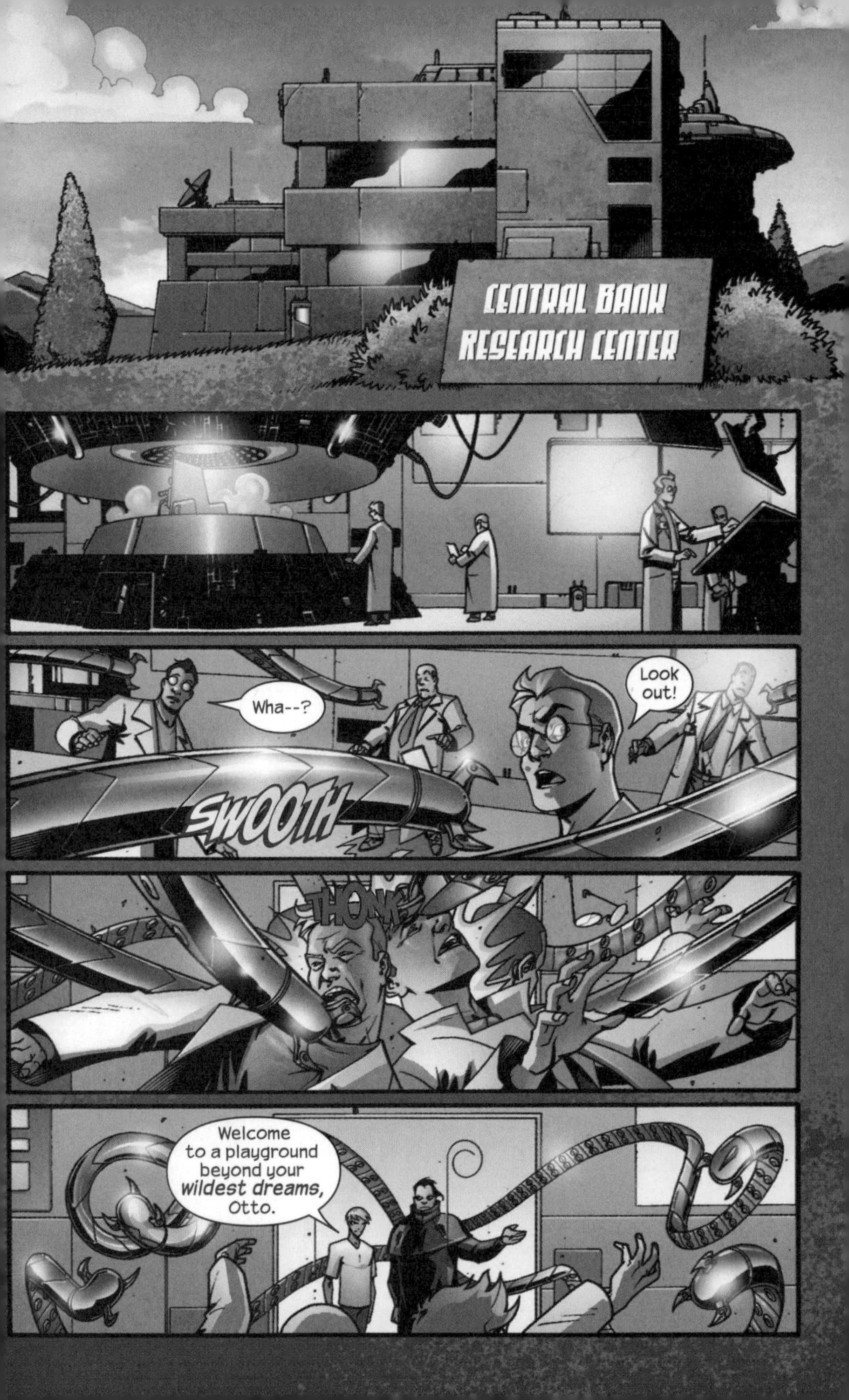
CENTRAL BANK
RESEARCH CENTER
Wha--?
Look out!
SWOOTH
THONK
Welcome to a playground beyond your *wildest dreams,* Otto.

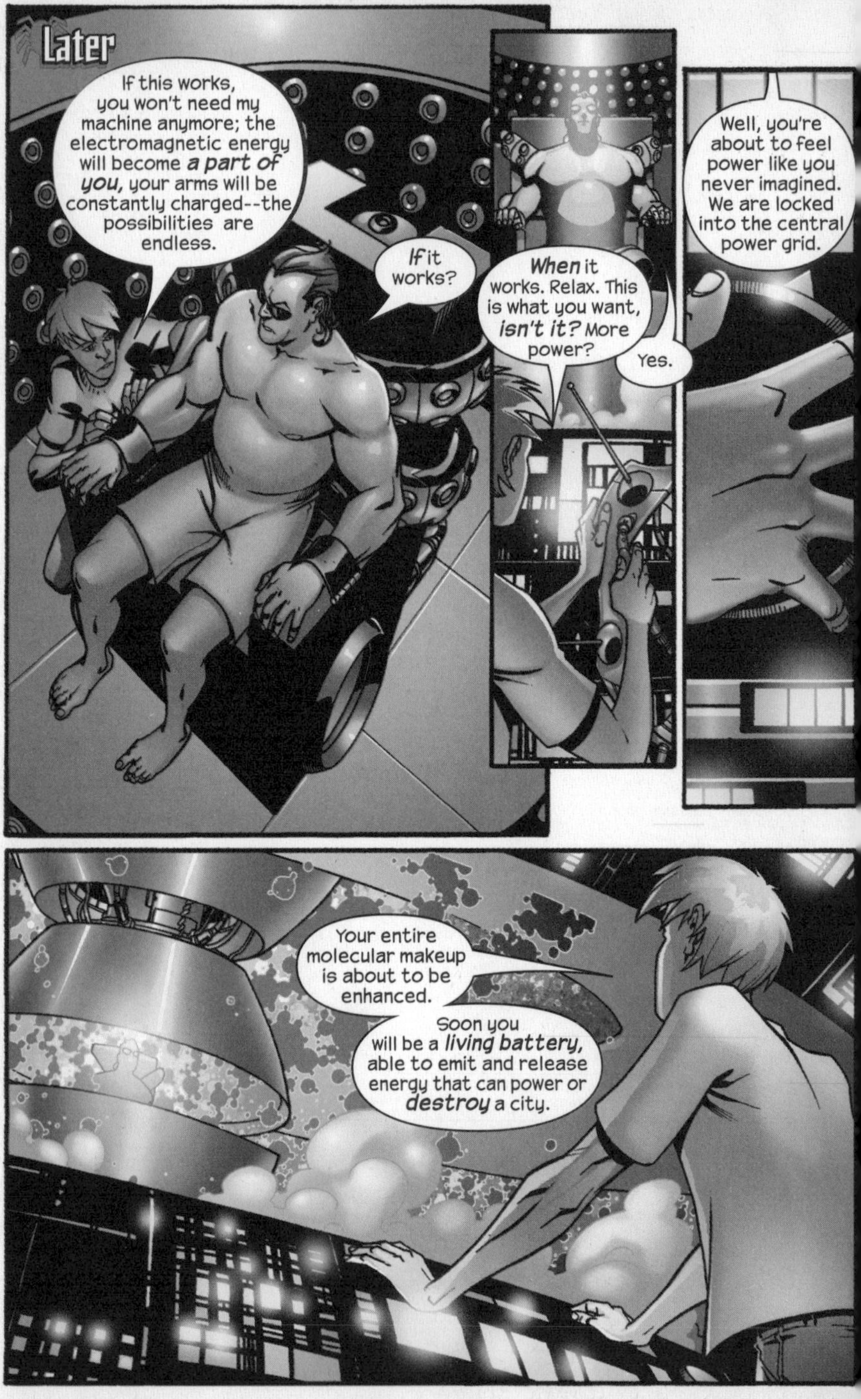
Later
If this works, you won't need my machine anymore; the electromagnetic energy will become a part of you, your arms will be constantly charged--the possibilities are endless.
If it works?
When it works. Relax. This is what you want, isn't it? More power?
Yes.
Well, you're about to feel power like you never imagined. We are locked into the central power grid.
Your entire molecular makeup is about to be enhanced.
Soon you will be a living battery, able to emit and release energy that can power or destroy a city.

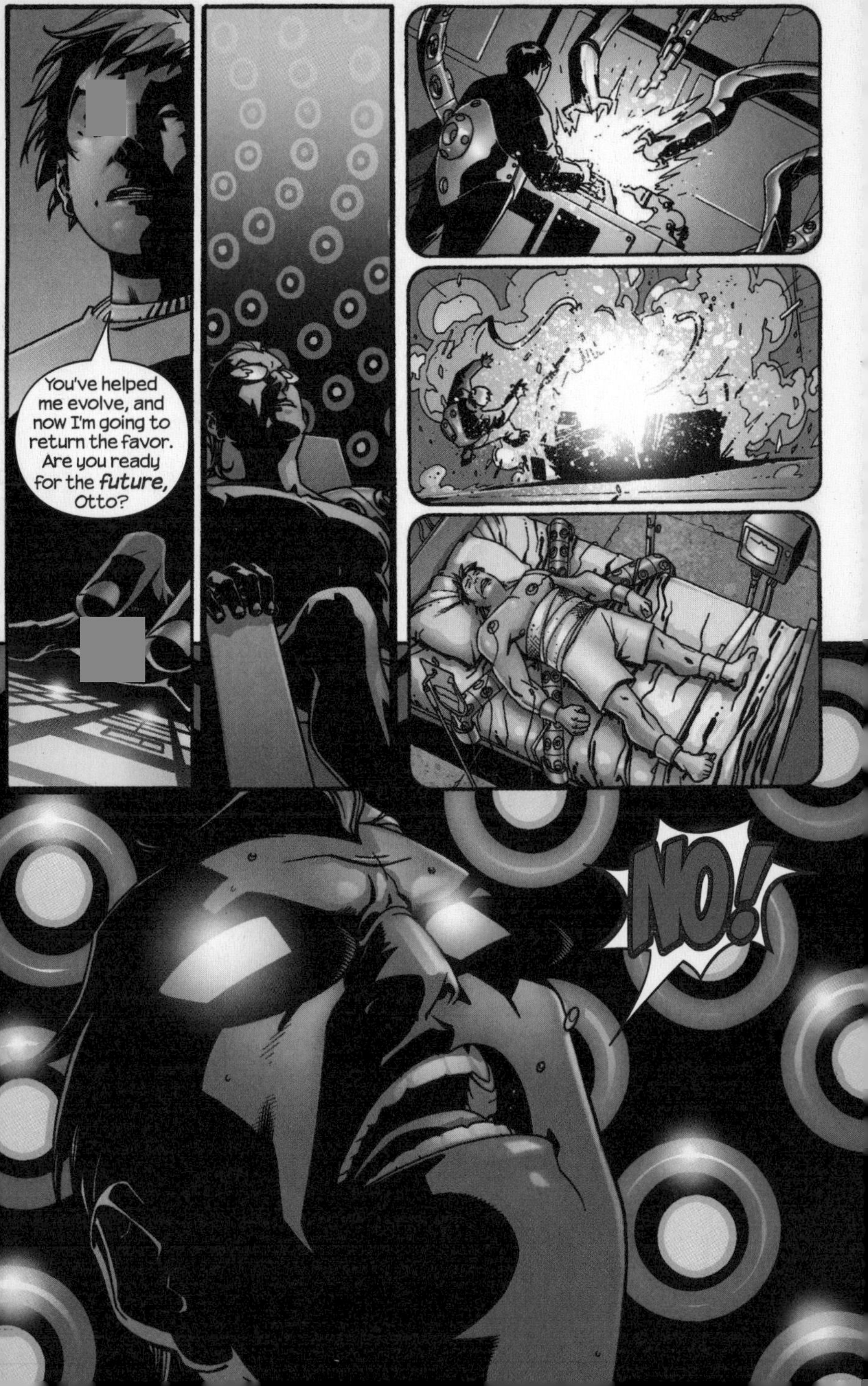
You've helped me evolve, and now I'm going to return the favor. Are you ready for the *future,* Otto?
NO!

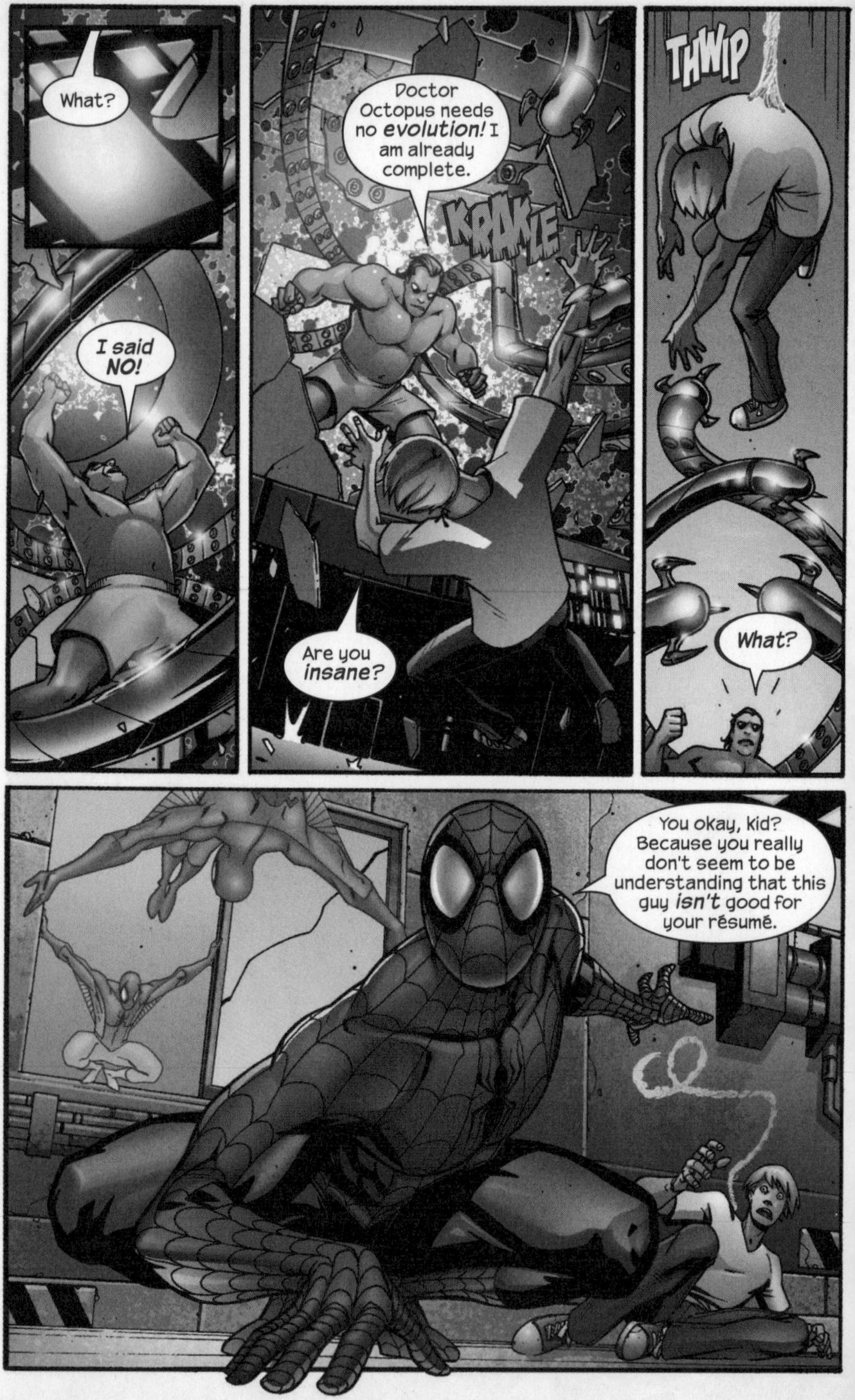
What?
I said NO!
Doctor Octopus needs no evolution! I am already complete.
KRAKLE
Are you insane?
THWIP
What?
You okay, kid? Because you really don't seem to be understanding that this guy isn't good for your résumé.

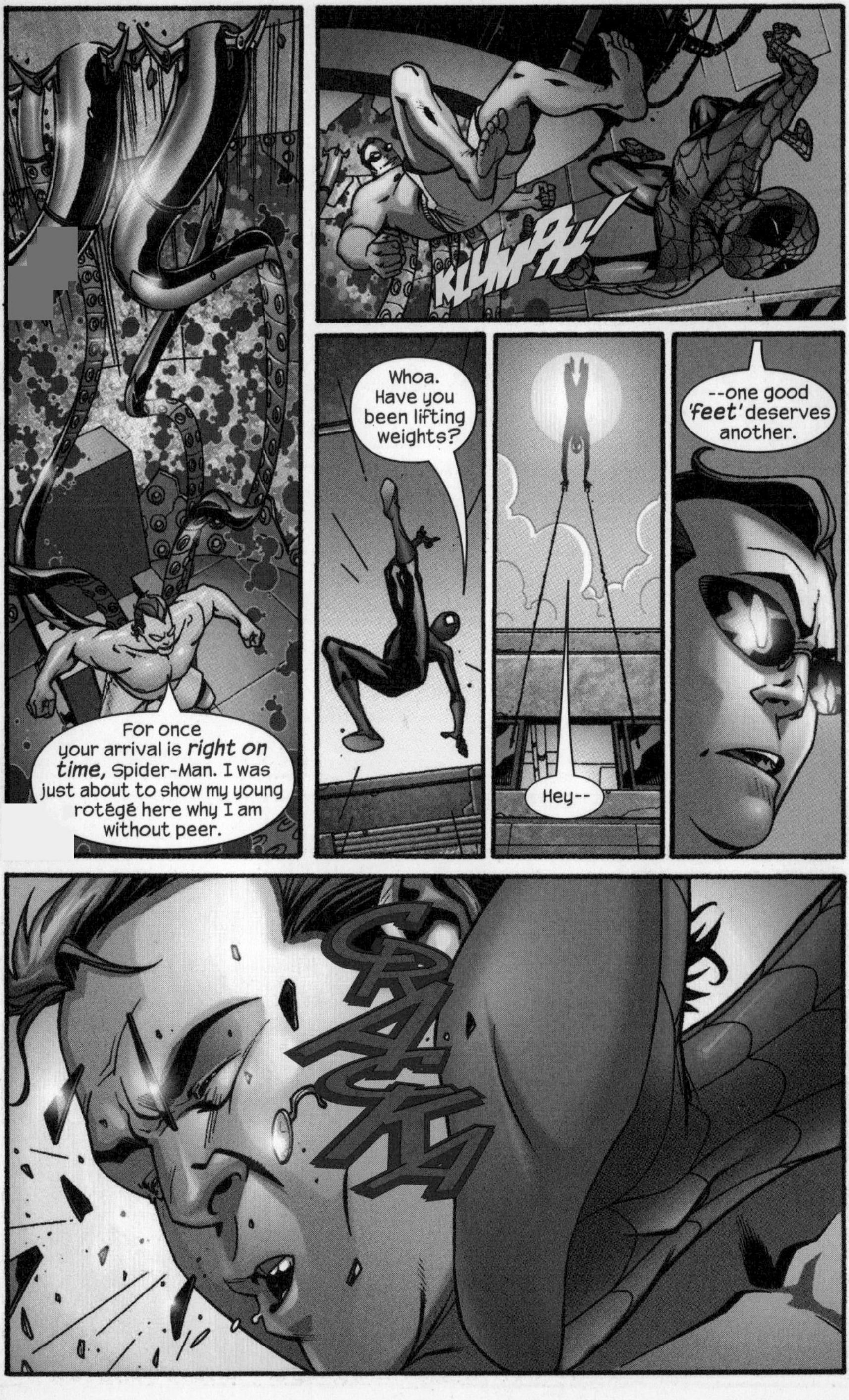
For once your arrival is *right on time,* Spider-Man. I was just about to show my young rotégé here why I am without peer.
KLUMPH!
Whoa. Have you been lifting weights?
Hey--
--one good *'feet'* deserves another.
CRACK

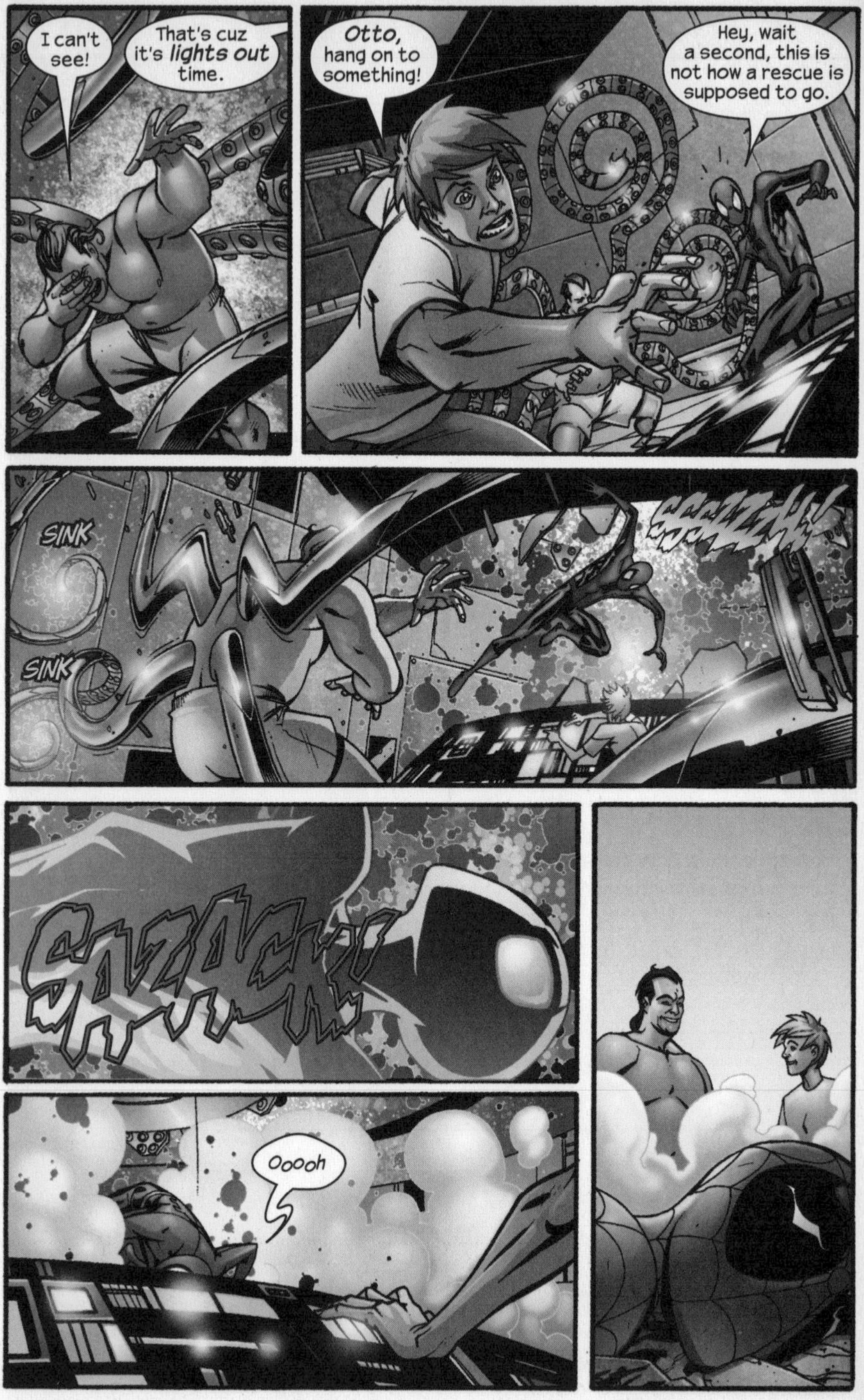
I can't see!
That's cuz it's *lights out* time.
Otto, hang on to something!
Hey, wait a second, this is not how a rescue is supposed to go.
SINK
SINK
Ooooh

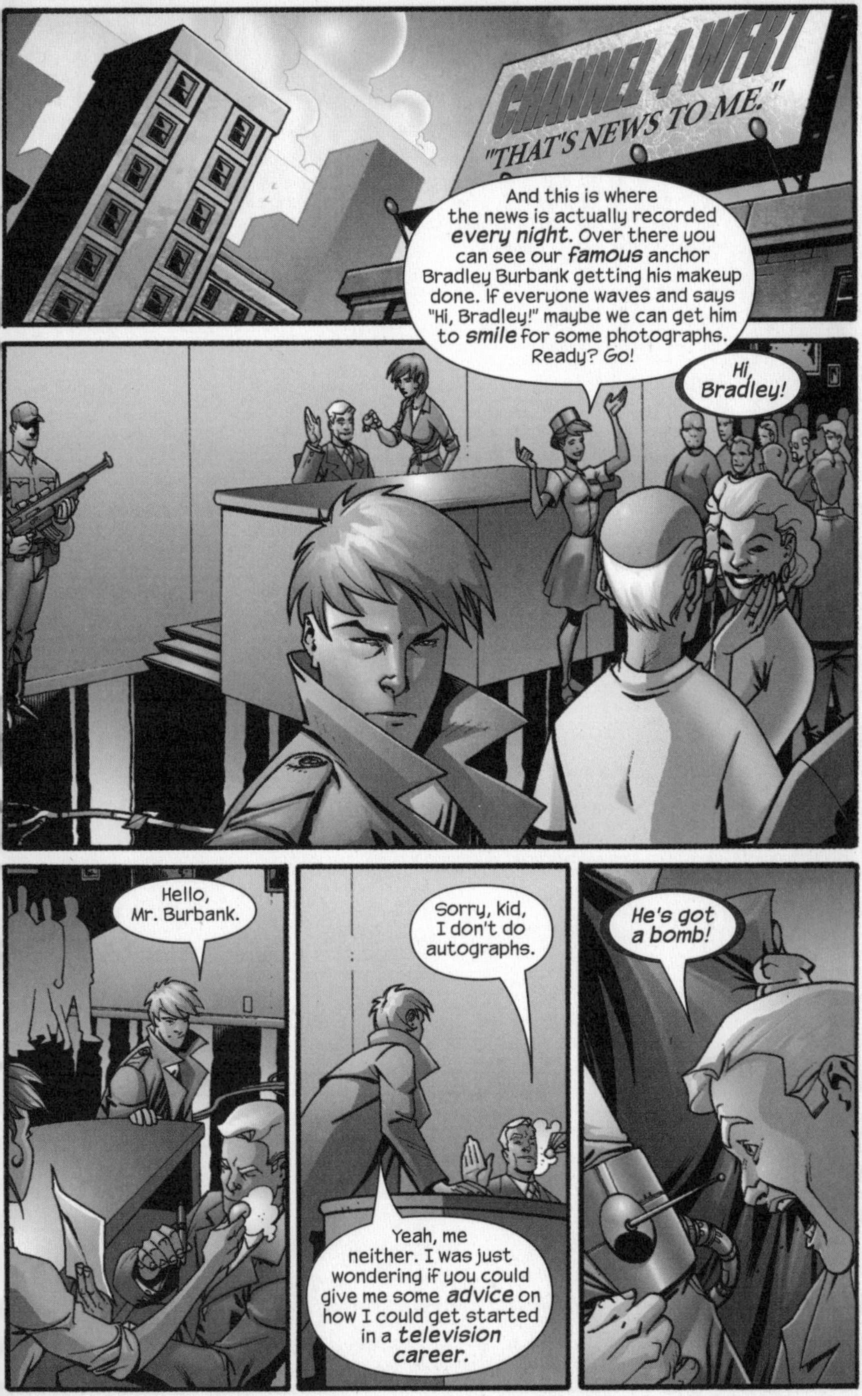
CHANNEL 4 WFRT
"THAT'S NEWS TO ME."
And this is where the news is actually recorded every night. Over there you can see our famous anchor Bradley Burbank getting his makeup done. If everyone waves and says "Hi, Bradley!" maybe we can get him to smile for some photographs. Ready? Go!
Hi, Bradley!
Hello, Mr. Burbank.
Sorry, kid, I don't do autographs.
Yeah, me neither. I was just wondering if you could give me some advice on how I could get started in a television career.
He's got a bomb!

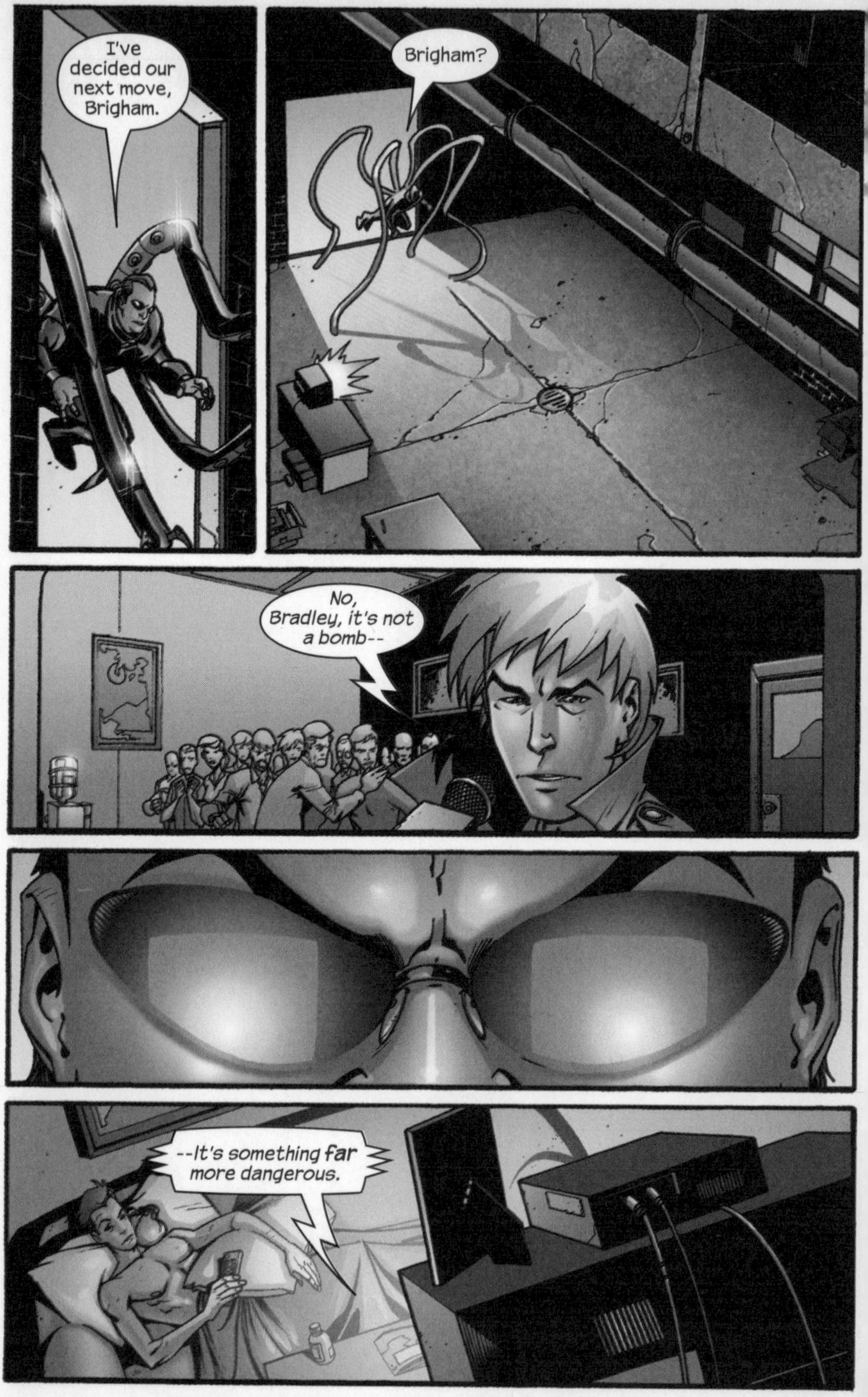
I've decided our next move, Brigham.
Brigham?
No, Bradley, it's not a bomb--
--It's something far more dangerous.

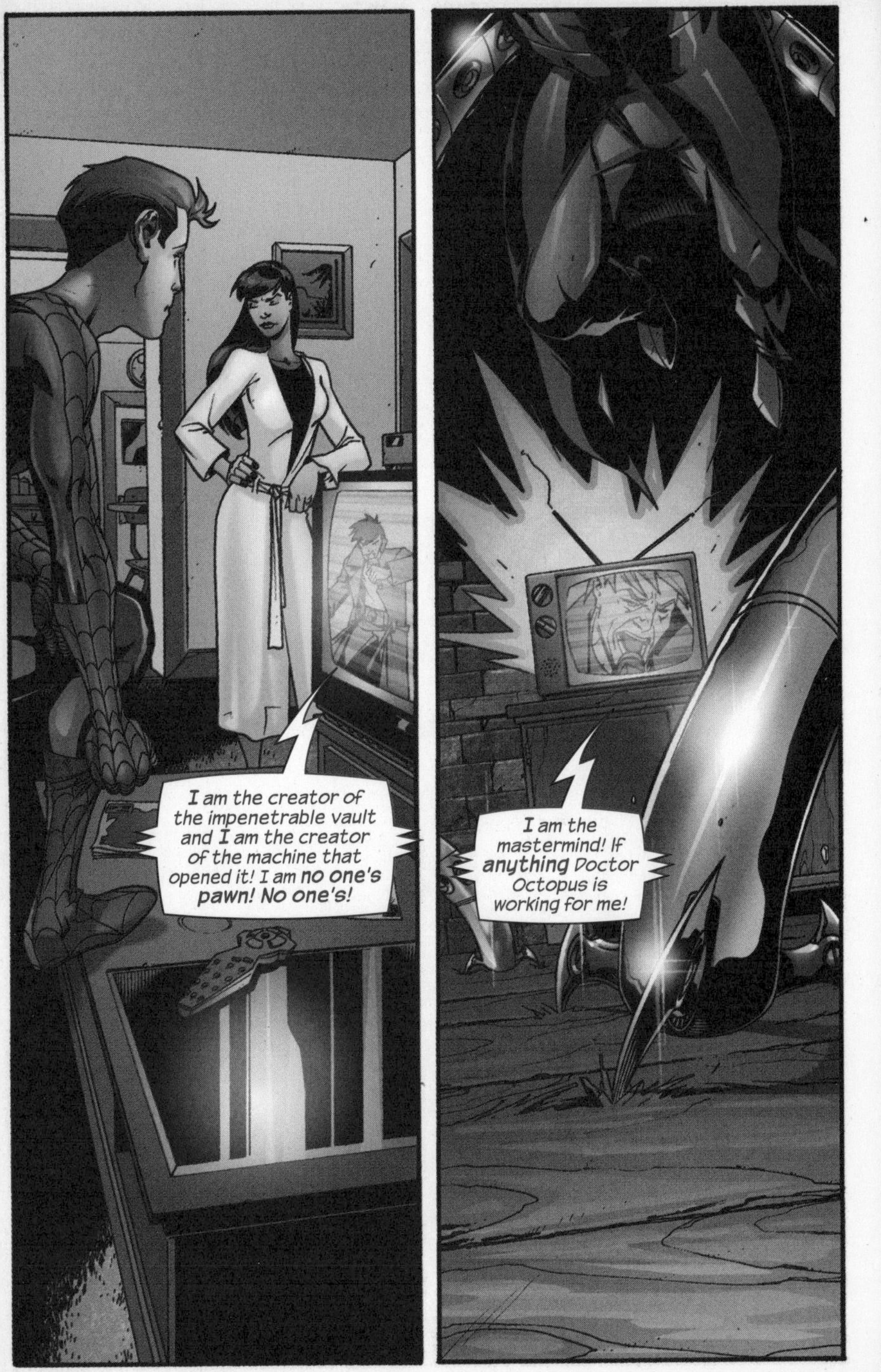
I am the creator of the impenetrable vault and I am the creator of the machine that opened it! I am no one's pawn! No one's!
I am the mastermind! If anything Doctor Octopus is working for me!

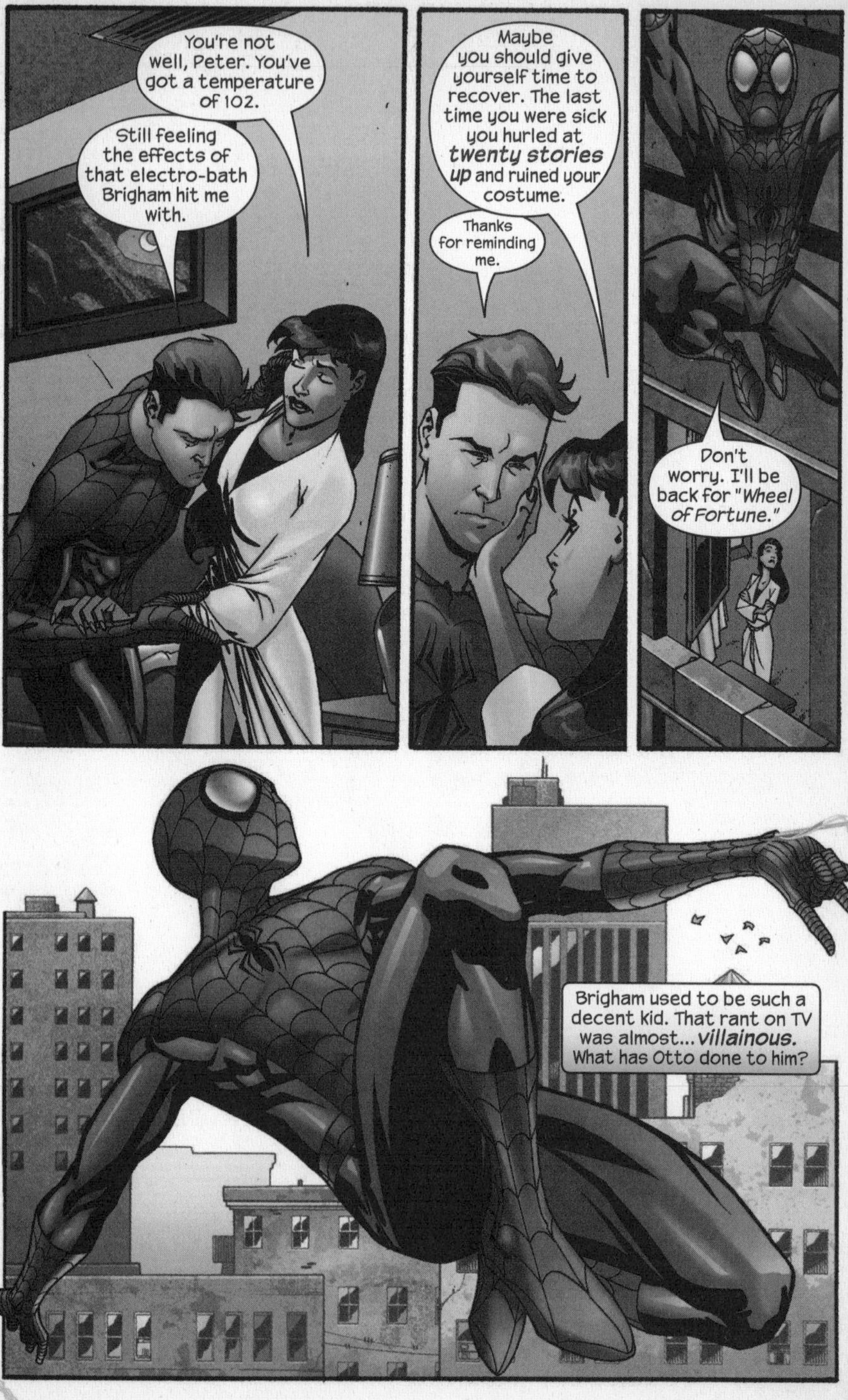
You're not well, Peter. You've got a temperature of 102.
Still feeling the effects of that electro-bath Brigham hit me with.
Maybe you should give yourself time to recover. The last time you were sick you hurled at *twenty stories up* and ruined your costume.
Thanks for reminding me.
Don't worry. I'll be back for "*Wheel of Fortune.*"
Brigham used to be such a decent kid. That rant on TV was almost... *villainous.* What has Otto done to him?

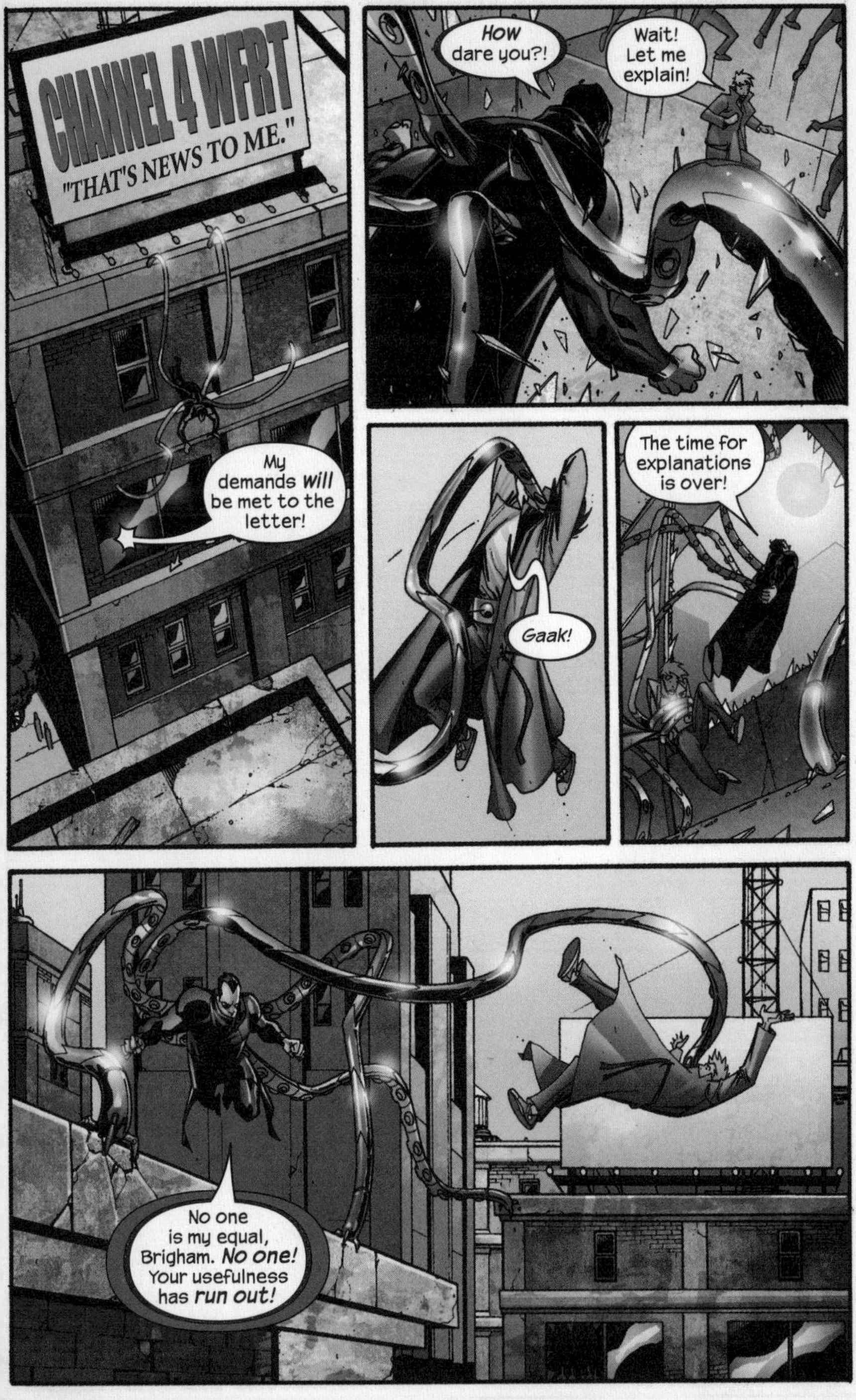
CHANNEL 4 WFRT
"THAT'S NEWS TO ME."
My demands will be met to the letter!
How dare you?!
Wait! Let me explain!
Gaak!
The time for explanations is over!
No one is my equal, Brigham. No one! Your usefulness has run out!

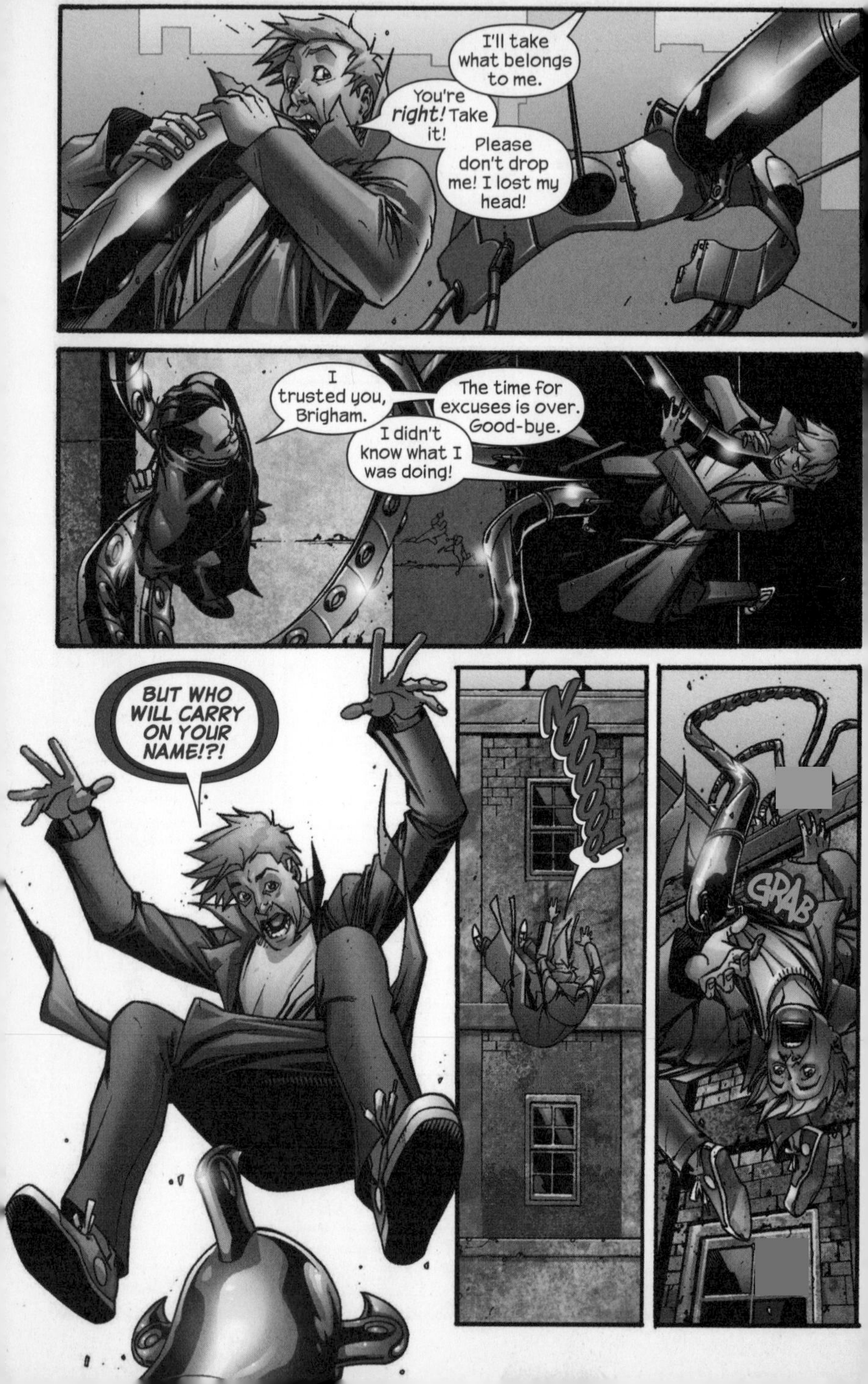

I'll take what belongs to me.
You're *right!* Take it!
Please don't drop me! I lost my head!
I trusted you, Brigham.
The time for excuses is over. Good-bye.
I didn't know what I was doing!
BUT WHO WILL CARRY ON YOUR NAME!?!
NOOOOOO!
GRAB

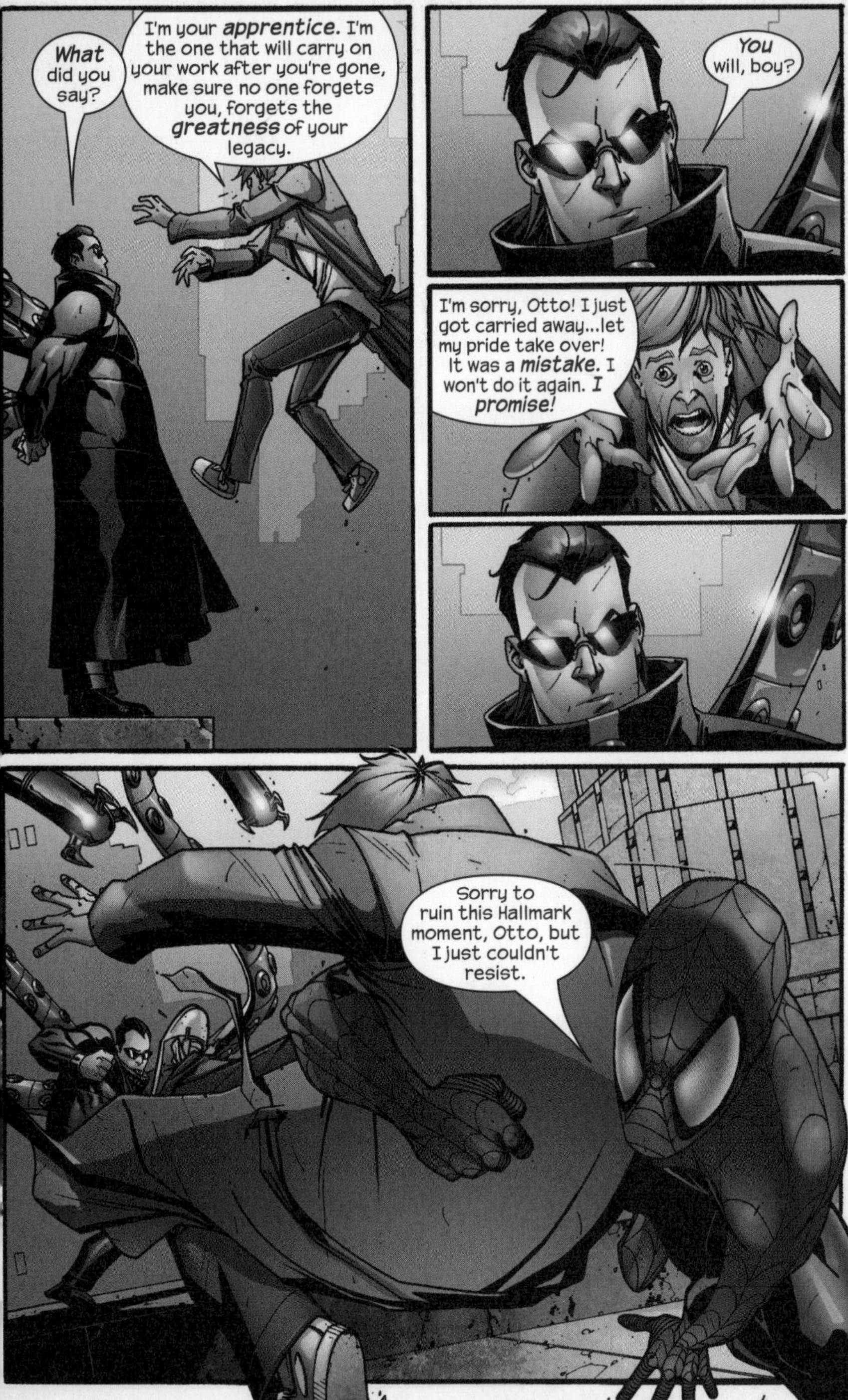
What did you say?
I'm your apprentice. I'm the one that will carry on your work after you're gone, make sure no one forgets you, forgets the greatness of your legacy.
You will, boy?
I'm sorry, Otto! I just got carried away...let my pride take over! It was a mistake. I won't do it again. I promise!
Sorry to ruin this Hallmark moment, Otto, but I just couldn't resist.

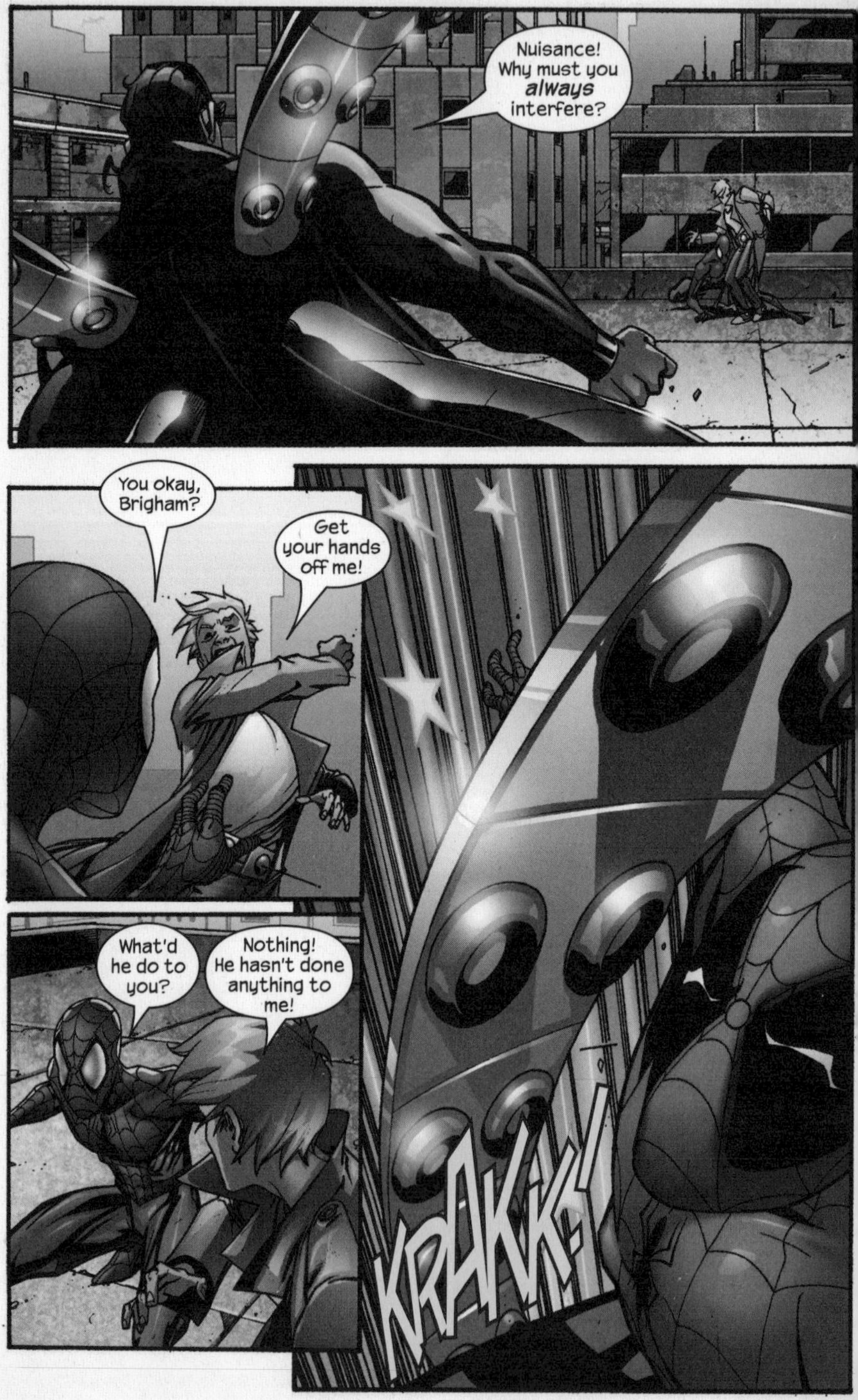
Nuisance! Why must you *always* interfere?
You okay, Brigham?
Get your hands off me!
What'd he do to you?
Nothing! He hasn't done anything to me!
KRAKK!

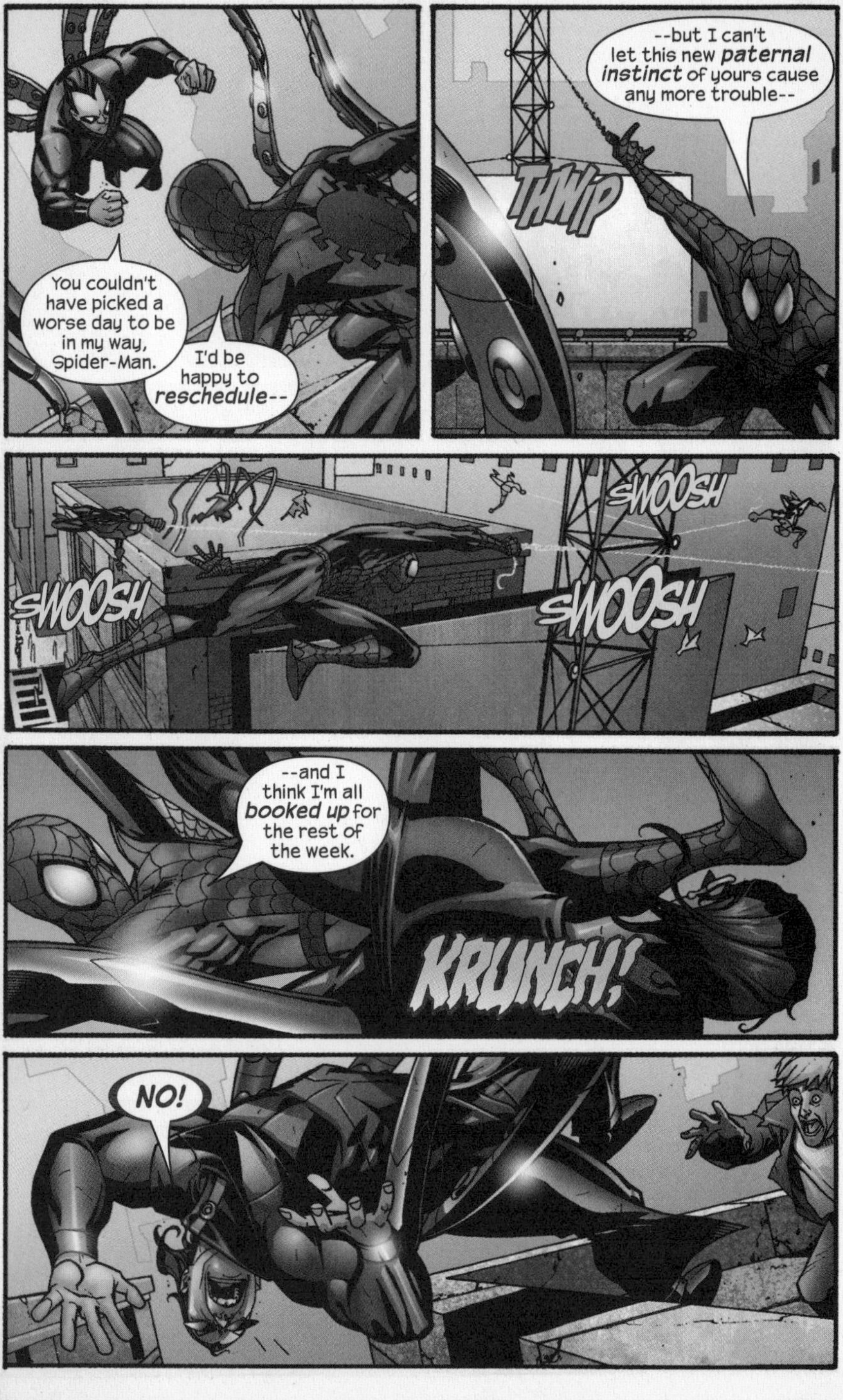
You couldn't have picked a worse day to be in my way, Spider-Man.
I'd be happy to reschedule--
--but I can't let this new paternal instinct of yours cause any more trouble--
THWIP
SWOOSH
SWOOSH
SWOOSH
--and I think I'm all booked up for the rest of the week.
KRUNCH!
NO!

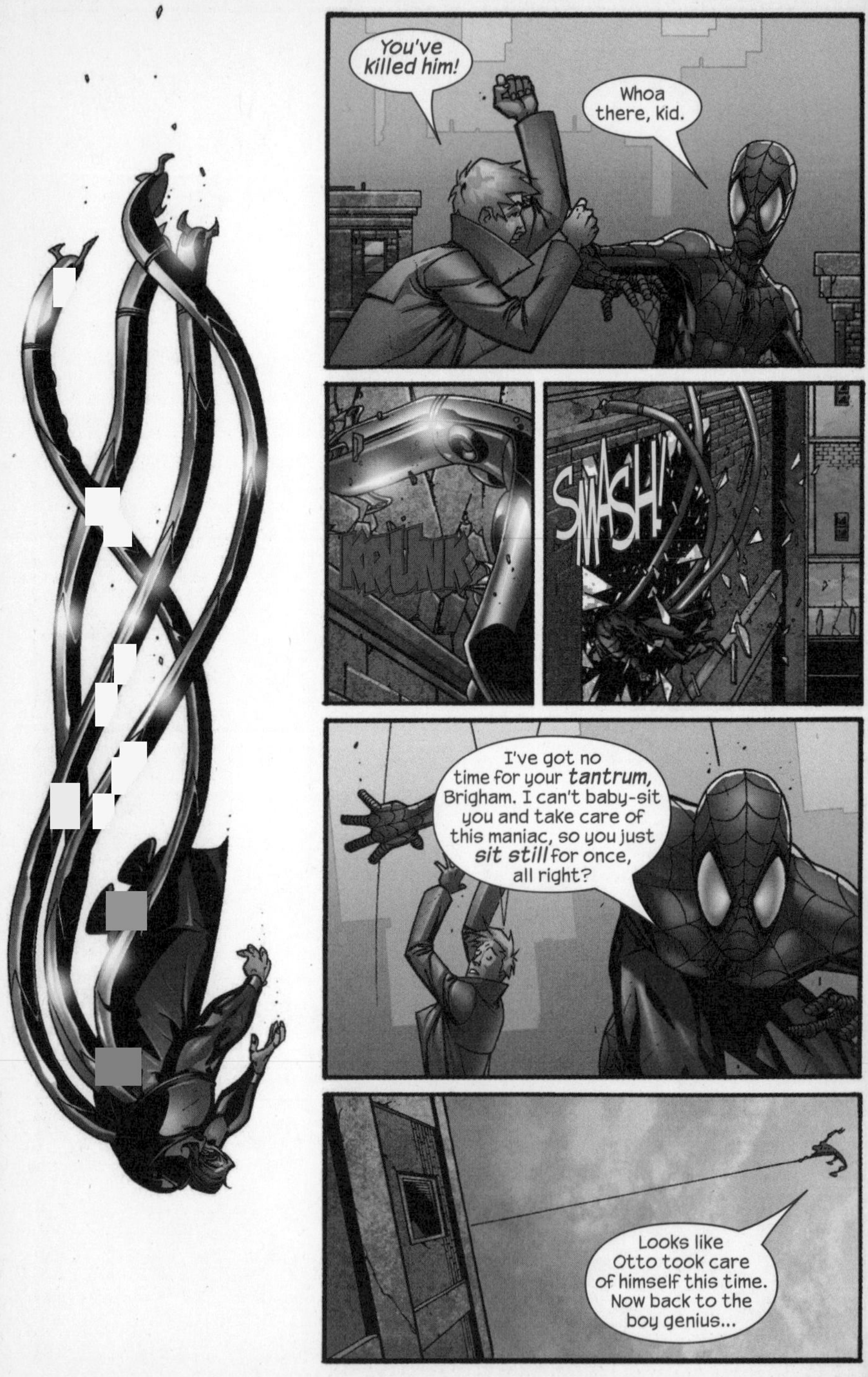

You've killed him!
Whoa there, kid.
KRUNK
SMASH!
I've got no time for your tantrum, Brigham. I can't baby-sit you and take care of this maniac, so you just sit still for once, all right?
Looks like Otto took care of himself this time. Now back to the boy genius...

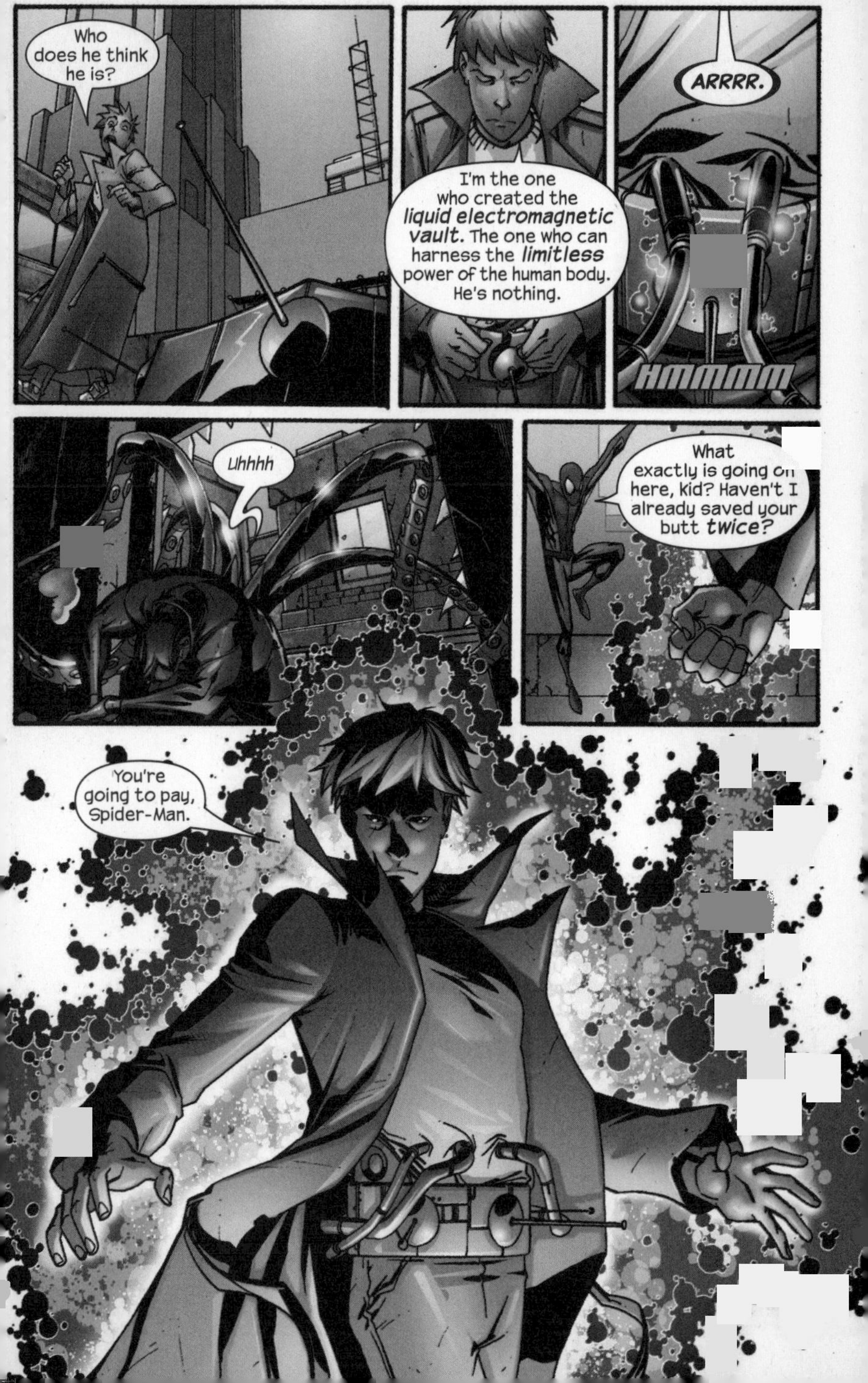
Who does he think he is?
I'm the one who created the liquid electromagnetic vault. The one who can harness the limitless power of the human body. He's nothing.
ARRRR.
HMMMM
Uhhhh
What exactly is going on here, kid? Haven't I already saved your butt twice?
You're going to pay, Spider-Man.

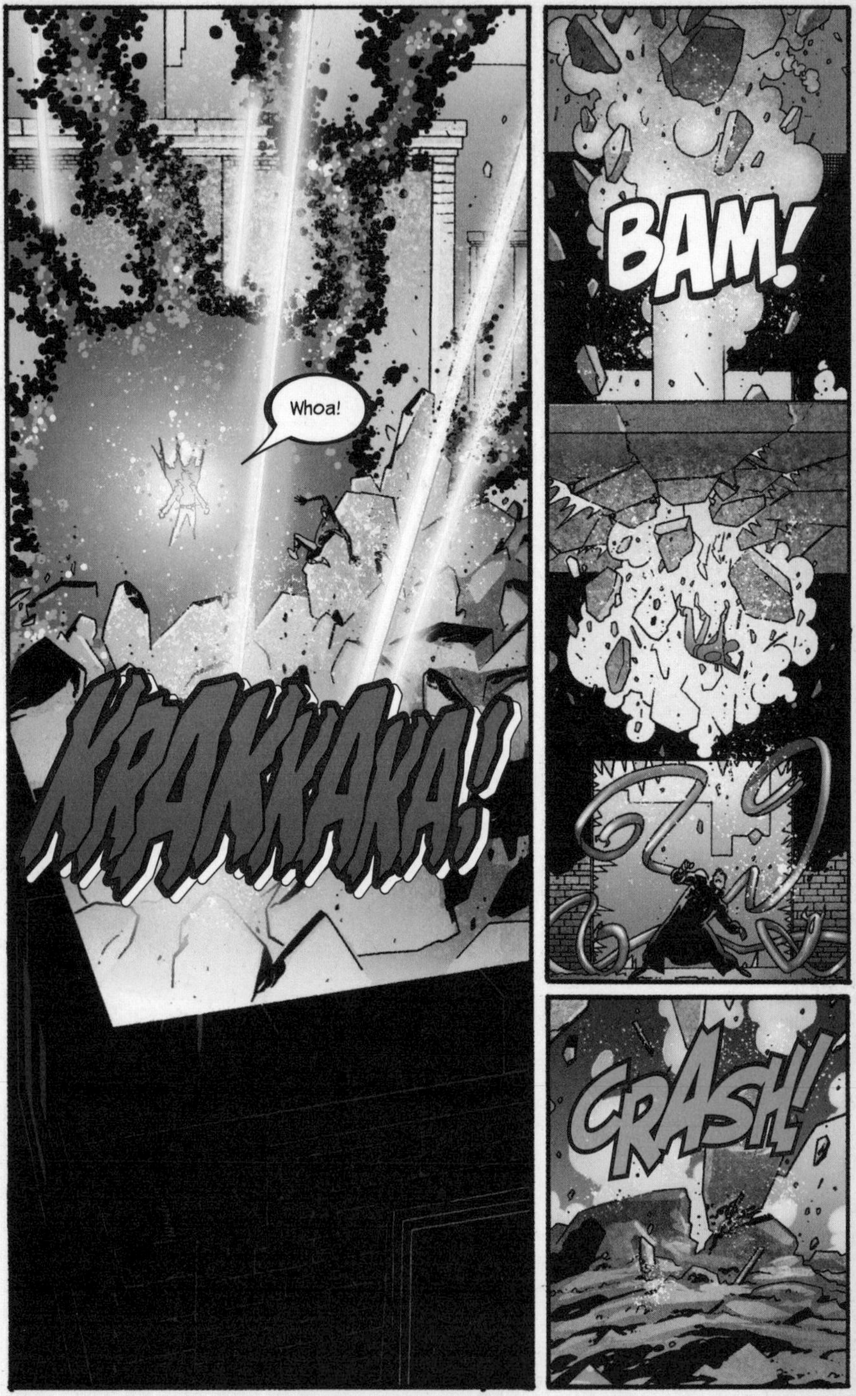
Whoa!
KRAKKAKA!
BAM!
CRASH!

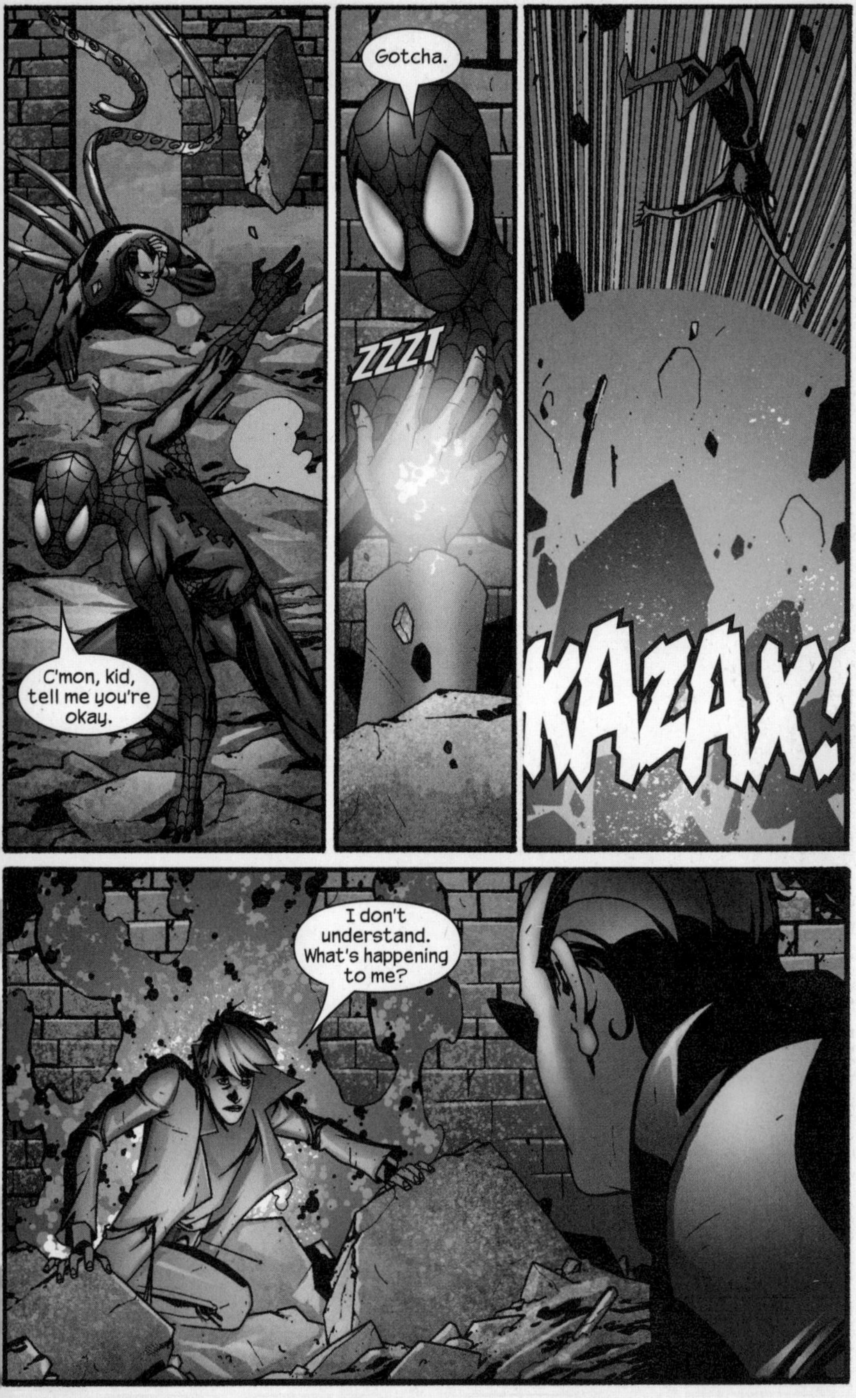
C'mon, kid, tell me you're okay.
Gotcha.
ZZZT
KAZAX!
I don't understand. What's happening to me?

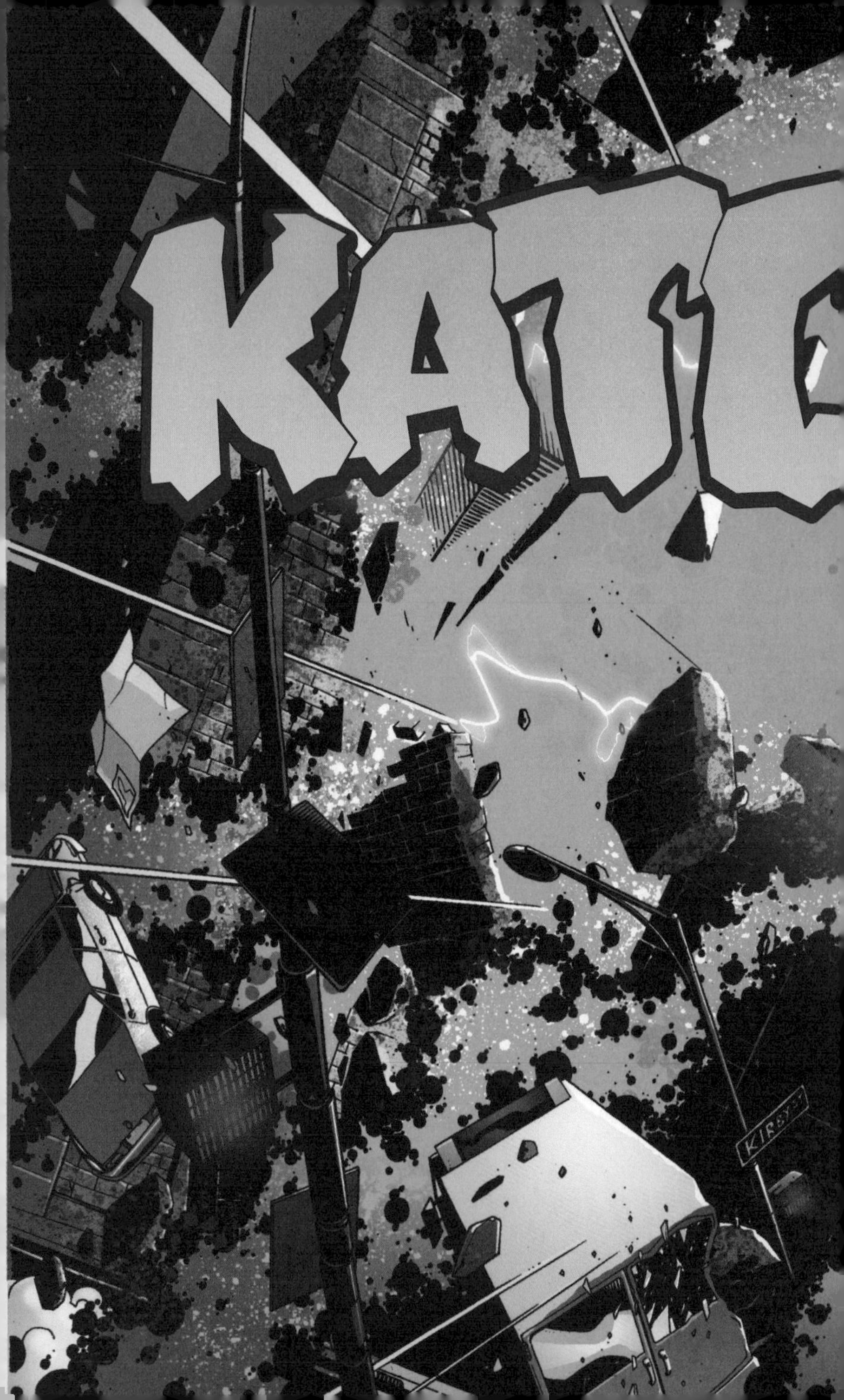
KAT
KIRBY

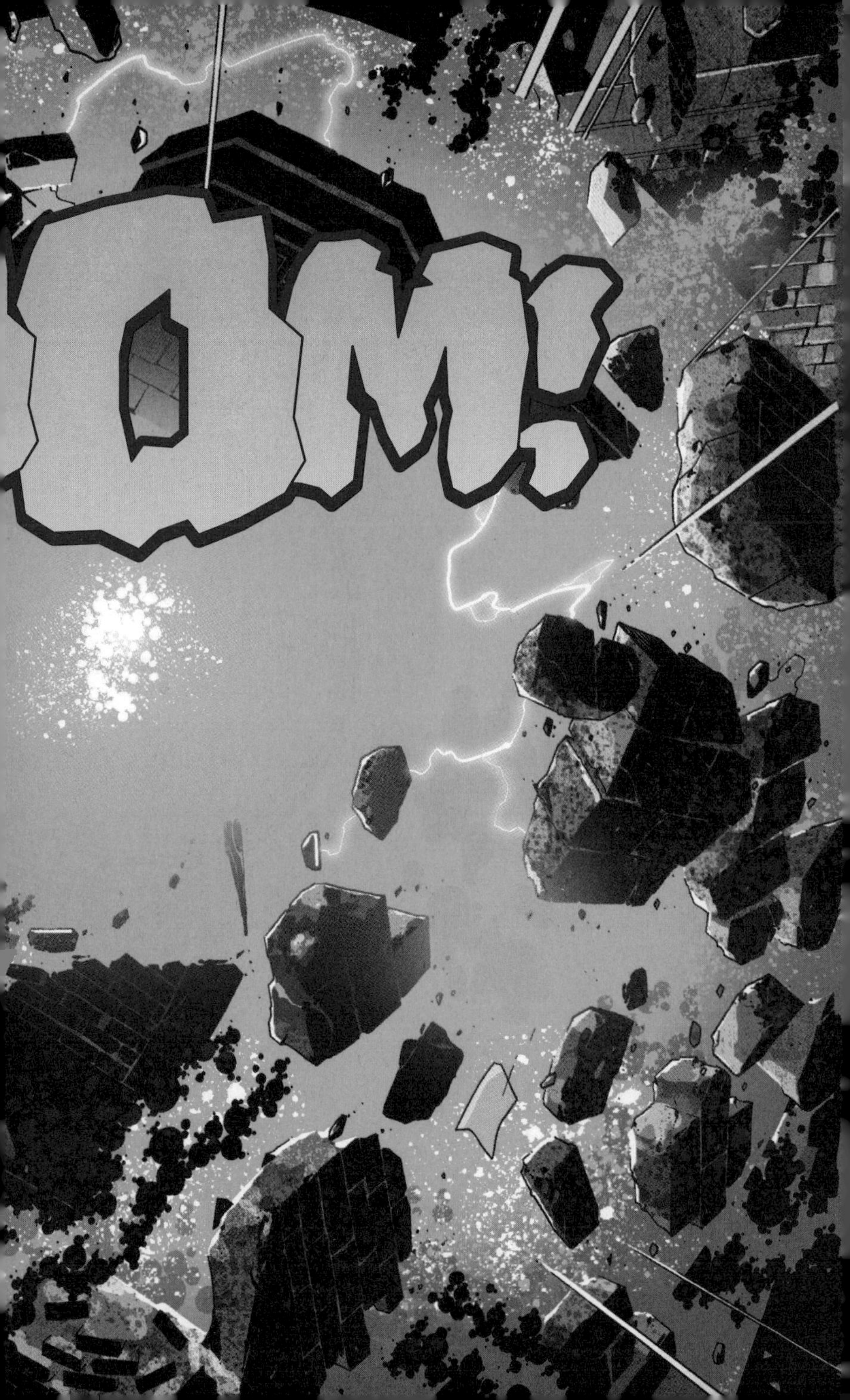
OM!

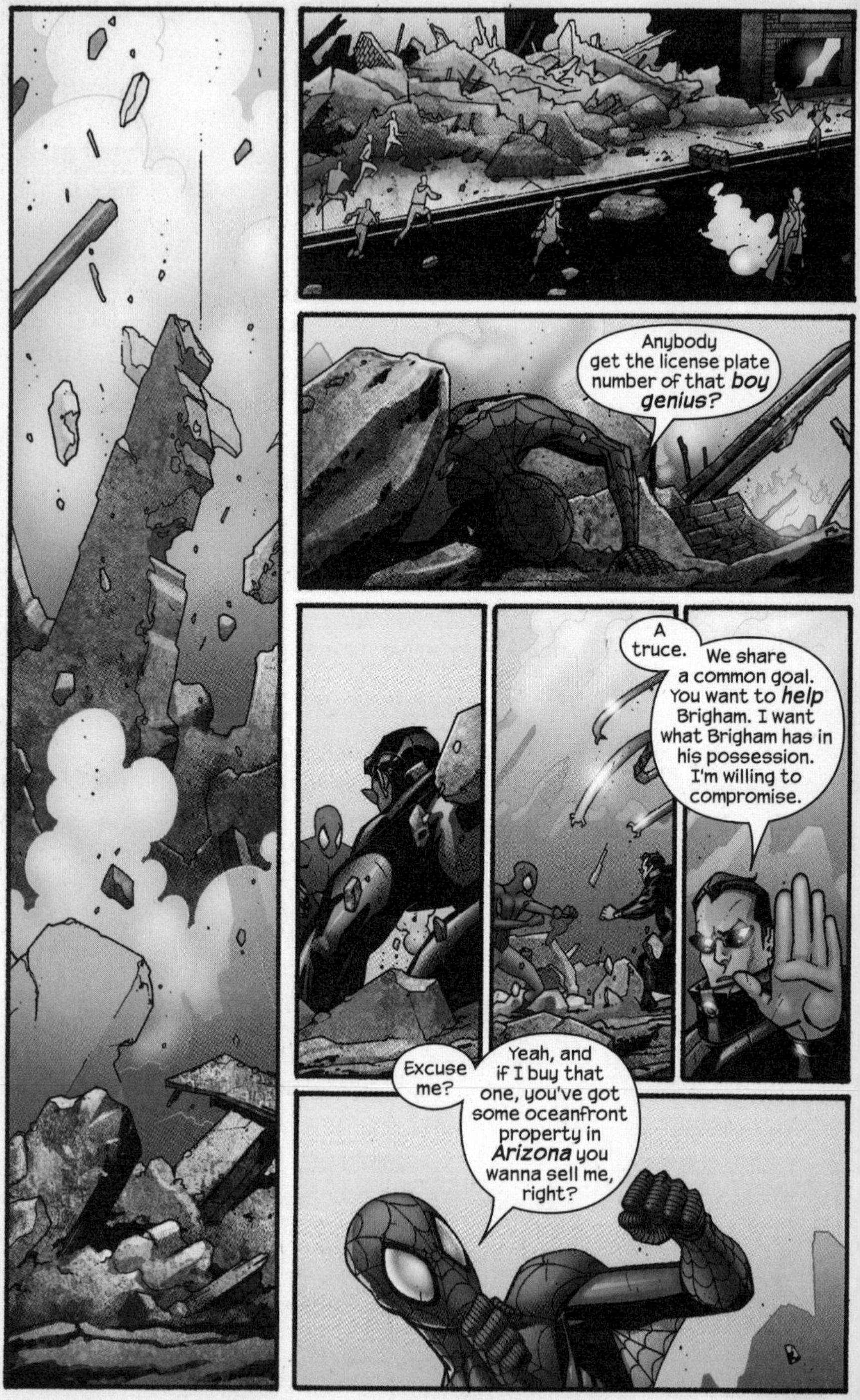
Anybody get the license plate number of that boy genius?
A truce.
We share a common goal. You want to help Brigham. I want what Brigham has in his possession. I'm willing to compromise.
Excuse me?
Yeah, and if I buy that one, you've got some oceanfront property in Arizona you wanna sell me, right?

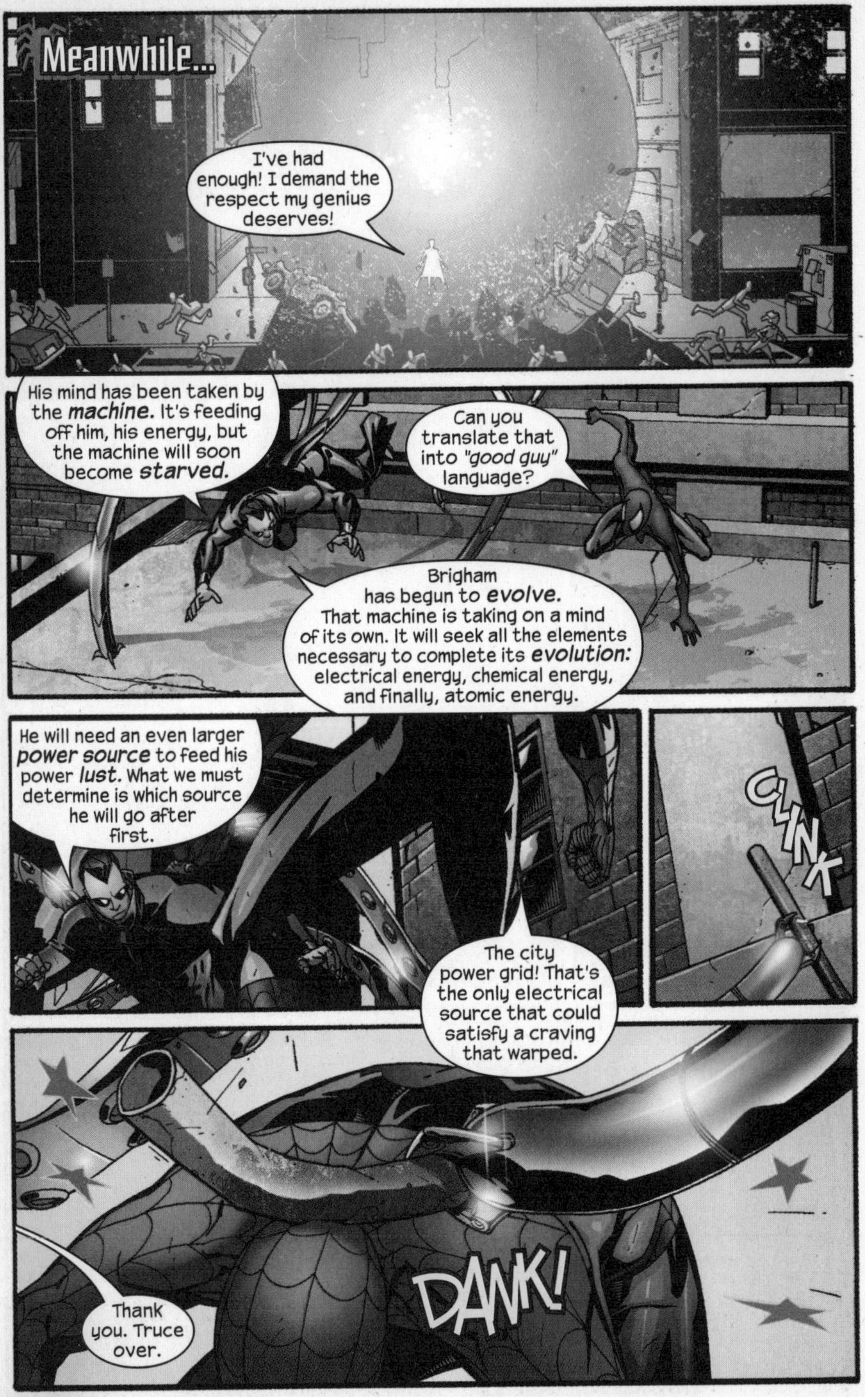
Meanwhile...
I've had enough! I demand the respect my genius deserves!
His mind has been taken by the machine. It's feeding off him, his energy, but the machine will soon become starved.
Can you translate that into "good guy" language?
Brigham has begun to evolve. That machine is taking on a mind of its own. It will seek all the elements necessary to complete its evolution: electrical energy, chemical energy, and finally, atomic energy.
He will need an even larger power source to feed his power lust. What we must determine is which source he will go after first.
The city power grid! That's the only electrical source that could satisfy a craving that warped.
CLINK
DANK!
Thank you. Truce over.

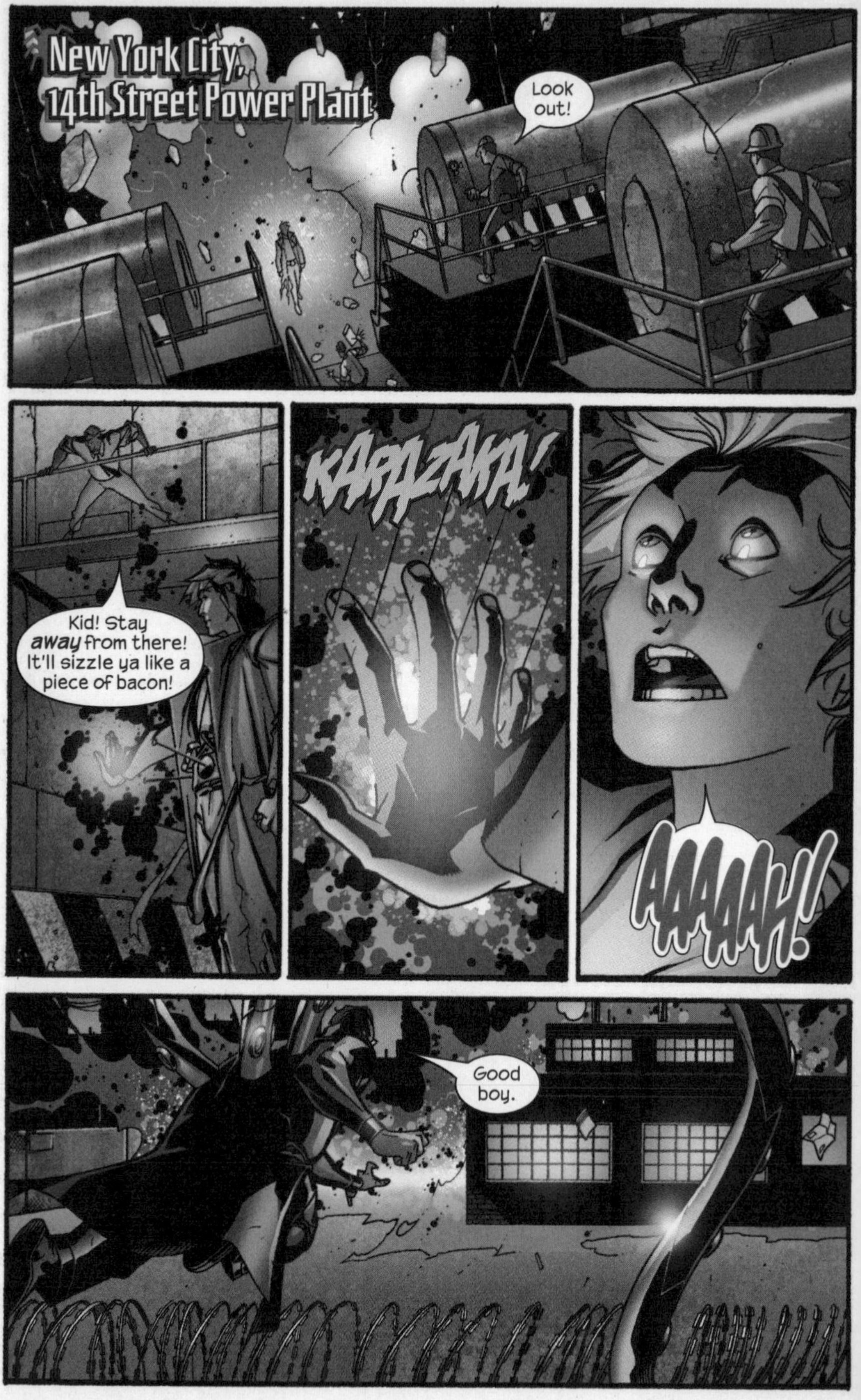
New York City,
14th Street Power Plant
Look out!
Kid! Stay *away* from there! It'll sizzle ya like a piece of bacon!
KARAZAKA!
AAAAAH!
Good boy.

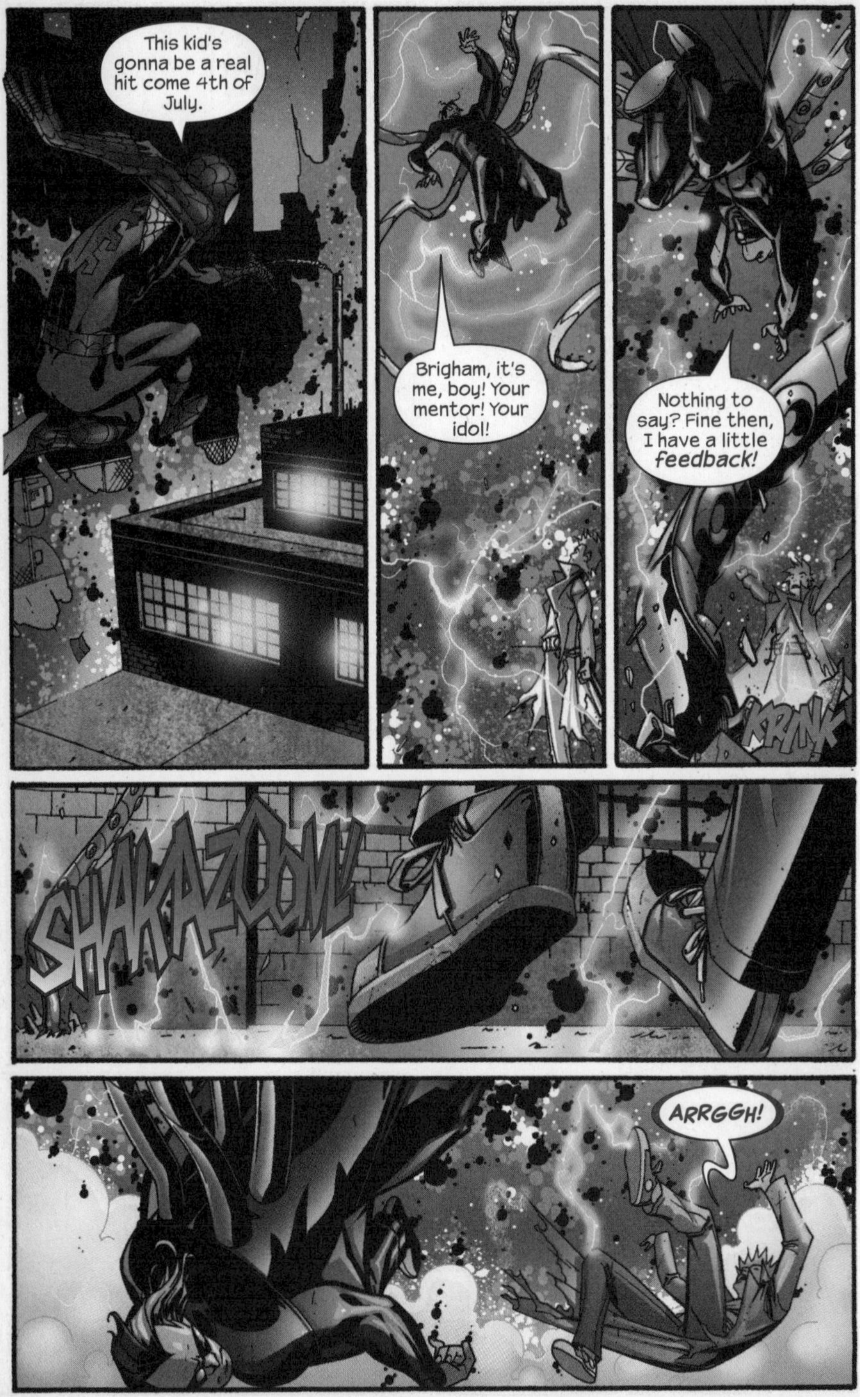
This kid's gonna be a real hit come 4th of July.
Brigham, it's me, boy! Your mentor! Your idol!
Nothing to say? Fine then, I have a little *feedback!*
KRNK
SHAKAZOOM!
ARRGGH!

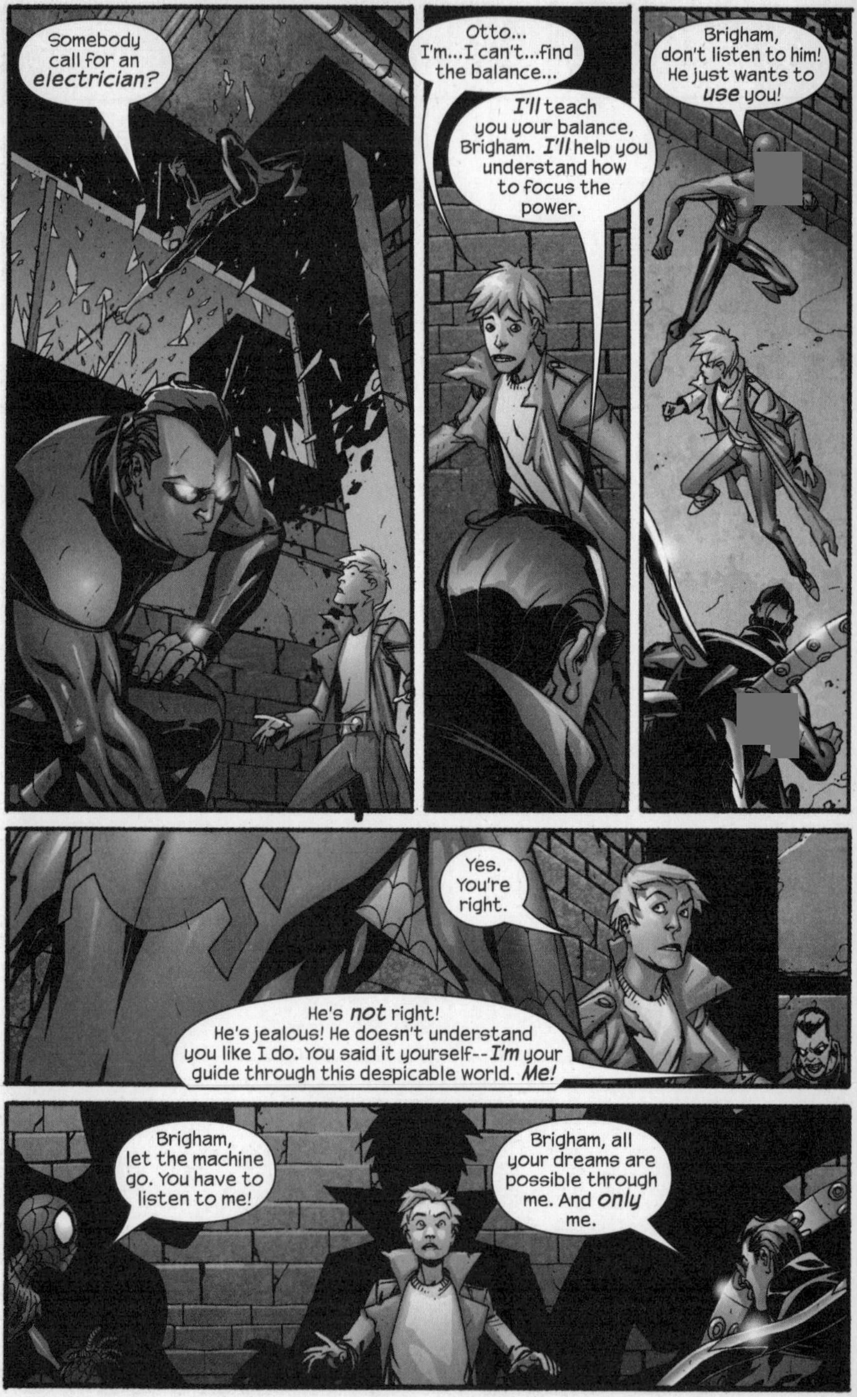
Somebody call for an *electrician?*
Otto... I'm...I can't...find the balance...
I'll teach you your balance, Brigham. *I'll* help you understand how to focus the power.
Brigham, don't listen to him! He just wants to *use* you!
Yes. You're right.
He's *not* right! He's jealous! He doesn't understand you like I do. You said it yourself--*I'm* your guide through this despicable world. *Me!*
Brigham, let the machine go. You have to listen to me!
Brigham, all your dreams are possible through me. And *only* me.

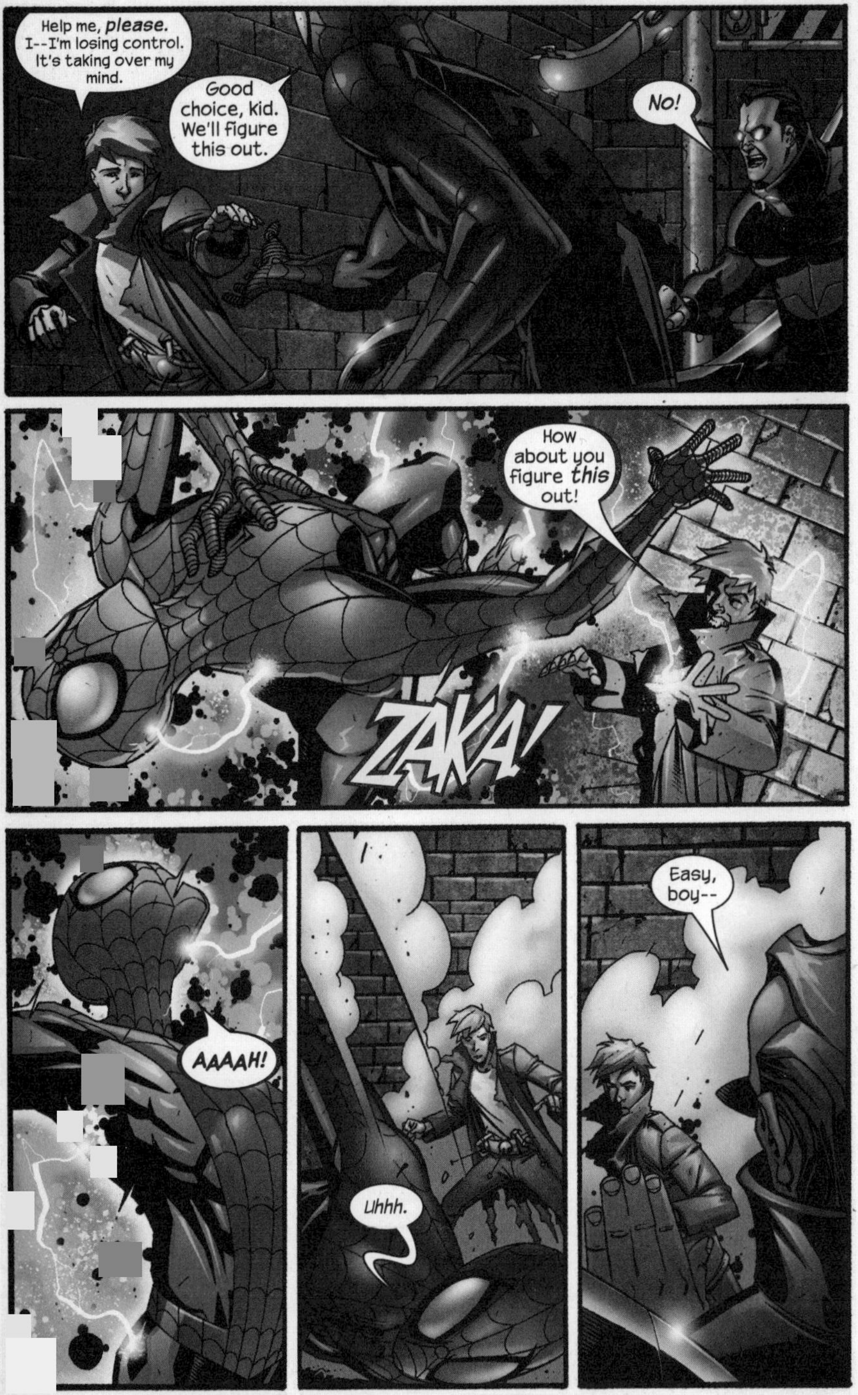
Help me, please. I--I'm losing control. It's taking over my mind.
Good choice, kid. We'll figure this out.
No!
How about you figure this out!
ZAKA!
AAAAH!
Uhhh.
Easy, boy--

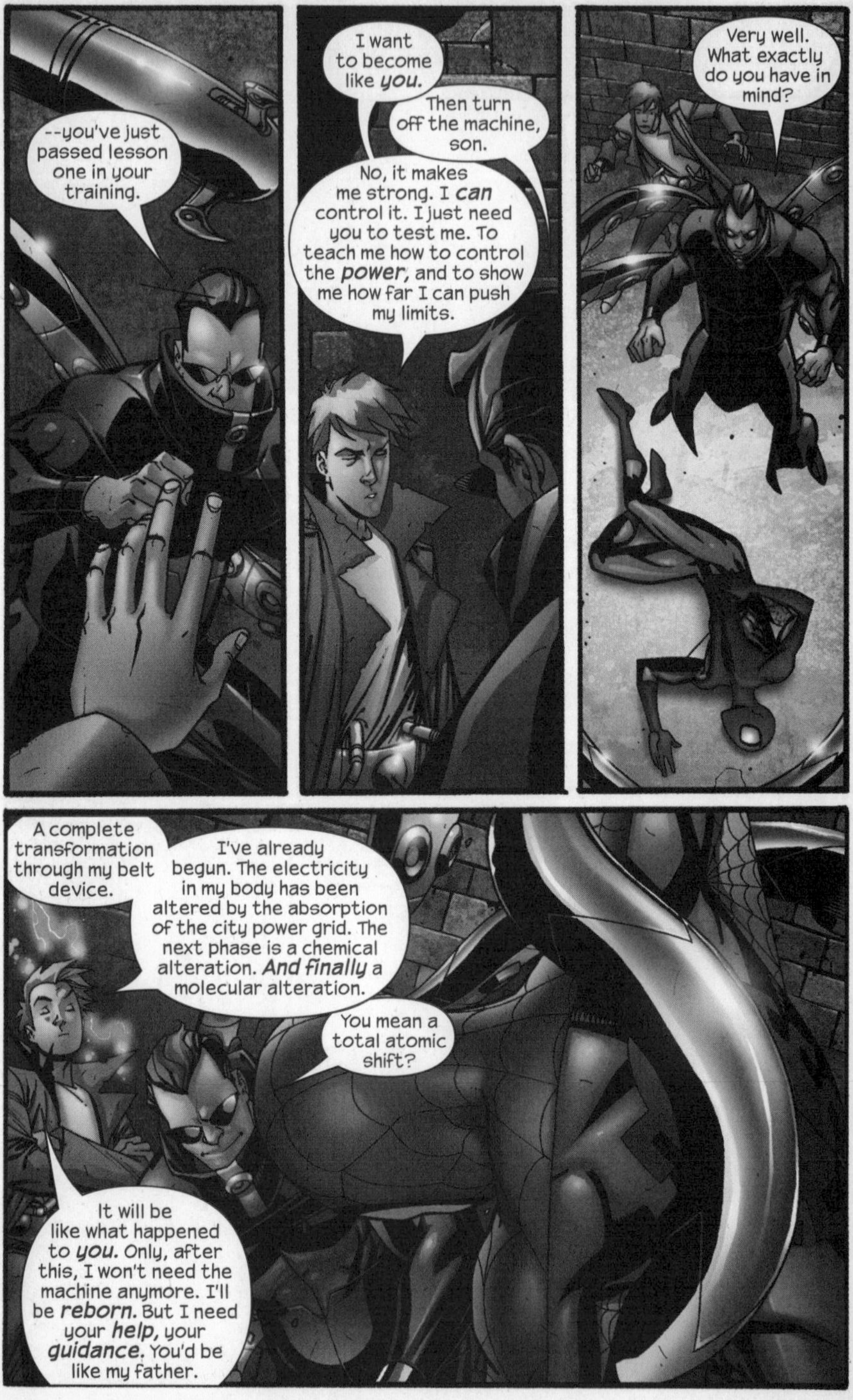
--you've just passed lesson one in your training.
I want to become like *you.*
Then turn off the machine, son.
No, it makes me strong. I *can* control it. I just need you to test me. To teach me how to control the *power,* and to show me how far I can push my limits.
Very well. What exactly do you have in mind?
A complete transformation through my belt device.
I've already begun. The electricity in my body has been altered by the absorption of the city power grid. The next phase is a chemical alteration. *And finally* a molecular alteration.
You mean a total atomic shift?
It will be like what happened to *you.* Only, after this, I won't need the machine anymore. I'll be *reborn.* But I need your *help,* your *guidance.* You'd be like my father.

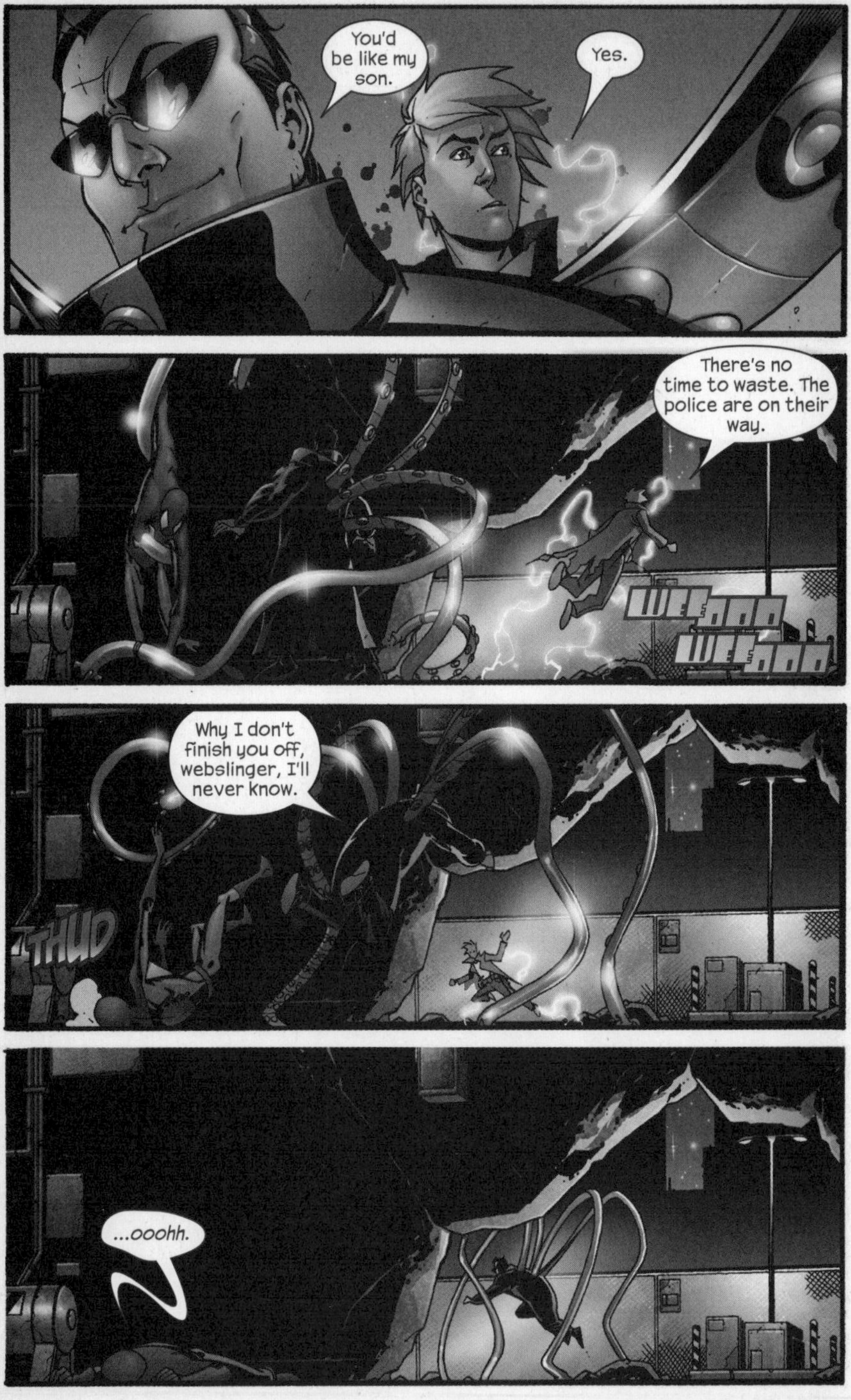
You'd be like my son.
Yes.
There's no time to waste. The police are on their way.
WEEOOO
WEEOOO
Why I don't finish you off, webslinger, I'll never know.
THUD
...ooohh.

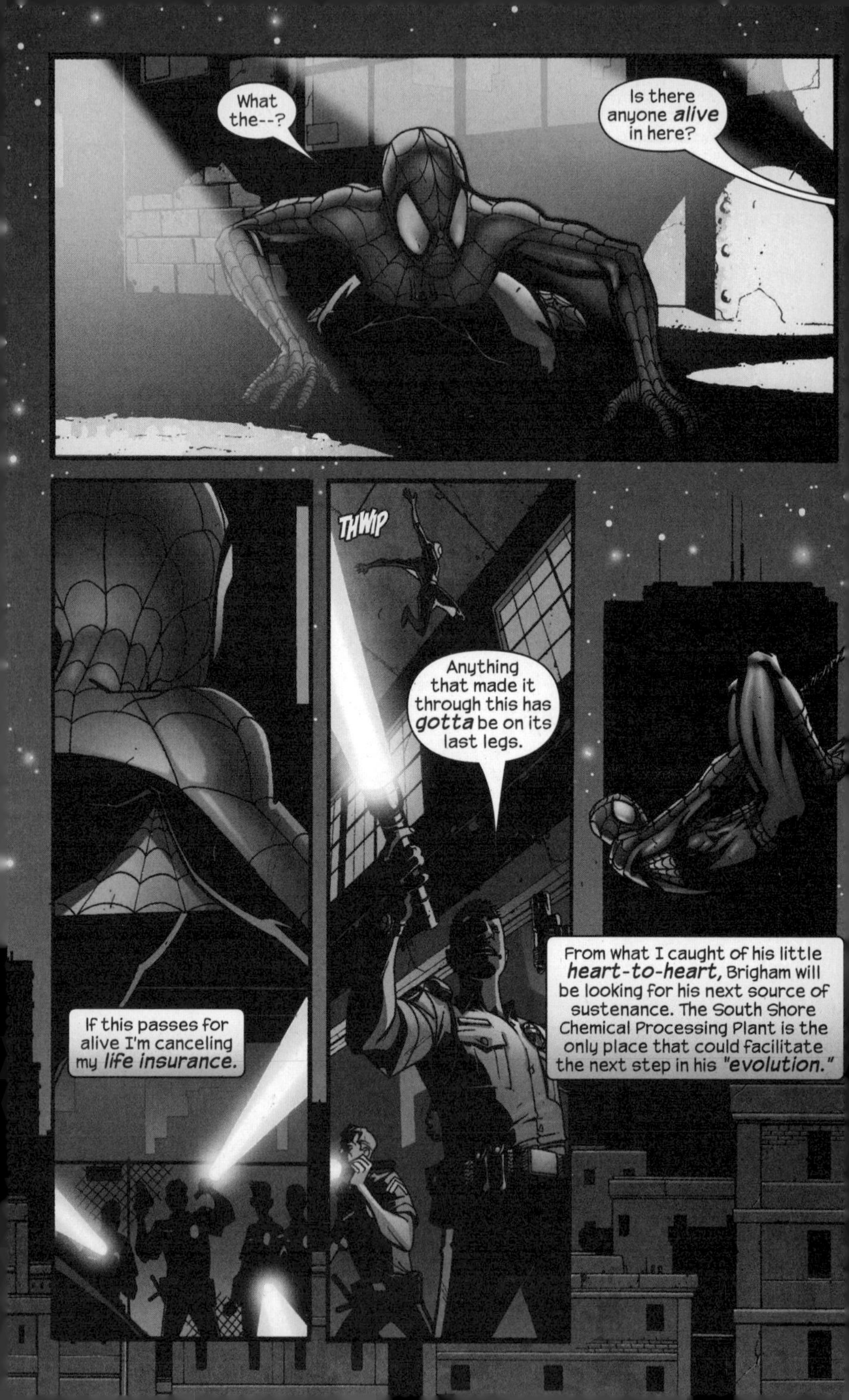
What the--?
Is there anyone *alive* in here?
If this passes for alive I'm canceling my *life insurance.*
THWIP
Anything that made it through this has *gotta* be on its last legs.
From what I caught of his little *heart-to-heart,* Brigham will be looking for his next source of sustenance. The South Shore Chemical Processing Plant is the only place that could facilitate the next step in his *"evolution."*

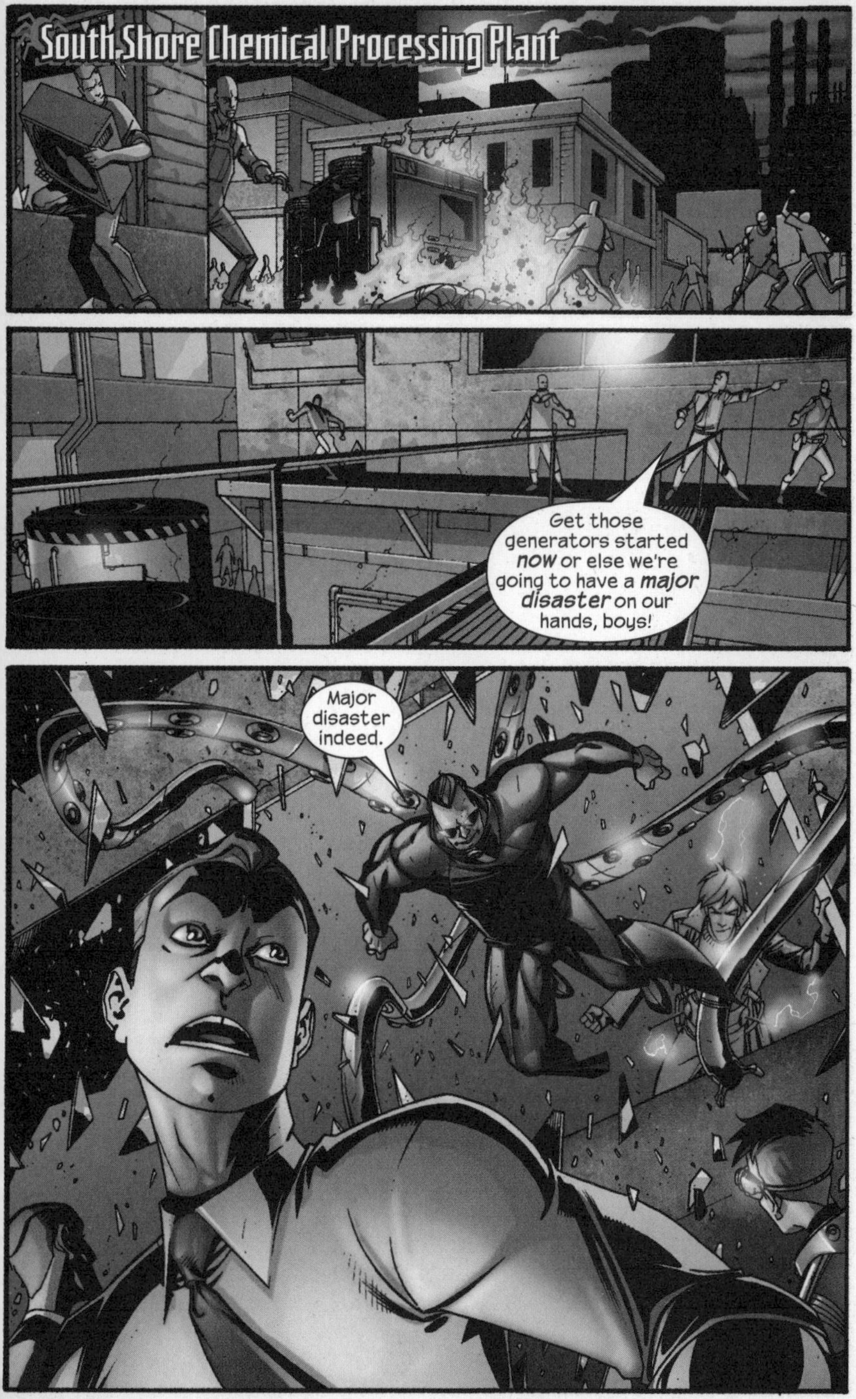
South Shore Chemical Processing Plant
Get those generators started *NOW* or else we're going to have a *major disaster* on our hands, boys!
Major disaster indeed.

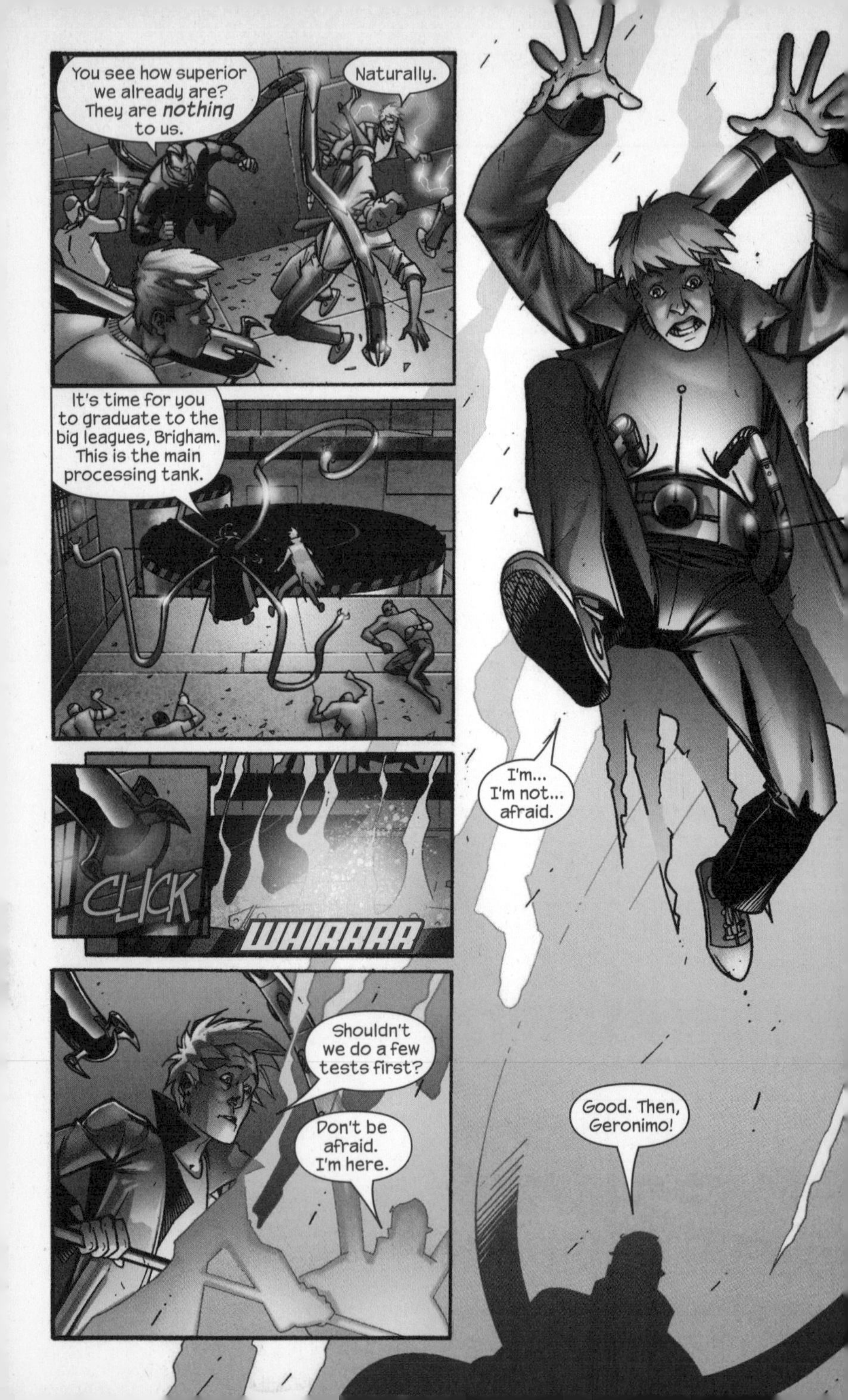
You see how superior we already are? They are *nothing* to us.
Naturally.
It's time for you to graduate to the big leagues, Brigham. This is the main processing tank.
CLICK
WHIRRRR
Shouldn't we do a few tests first?
Don't be afraid. I'm here.
I'm... I'm not... afraid.
Good. Then, Geronimo!

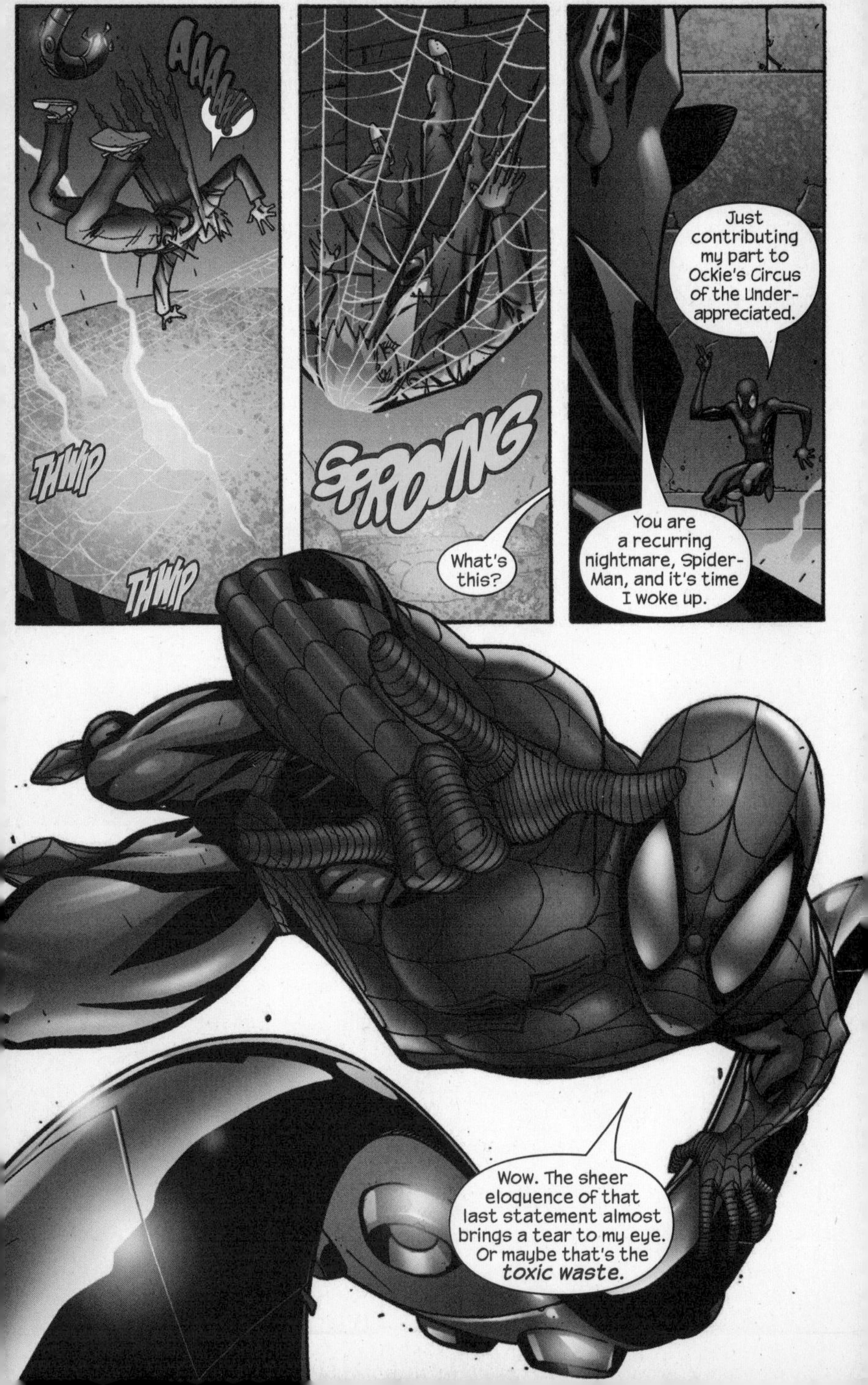
AAAAAK!
THWIP
THWIP
SPROING
What's this?
Just contributing my part to Ockie's Circus of the Under-appreciated.
You are a recurring nightmare, Spider-Man, and it's time I woke up.
Wow. The sheer eloquence of that last statement almost brings a tear to my eye. Or maybe that's the *toxic waste.*

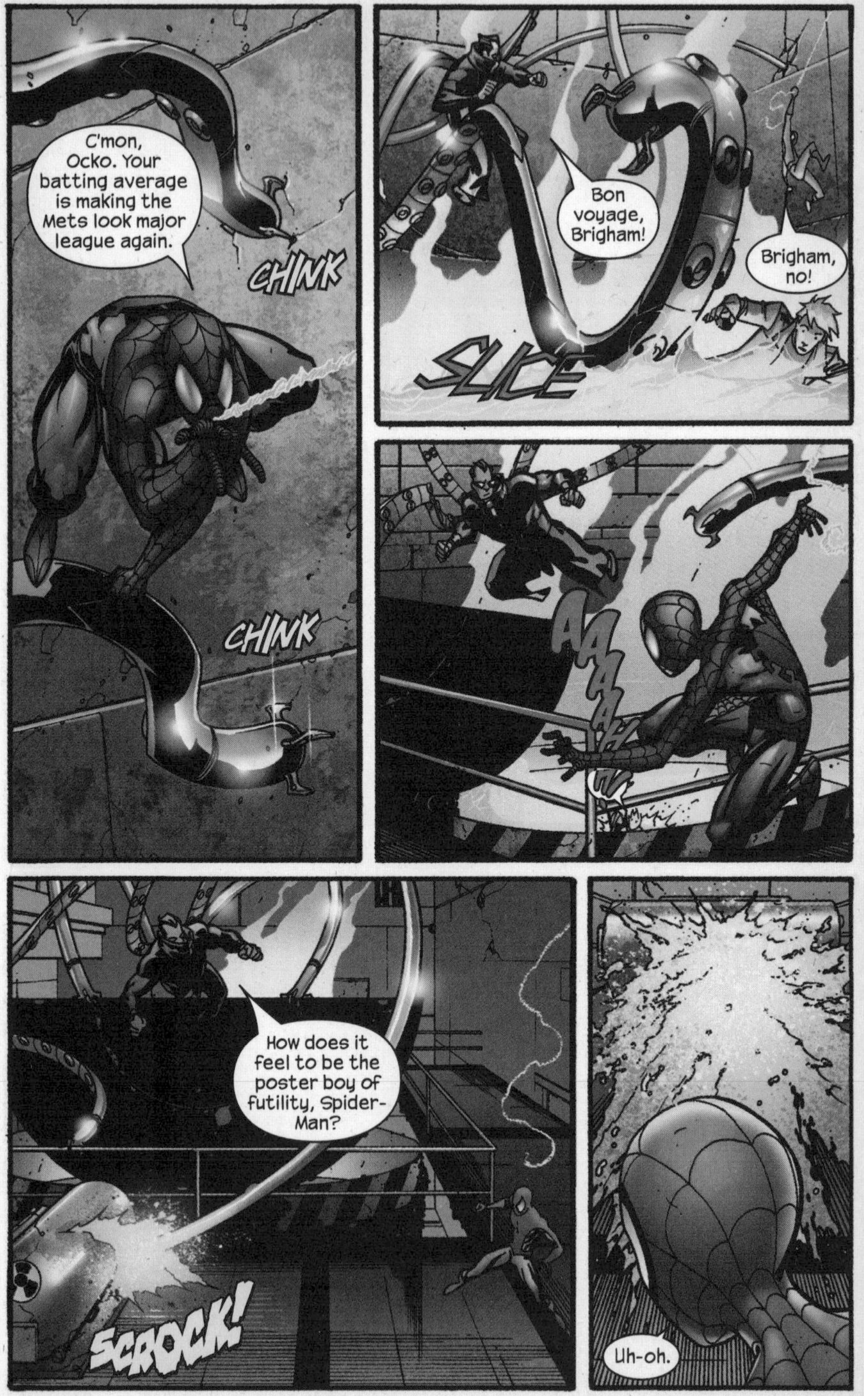
C'mon, Ocko. Your batting average is making the Mets look major league again.
CHINK
CHINK
Bon voyage, Brigham!
Brigham, no!
SLICE
How does it feel to be the poster boy of futility, Spider-Man?
SCROCK!
Uh-oh.

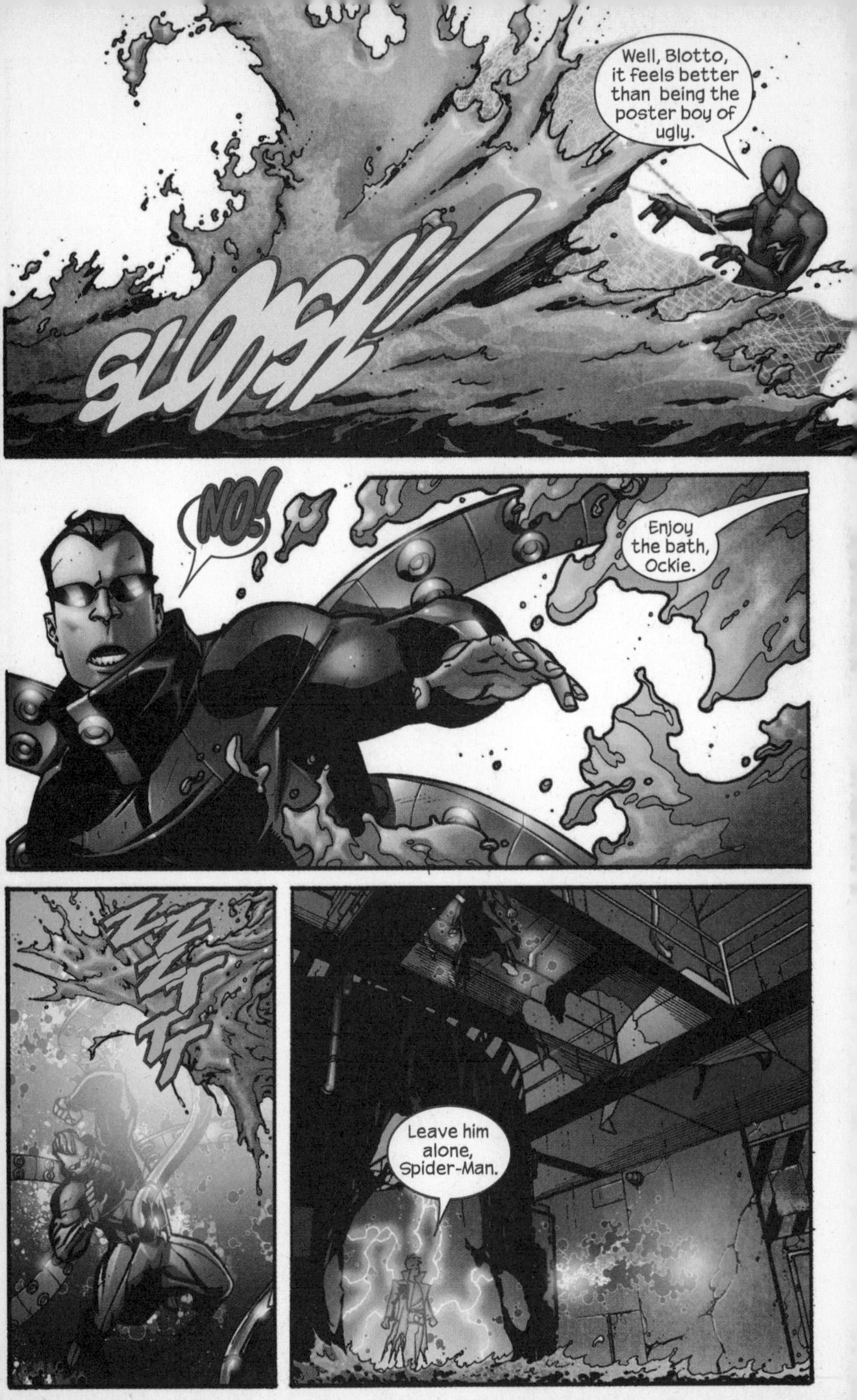
Well, Blotto, it feels better than being the poster boy of ugly.
SLOOSH
NO!
Enjoy the bath, Ockie.
Leave him alone, Spider-Man.

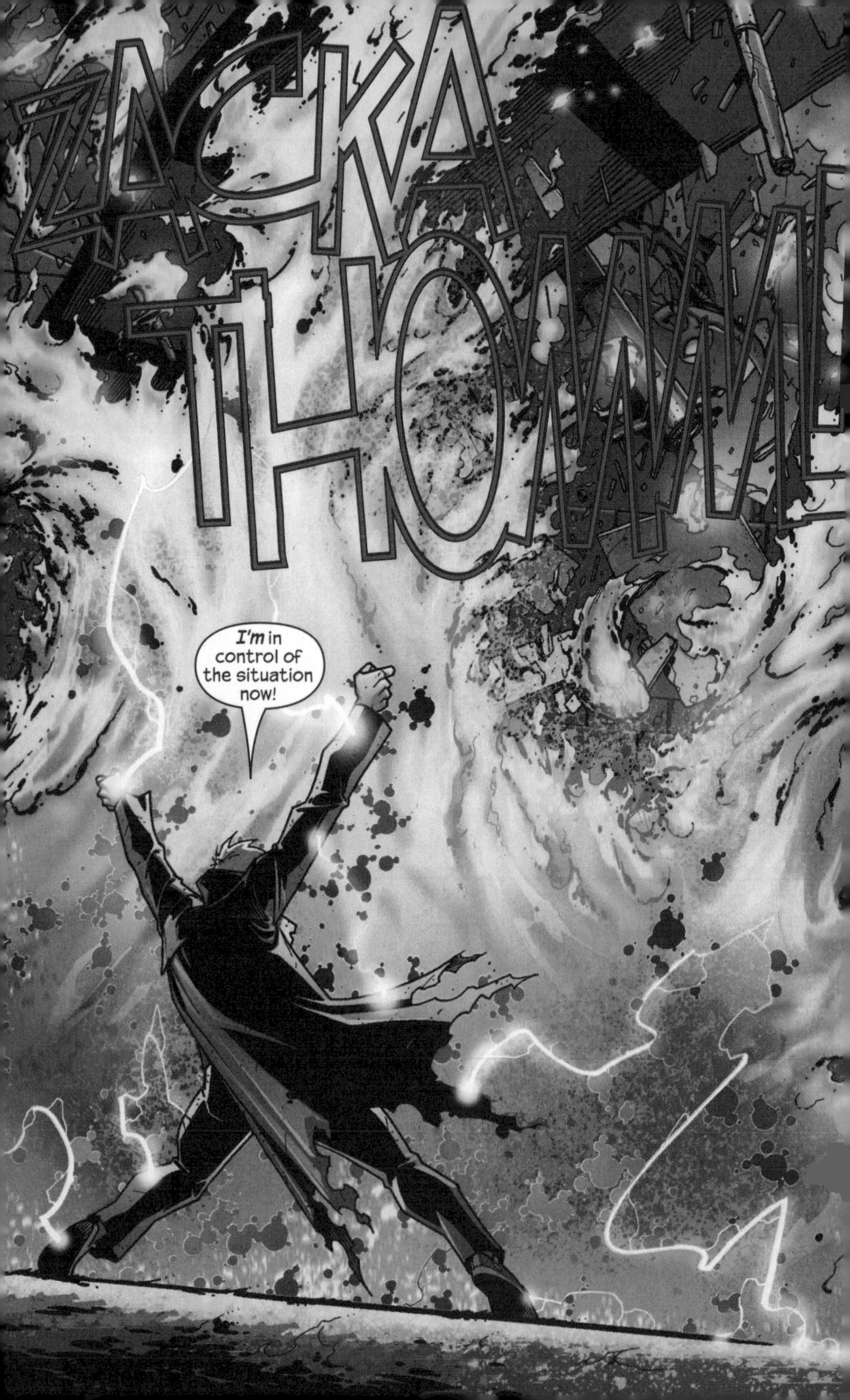
ZZACKA THOOM!
I'm in control of the situation now!

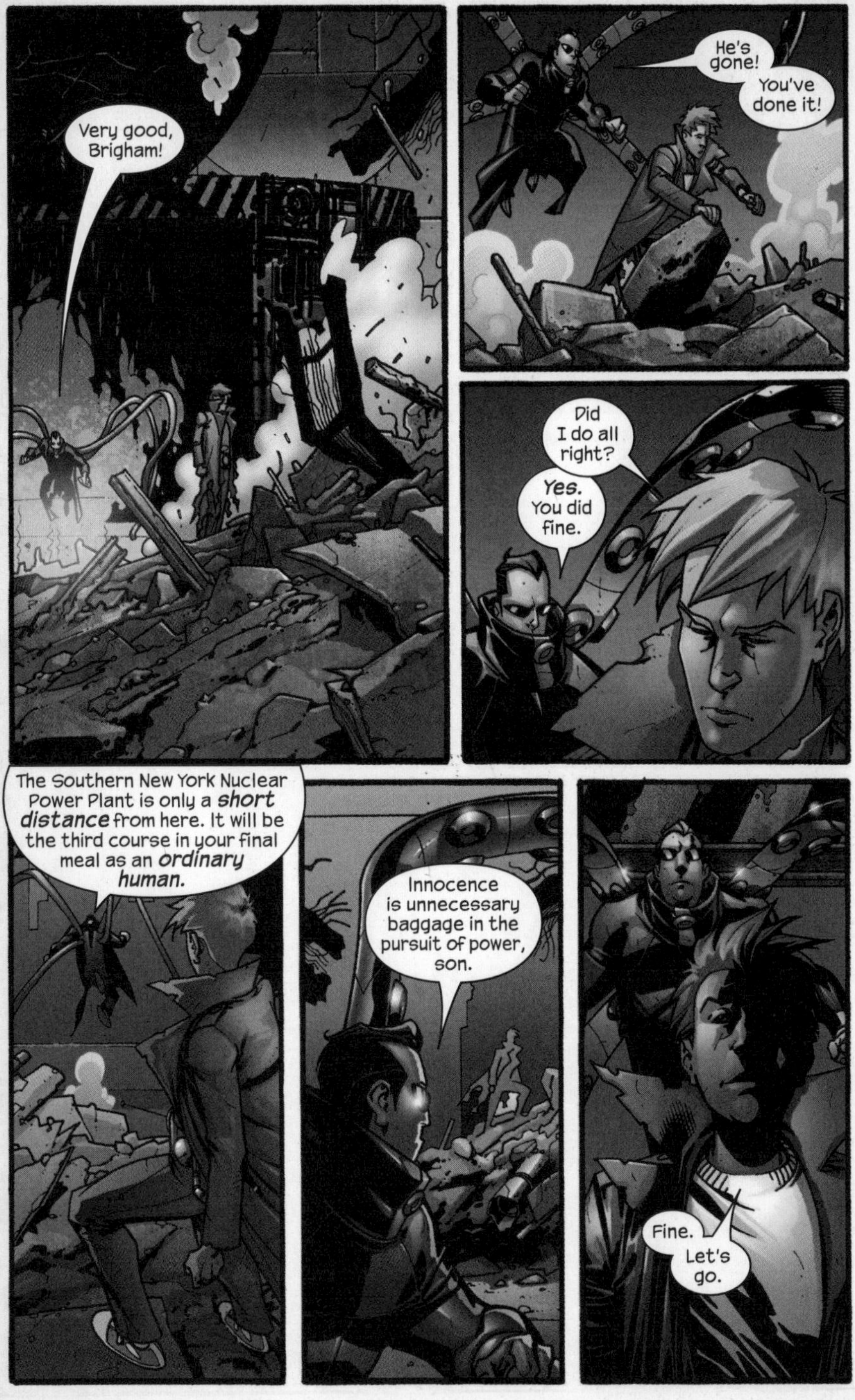
Very good, Brigham!
He's gone!
You've done it!
Did I do all right?
Yes. You did fine.
The Southern New York Nuclear Power Plant is only a short distance from here. It will be the third course in your final meal as an ordinary human.
Innocence is unnecessary baggage in the pursuit of power, son.
Fine.
Let's go.

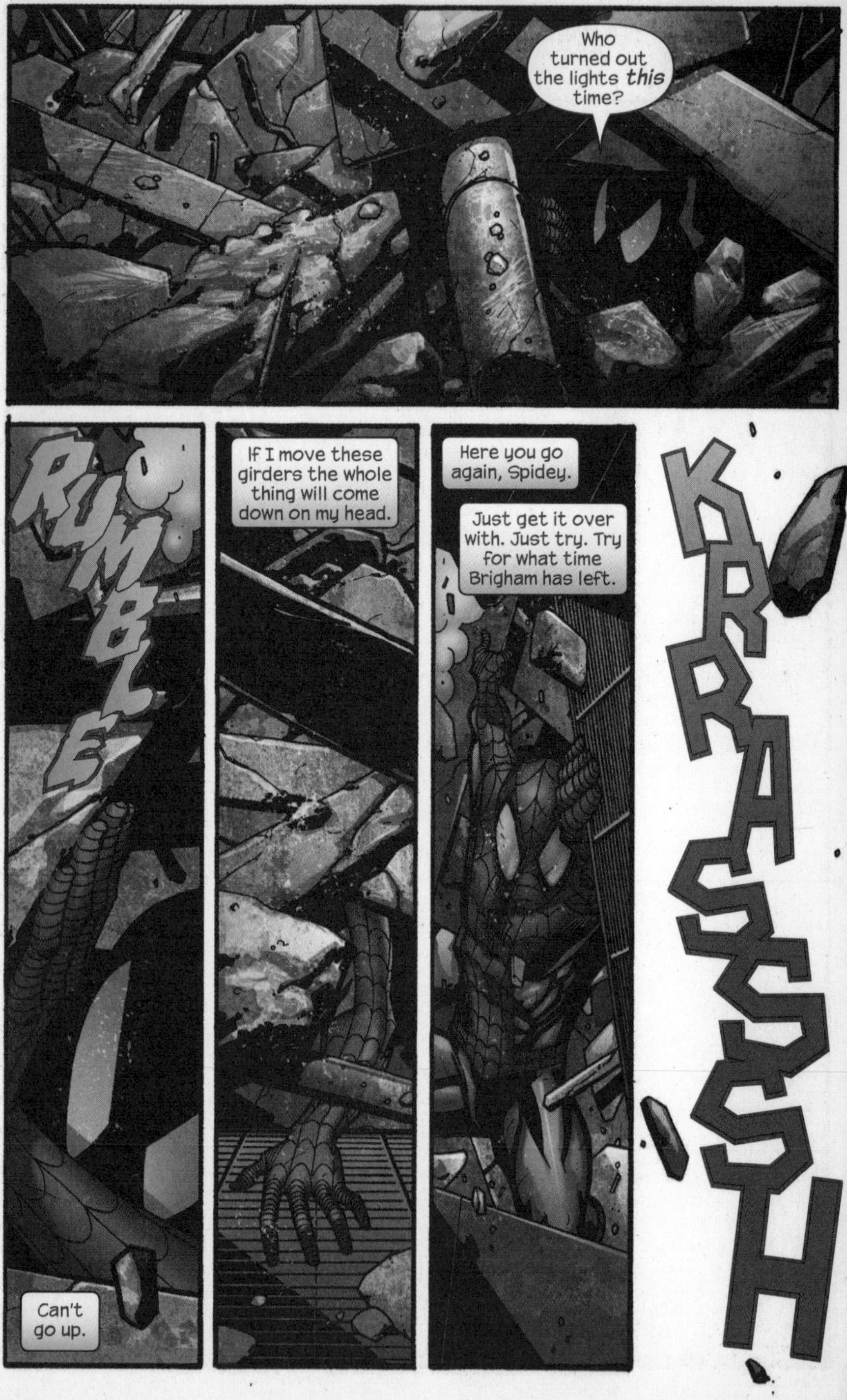
Who turned out the lights *this* time?
RUMBLE
Can't go up.
If I move these girders the whole thing will come down on my head.
Here you go again, Spidey.
Just get it over with. Just try. Try for what time Brigham has left.
KRRRASSSH

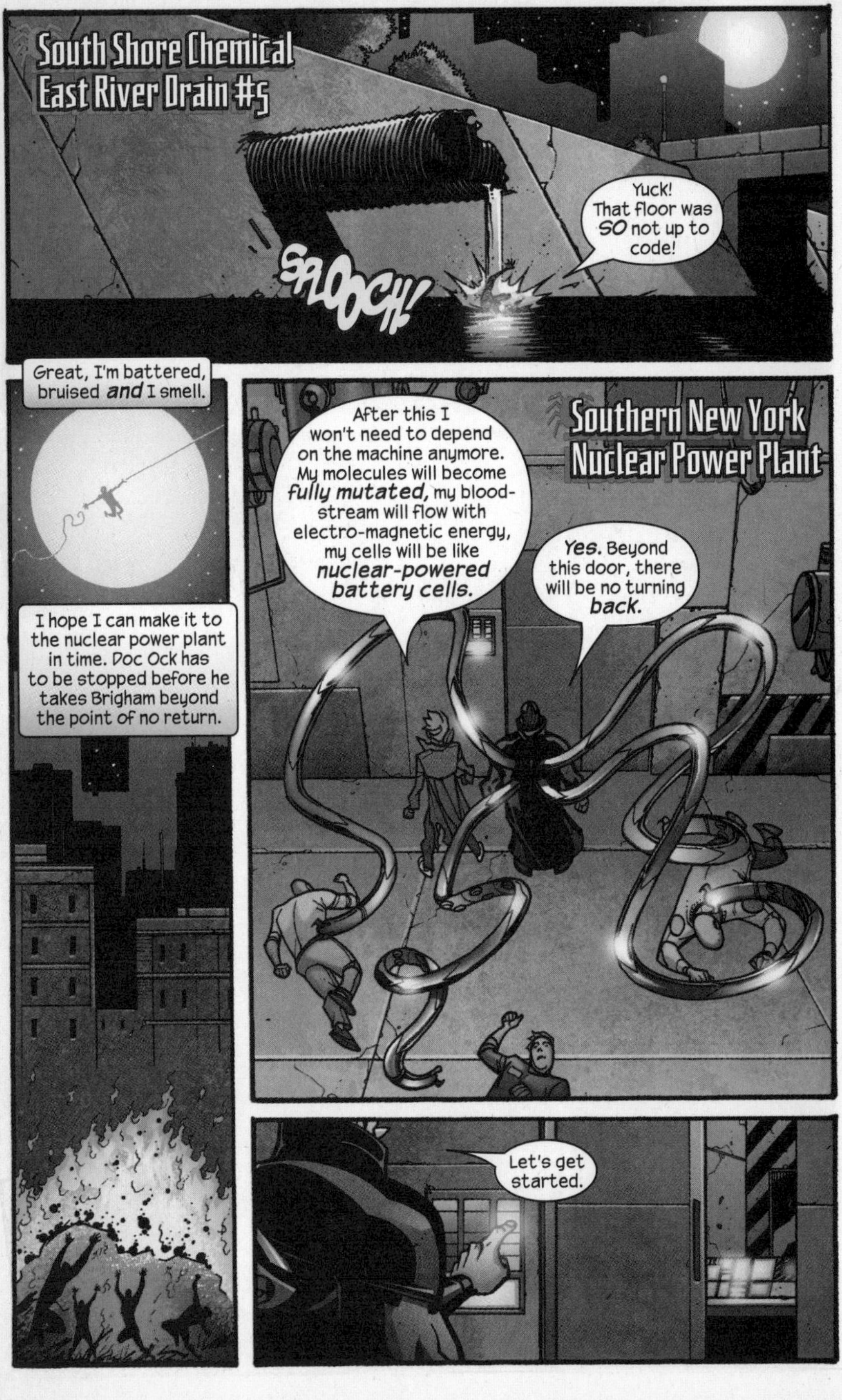
South Shore Chemical
East River Drain #5
Yuck! That floor was SO not up to code!
SPLOOCH!
Great, I'm battered, bruised and I smell.
I hope I can make it to the nuclear power plant in time. Doc Ock has to be stopped before he takes Brigham beyond the point of no return.
Southern New York
Nuclear Power Plant
After this I won't need to depend on the machine anymore. My molecules will become fully mutated, my blood-stream will flow with electro-magnetic energy, my cells will be like nuclear-powered battery cells.
Yes. Beyond this door, there will be no turning back.
Let's get started.

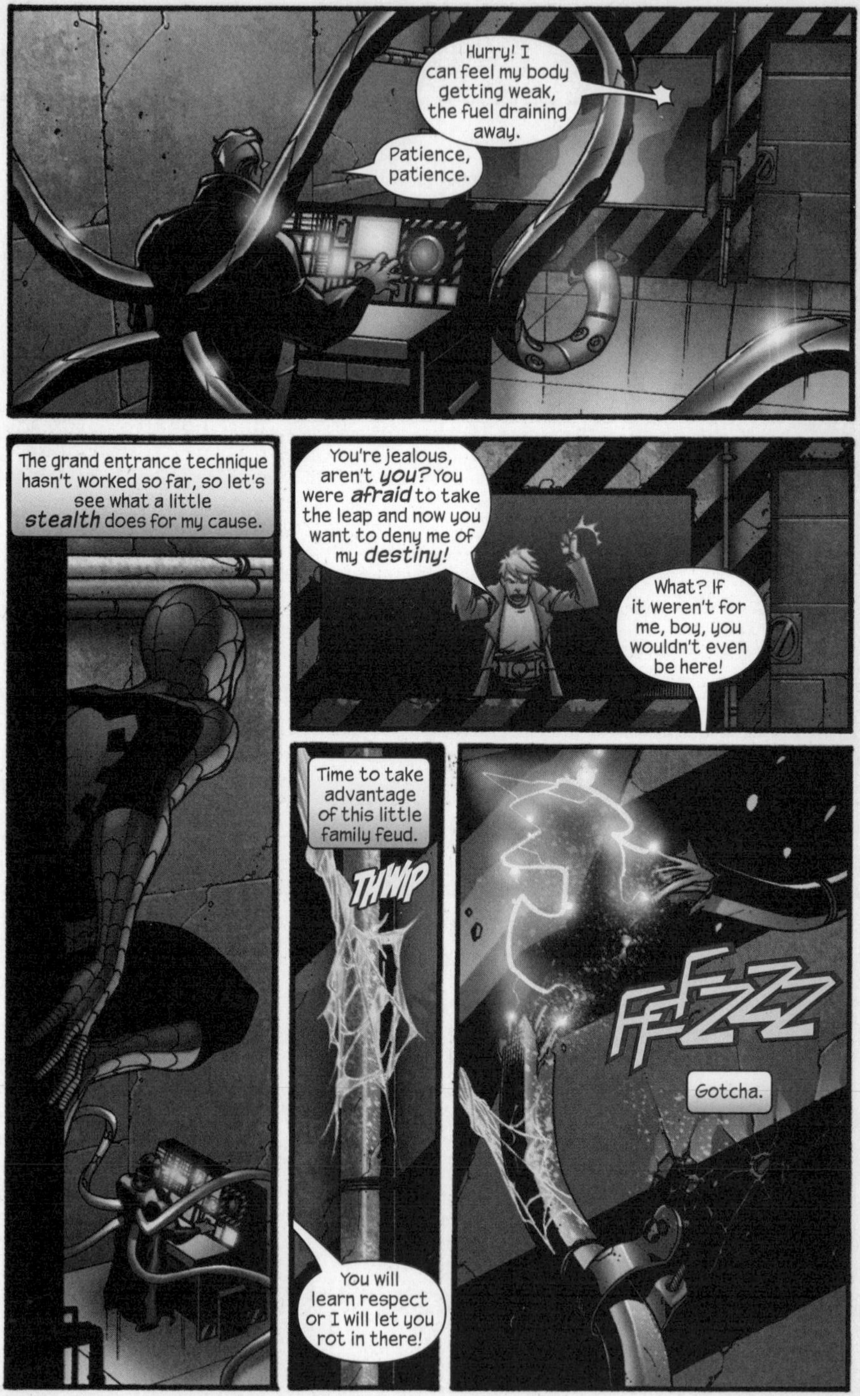
Hurry! I can feel my body getting weak, the fuel draining away.
Patience, patience.
The grand entrance technique hasn't worked so far, so let's see what a little stealth does for my cause.
You're jealous, aren't you? You were afraid to take the leap and now you want to deny me of my destiny!
What? If it weren't for me, boy, you wouldn't even be here!
Time to take advantage of this little family feud.
THWIP
You will learn respect or I will let you rot in there!
FFFZZZ
Gotcha.

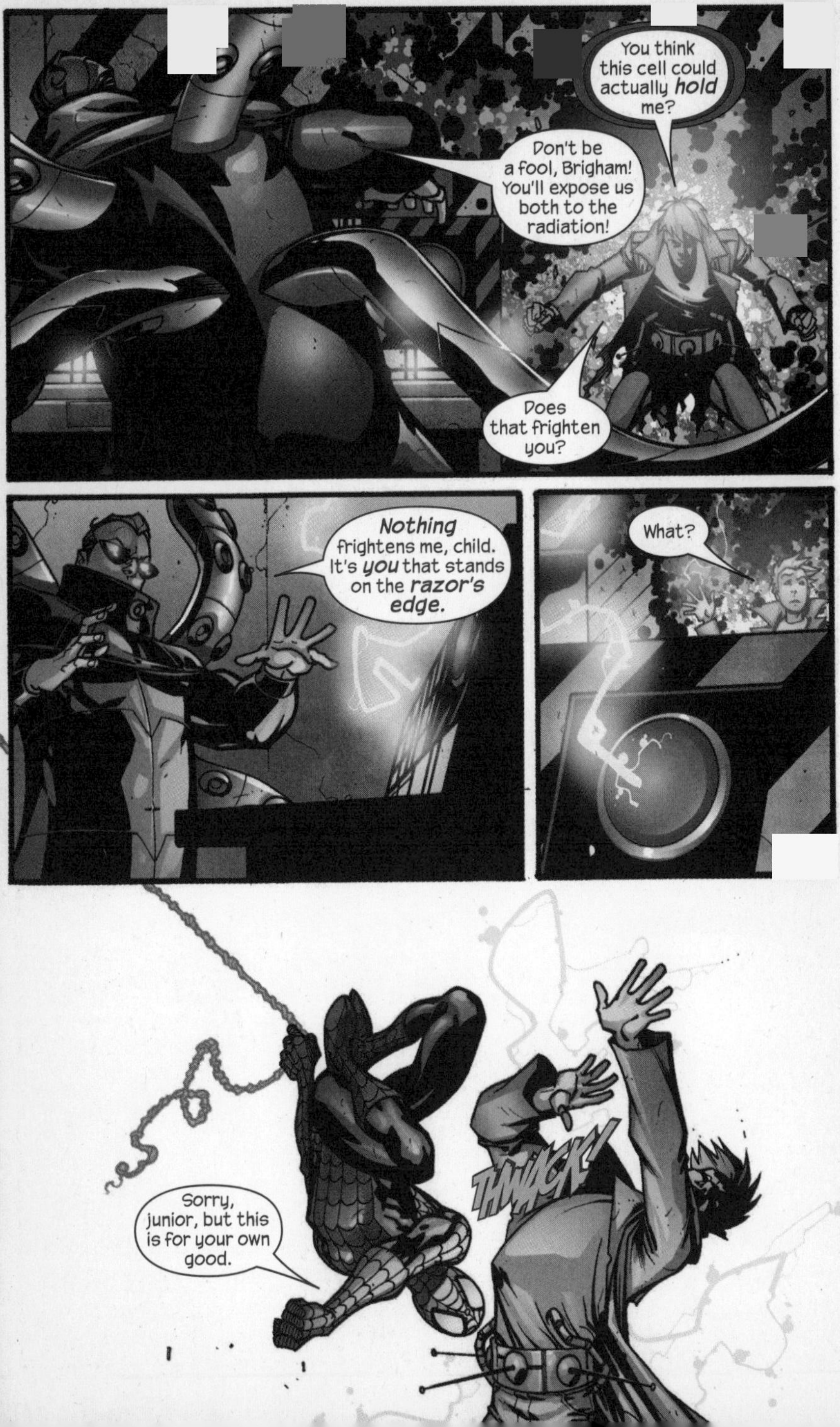
You think this cell could actually *hold* me?
Don't be a fool, Brigham! You'll expose us both to the radiation!
Does that frighten you?
Nothing frightens me, child. It's *you* that stands on the *razor's edge.*
What?
THWACK!
Sorry, junior, but this is for your own good.

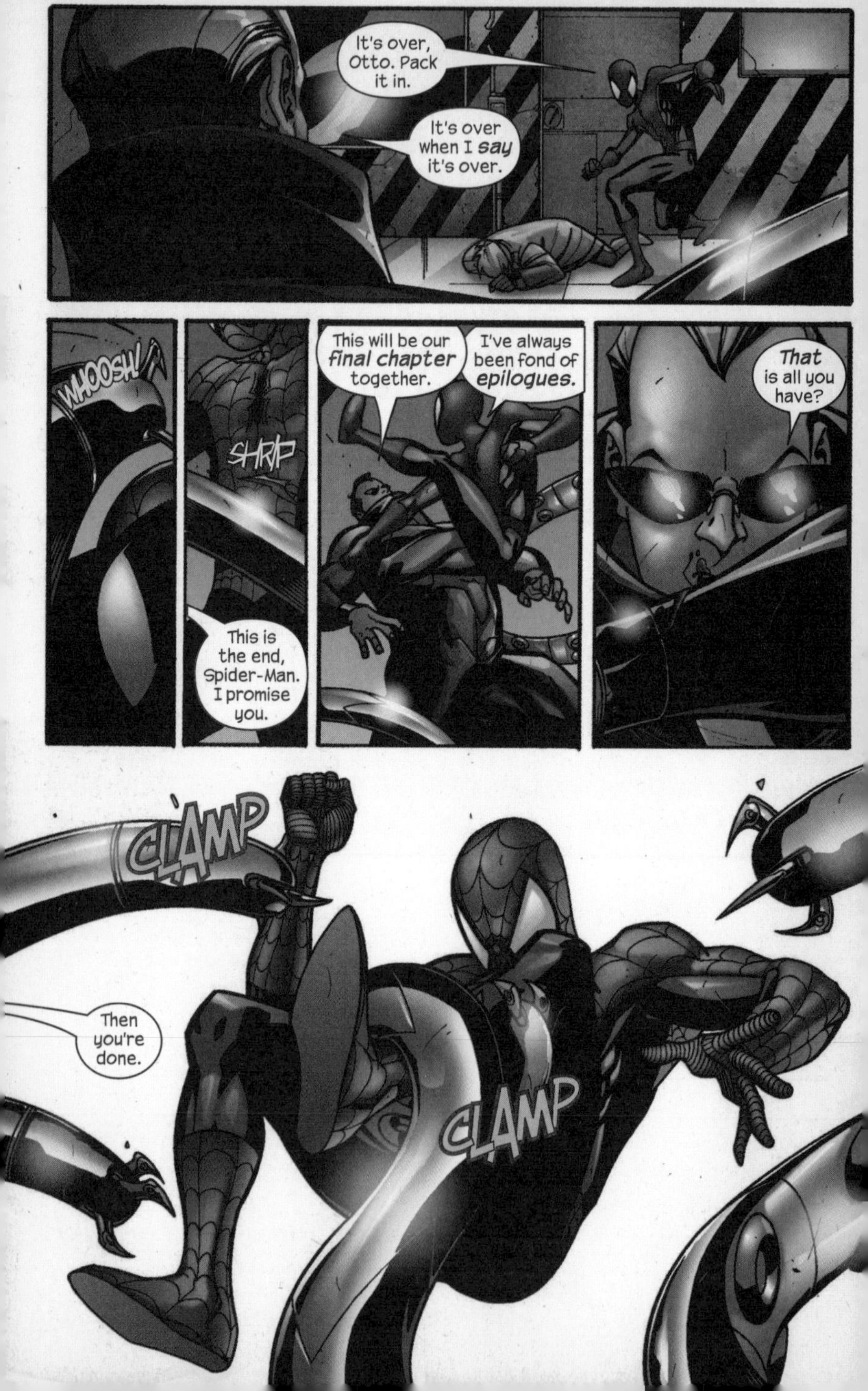
It's over, Otto. Pack it in.
It's over when I *say* it's over.
WHOOSH!
SHRIP
This is the end, Spider-Man. I promise you.
This will be our *final chapter* together.
I've always been fond of *epilogues.*
That is all you have?
CLAMP
Then you're done.
CLAMP

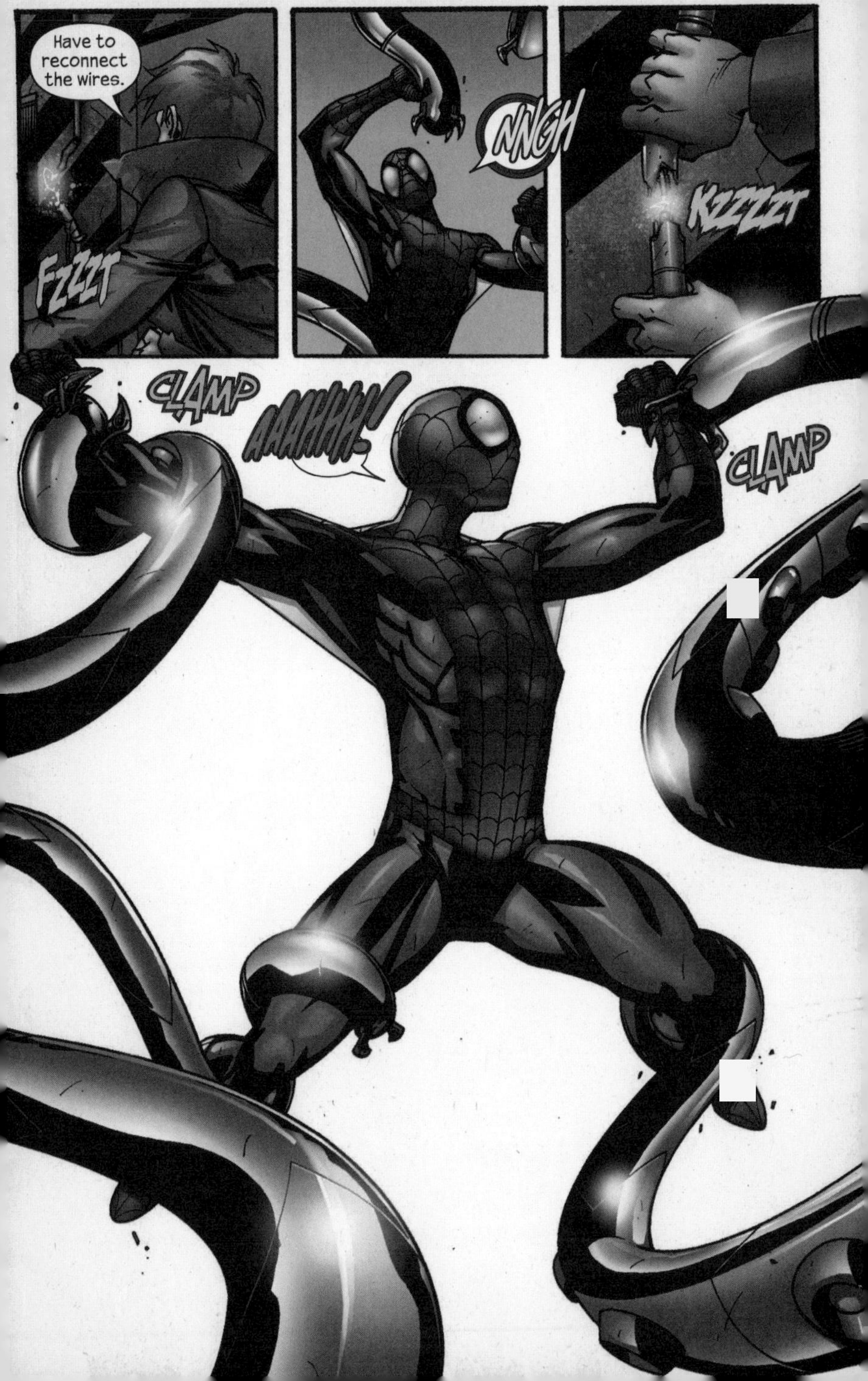
Have to reconnect the wires.
FZZZT
NNGH
KZZZZT
CLAMP
AAAHHH!
CLAMP

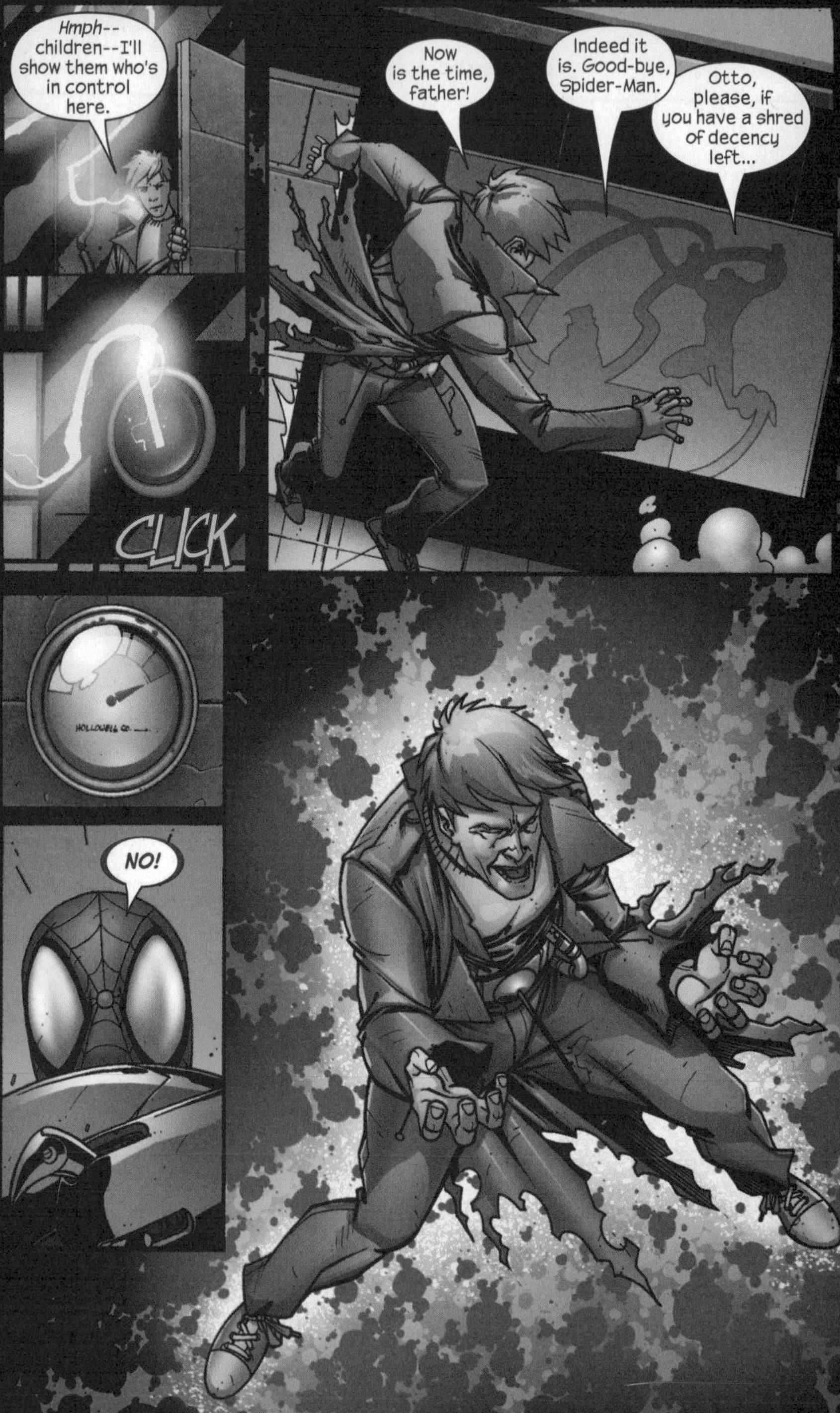
Hmph--children--I'll show them who's in control here.
Now is the time, father!
Indeed it is. Good-bye, Spider-Man.
Otto, please, if you have a shred of decency left...
CLICK
HOLLOWELL CO.
NO!

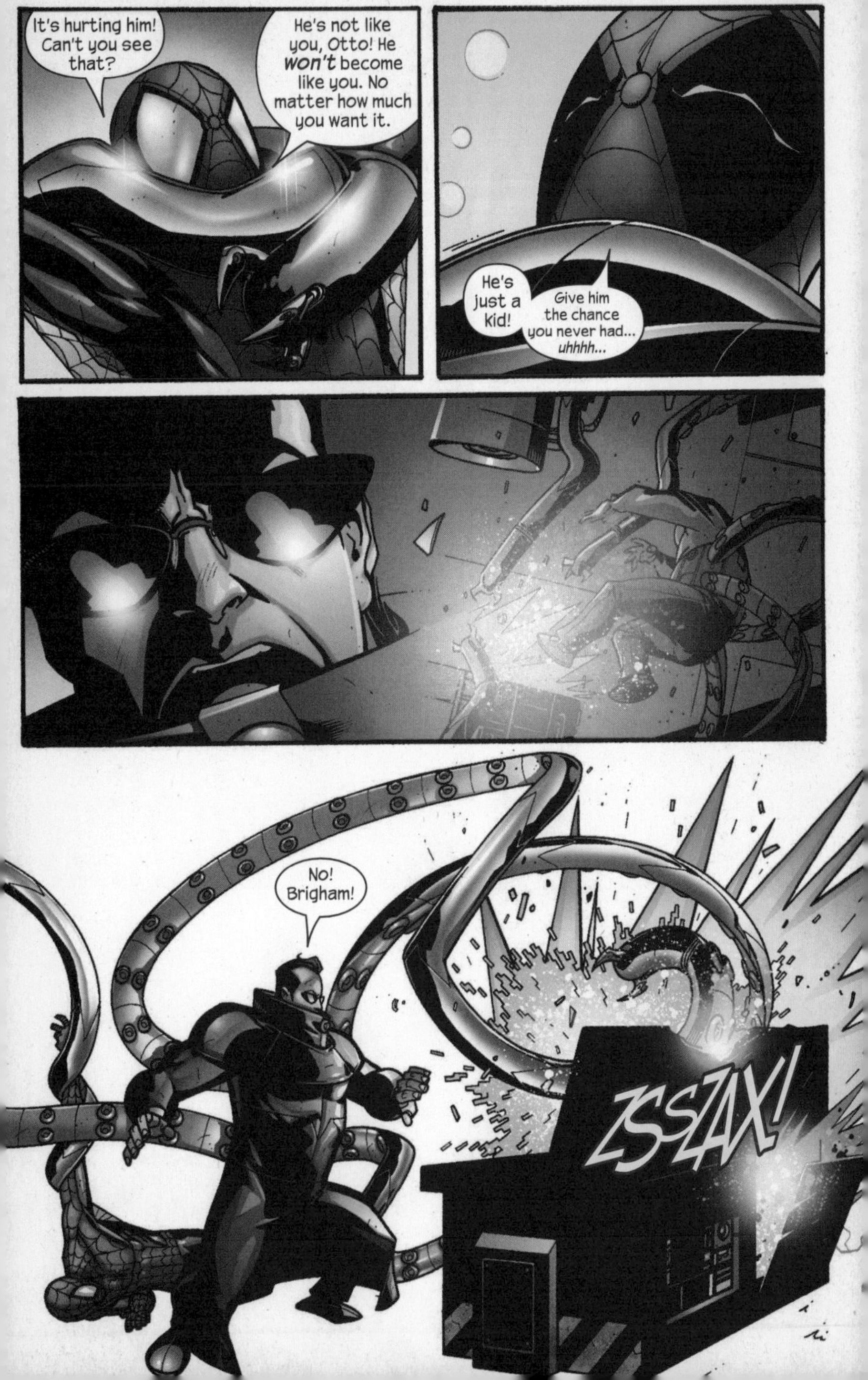
It's hurting him! Can't you see that?
He's not like you, Otto! He *won't* become like you. No matter how much you want it.
He's just a kid!
Give him the chance you never had... *uhhhh...*
No! Brigham!
ZSSZAX!

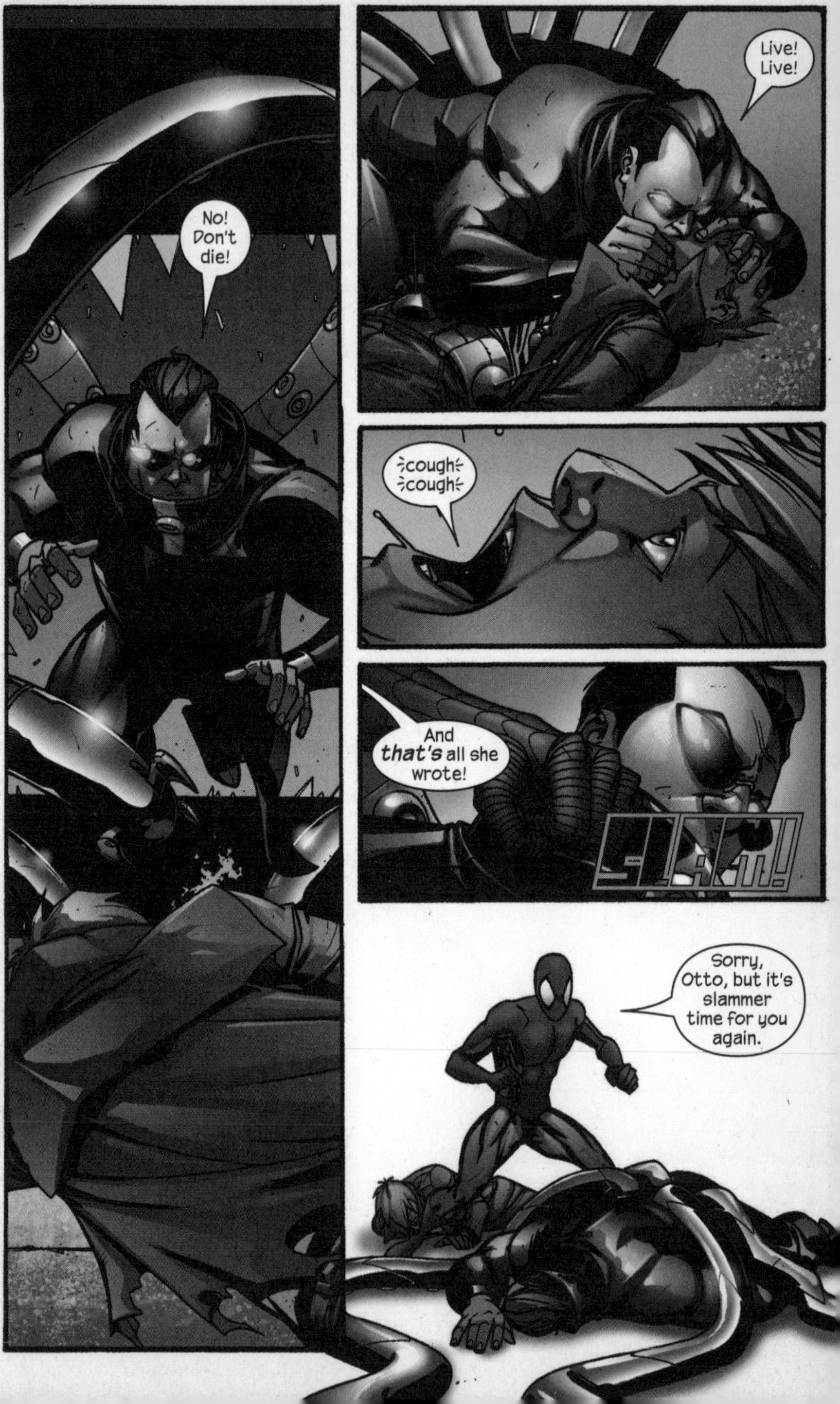
No! Don't die!
Live! Live!
cough cough
And that's all she wrote!
SLAM!
Sorry, Otto, but it's slammer time for you again.

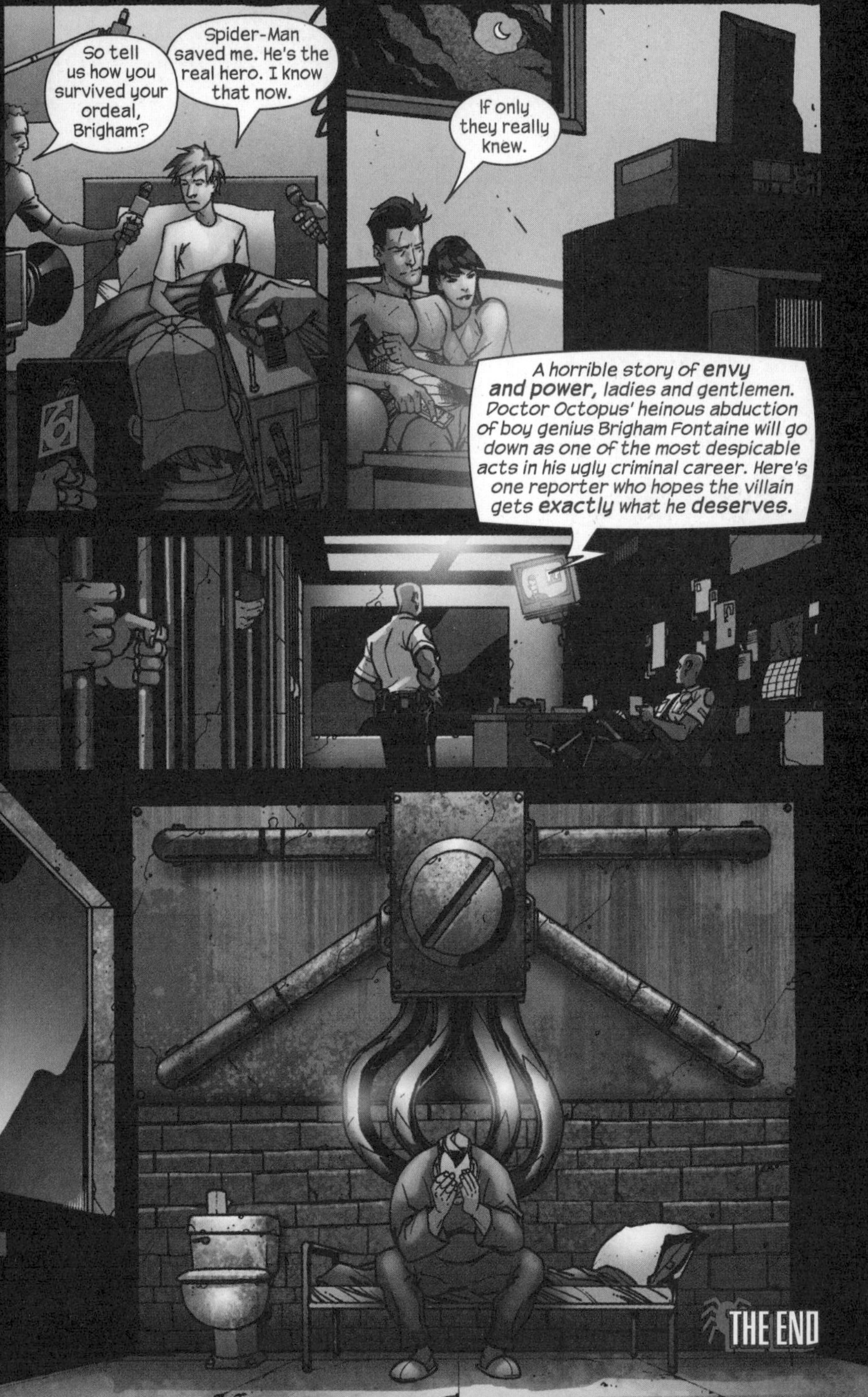
So tell us how you survived your ordeal, Brigham?
Spider-Man saved me. He's the real hero. I know that now.
If only they really knew.
A horrible story of envy and power, ladies and gentlemen. Doctor Octopus' heinous abduction of boy genius Brigham Fontaine will go down as one of the most despicable acts in his ugly criminal career. Here's one reporter who hopes the villain gets exactly what he deserves.
THE END

COVER GALLERY

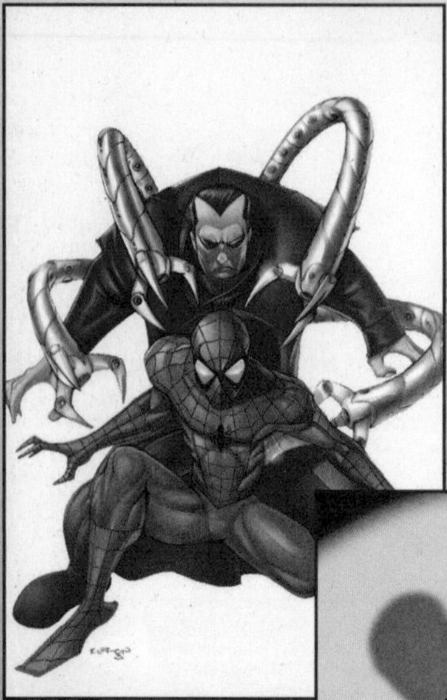

ONE

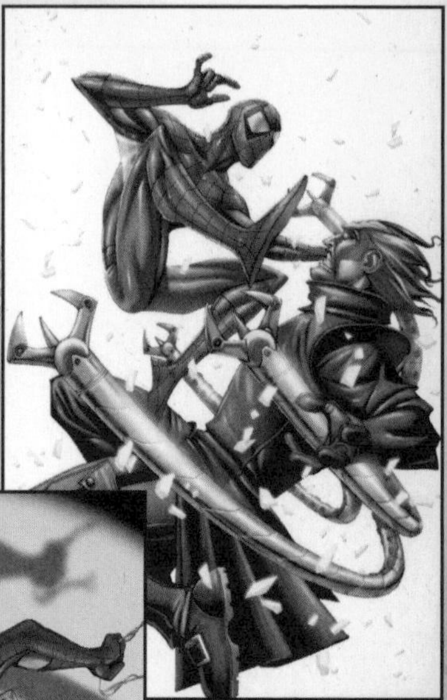

TWO

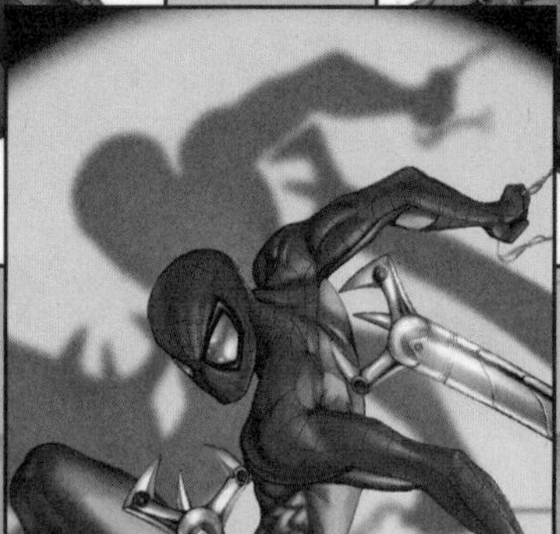

THREE

FOUR

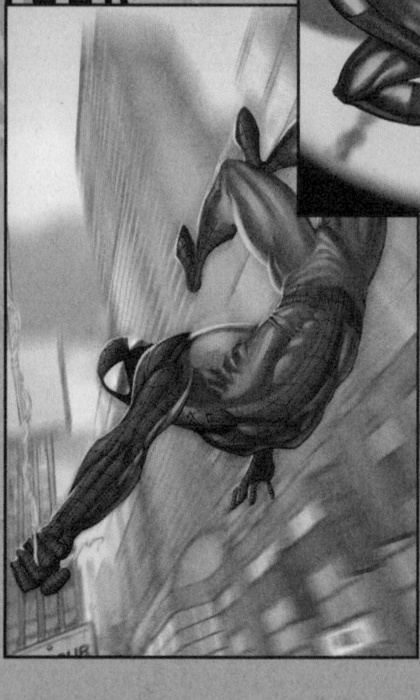

FIVE

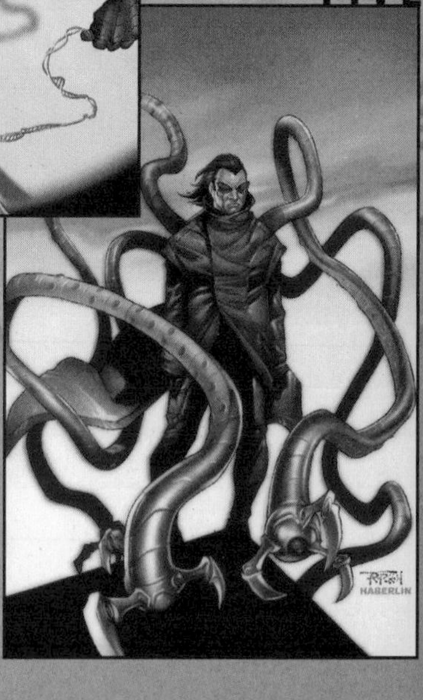
HABERLIN